The Author

Norman Brooke was born in Wensleydale, and educated in the West Riding of Yorkshire. He entered H.M. Customs & Excise after success in the first round of "Open" entrance examinations after WWII.

National Service in 1951 found him in the ranks of his father's old regiment, the West Yorkshires. He was transferred to the Royal Northumberland Fusiliers for service in Korea. Whilst on embarkation leave, as he had reasonable fluency in French, he was interviewed as a potential trainee at a military language school to be established in Cornwall. Twelve months later, having learnt to speak Russian, he was transferred to the Intelligence Corps.

"Demob" in 1953 saw him back with H.M. Customs & Excise for 39 years, serving in various parts of the United Kingdom. In Scotland, he met and married his wife before coming to the port of Harwich in 1962. Having retired in 1990, over the next ten years he became involved in tracing the war record of his father in WWI. This produced the valuable piece of family history which has been used as the basis of this story.

Both the author and his wife still live in Dovercourt within easy distance of their two sons and their families.

Bloodied, but Unbowed
A Story of Two Yorkshire Bantams in World War I

– NORMAN A. BROOKE –

An environmentally friendly book printed and bound in England by
www.printondemand-worldwide.com

This book is made entirely of chain-of-custody materials

www.fast-print.net/store.php

BLOODIED, BUT UNBOWED
Copyright © Norman A. Brooke 2014
Jacket photograph © Imperial War Museum (Q3014)

All rights reserved

No part of this book may be reproduced in any form by photocopying or any electronic or mechanical means, including information storage or retrieval systems, without permission in writing from both the copyright owner and the publisher of the book.

The right of Norman A. Brooke to be identified as the author of this work has been asserted by him in accordance with the Copyright, Designs and Patents Act 1988 and any subsequent amendments thereto.

A catalogue record for this book is available from the British Library

ISBN 978-178035-777-5

First published 2014 by
FASTPRINT PUBLISHING
Peterborough, England.

This book is dedicated to the memory of
17/541 Pte. N.F.Brooke
of the
17th West Yorkshire Regiment (The 2nd LEEDS)
otherwise known as
"The Yorkshire Bantams",
and also to that of all the other original "Bantams".

★★★★★★★★★★★★★★★★★

"What of the faith and fire within us
Men who march away
Ere the barncocks say
Night is growing grey,
To hazards whence no tears can win us;
What of the faith and fear within us
Men who march away".

Written in September, 1914
Thomas Hardy. (1840 – 1928)

Author's Note

"*BLOODIED, but UNBOWED*" although fiction, is based solidly on fact. All the characters in the story are figments of my imagination although some of them are based on real people. One of them follows the footsteps of my father.

All the places mentioned are those he visited on his travels during the Great War and have been located, with the exception of the hospital near Folkestone. This was probably a temporary extension to Shorncliffe Military Hospital built to handle the vast numbers of casualties coming back from the Western Front. As such, at the end of the war when there was no longer the demand for this extra capacity, it would be dismantled. Likewise, some of the actions described are those in which he was actively involved and experienced during his time in uniform. The wounding described is what he suffered.

Any credit which may accrue from this narrative should be given to the original "Bantams", volunteers to a man, who so proudly wore the emblem of the 35th (Bantam) Division, the "Fighting Cock".

Any errors or inaccuracies are mine, and mine alone.
Norman A. Brooke.

Acknowledgement

The research which went into the background for this book was spread over some ten years following the initial curiosity roused by my reading of the letter from the Somme, (shown as Appendix I). This curiosity became a challenge on discovering that the official records of my father's service in the Great War had been destroyed when the Public Records Office was fire-bombed during the London *blitz* in WW2.

As I gradually collected scraps of information from varied and obscure sources, I was to find that my quest was becoming more of an obsession. Eventually, after ten years or so, I was in a position where I could compile a reasonably complete service record.

It was at this point that I came to realise just how tolerant and patient my wife must have been. All the time that I had been so totally immersed in what I was doing, she was living with the situation without complaining. I must have been taking her support for granted.

There is an old adage which says that it is easy to be wise after the event. As this is indeed the case, I must acknowledge the value of being free to pursue my "hobby horse" without any protest from Audrey, my wife. Her patience was to be tested even more whilst the writing of this book was under way.

Nor must I forget the invaluable help given to me by the friendly staff of the museum of the West Yorkshire Regiment (the Prince of Wales's Own) in York who made available to me the War Diaries of the 17th Battalion W.Y.R. together with

Everard Wyrell's tome, "The West Yorkshire Regiment in the War, 1914 – 1918".

As regards the photograph used in the design of the book-jacket, this was used by courtesy of the Imperial War Museum.

To all concerned, I proffer my grateful thanks.

Introduction

During the rush to enlist for service in the British Army in response to the Kitchener poster campaign in 1914, thousands of keen, would-be volunteers were being summarily rejected out of hand. At the time, the regulation minimum height for acceptance was five feet three inches. Those who failed in this respect were not even considered for service.

The existence of this (as yet) untapped source of potential fighting men was recognised by Lord Birkenhead who set about raising what were known initially as "B.B.B.", or, in full, "Birkenhead's Bantam Battalions". He had realised that the height requirement was excluding hardy little natural fighters. These came from such backgrounds as the mines, mills and factories of industrial Britain. The farms of the British Isles could also supply tough characters who were used to putting up with atrocious conditions working out-of-doors all the year round. All these were men who had had to endure very harsh formative years, and then, in effect, continue to fight for their very existence in the difficult working conditions of the time. These men were now being cast aside as useless simply because they were not tall enough.

Lord Birkenhead was authorised to go ahead with his scheme but only on condition that not only had he to recruit a battalion for active service in France, he also had to ensure that a second battalion was also recruited to provide replacements for those killed or wounded.

When the recruiting of "Bantams" got under way, the response was staggering, to say the least!

The first Bantam recruiting centre was at Chester. Among the first to enlist were two miners who had walked all the way from County Durham to do so. Such was the spirit of all the members of the new force.

The sheer enthusiasm of men volunteering for Bantam units was such that a song was regularly being sung in all the music halls in Britain, the first verse of which is quoted in Appendix III.

Twenty-two battalions would be raised including two from Canada.

One of the other twenty was the 17th Battalion, The West Yorkshire Regiment, one of whose titles was the "2nd. Leeds". The "1st Leeds" was the 15th Battalion W.Y.R.(The Leeds Pals) who were to be slaughtered at Serre along with the 16th and 18th Battalions W.Y.R. (The Bradford Pals). Ultimately, in 1917, the survivors of the 1st and 2nd Leeds would be amalgamated to become the 15 / 17th W.Y.R.

One volunteer would be my father. He had already been rejected as being too short.

Although this book is, in some part, a work of fiction, it is based on what I knew or had found out about his experiences and sufferings in World War 1, or "The Great War" as it is sometimes known.

By coincidence (or possibly intentionally) several Bantam battalions were numbered as the 17th of their parent regiments. Hence the fictitious 17th Mid-Yorkshire Regiment.

Fred Booth in the narrative is based loosely on my father.

Tom Gardiner is also based on a real character who was as large in life as he is in this story. The friendship established and tested during the war was still there after the fighting was over and done with. I was privileged to meet the real "Tom" when I was a small boy in Wensleydale. He was once again a gamekeeper, but this time in the legal sense of the word.

The other stalwarts in Fred's half-section are also products of my imagination, although there is more than a passing resemblance to men I served with in the W.Y.R. during my National Service in the 1950's.

Lt. Richardson on the other hand is wholly imaginary. With the lieutenant, I have tried to give him the character and personality of the 2nd Lieutenant O'Brien who wrote to my grandmother when my father was wounded during the Somme offensive. This letter is reproduced verbatim elsewhere in this book. When I first came across this letter, and read it, I was amazed at the wording of the first two sentences. I still am!

The fact is that this officer found the time to write telling her of Dad's wounding, but at the same time, reassuring her. Bearing in mind what they had just been through, and the conditions prevailing at the Front at the time, Lt. O'Brien comes over as an officer who not only cared about the wellbeing of his men, but who took his responsibilities in this area very seriously. He even remembered to explain the disposal of a parcel she had just sent to Dad, but which had arrived after he had been taken to hospital.

The disposal of packages in this manner in the absence of the intended recipient was done as normal procedure in Dad's lot, and was based on common sense in order to avoid the waste not only of the contents of the parcel, but also of the sheer effort expended in actually getting it up to the forward areas.

I have tried to portray such an officer.

I recently checked the War Graves Commission website in attempt to find out if he survived. As I could find no reference to either grave or memorial, I can only conclude, happily, that he probably came though it all.

The Leeds Bantams (also known as The Yorkshire Bantams) typified the spirit and nature of these battalions. Raised in December, 1914, after intensive training, they were on active service from February, 1916 until December of that year when the survivors were absorbed into other units of their parent regiments.

During those ten months that the Leeds "Bantams" existed as a separate entity, eleven officers as well as two hundred and seventy men lost their lives together with a commensurate number wounded. The death rate alone stood at over twenty five per cent.

Medals awarded to them were two V.C.'s, one D.S.O., three M.C.'s, and getting on for thirty M.M.'s and D.C.M.'s. Not a bad haul, one might say. In fact, they were the most decorated of all the Bantam battalions.

However, the high rate of attrition was to sound the final knell for the Bantams. With the arrival of conscription in January, 1916, recruiting officers were now taking any man who could see the door, was fit enough to walk through it, and was still able to stand when he got inside. This is certainly exaggeration, but the truth remains that very weedy specimens were being accepted without hesitation. If under height or below standard in any respect, they were automatically graded 'bantam'.

It should be stressed at this juncture that "Bantam" is a title, an honorific, whilst "bantam" (with the lower case 'b') is a classification of physical stature. The fact that a "Bantam" could be said to be of bantam build is irrelevant in the main. The original requirement of strong build plus at least one inch over the average chest measurement was now being totally ignored.

These so-called 'replacements' for Bantam regiments resulted in a drastic and disastrous reduction in the quality of these units. As well as not meeting the physical requirements, the newcomers also lacked the drive and the flair of the original Bantams.

The men now being posted to Bantam units which were under strength due to the casualties they had taken were conscripts, not volunteers as had been the original Bantams.

They were in the army because they had to be, they had no choice.

The inevitable outcome was that these 'non-Bantams' were weeded out and sent to areas where they could pull what little weight they possessed. This released for service in the front line fitter men currently in the rear echelons.

This 'weeding-out' process left many battalions under strength. They would ultimately be amalgamated with similarly decimated units of their parent regiments.

Such then were the "Bantams", the original Bantams, who would be so contemptuously dismissed by Lt.General Sir A. Haldane, commander of VI Corps. He would write them off as "under-sized, sub-standard troops".

In truth, the Bantams by their very nature could only be expected to have a limited life considering the terrible casualties that all regiments were taking at the time. There was, after all, a limit to the number of men who could be classified as a "Bantam".

In all fairness to the Lt. General, the slighting remarks he is said to have made with regard to the Bantams may well have been quoted out of context. It is more than likely that he was referring to the so-called 'replacements' when he made his scathing comments. Be that as it may, the slur it cast on the reputation and history of Bantam units is still evident today.

The troops weeded out as lacking the necessary attributes of front-line fighting troops, and sent back to the rear areas were the conscripted "bantams" NOT the original volunteers.

In December, 1916, the title "Bantam" was expunged. Henceforth, the division would be known simply as the "35th" with anyone being taken as replacements. Even the insignia was abolished. The Bantam "Fighting Cock" was replaced by seven 'fives' linked together in the form of a convoluted circle.

The 'flash' of the 40th Division was retained, however. Although this formation had never been 100% Bantam, its badge was also a fighting cock, but in a different style to that of the 35th. But now, superimposed on their version would be an oak leaf and acorn symbolising Bourlon wood where the 40th had won lasting fame in the fierce fighting for this strongpoint.

Were the Bantams sub-standard troops? I think not. Definitely not as far as the original Bantams were concerned.

"Under height, but otherwise fit for service" was the official verdict on thousands of potential fighting men who were under regulation height, and as a result were rejected when they volunteered for Kitchener's armies.

All this would change with the inception of formation of "Birkenhead's Bantam Battalions" in 1914 and early 1915.

One can be certain that during his time in uniform, the Bantam, as a consequence of his diminutive stature would be referred to as "half pint", if not worse. It is self-evident, however, that the prowess shown by the various units of the 35th (Bantam) Division when involved in the fighting on the Western front, earned them the respect of everyone with whom they came into contact.

Dramatis Personae

Fred Booth.   Age 19.
Home in Cleckmonsedge.
Mechanic in a woollen mill.

Tom Gardner.   Age 25.
Gamekeeper (poacher!).

Billy Cunliffe.   Age 21 "officially", but actually 16.
Ploughboy.

Bob Metcalfe.   Age 23.
Home in Ledford.

Would do anything legal for wages.

Charlie Ackroyd.   Age 24. Home in Ledford.
He too would turn his hand to anything.

William Sugden.   Age 22.
Home in Huddersfield.
Solicitor's secretary / clerk.

2nd. Lt. Richardson.   4 Platoon commander.

Capt. Yorke.   'C' Company commanding Officer

Bloodied, but Unbowed
– NORMAN A. BROOKE –

Part One
"A Clutch of Bantams"

Chapter 1

The summer of 1914 was very much like most English summers, hot, dry and dusty, the air redolent with the scent of newly-mown hay drying in the fields.

From the village green in front of the inn came the sounds of a cricket match. This was the annual contest between Cleckmonsedge and Scholesworth. From time to time, as well as the sound of leather on willow, there came a ripple of polite applause from one team's supporters or the other's as either side gained the upper hand.

As yet they were unaware that this match was to be the last for several years. Little did they realise that before the end of summer, this spirit of friendly rivalry would be violently thrust aside by a wave of animosity which, within the space of four years would engulf the world. The clouds of war were looming on the horizon.

A Serb patriot had assassinated the Austrian Archduke Franz Ferdinand whilst he was in Sarajevo. As a result, the might of the Austro-Hungarian Empire was now bearing down on the small Balkan state of Serbia.

As a friend and ally, Russia was threatening retaliation if Serbia was attacked.

Germany, being in alliance with the Austro-Hungarians would be drawn in. This in turn involved the French who were bound by treaty to support Russia.

Various belligerent attitudes had been taken up by the countries so far involved but up to now, the exchanges had been verbal, not physical. All this would change when Germany decided to invade France. They did this by moving troops through Belgium in order to by-pass French military defence-works.

Britain now became involved under her treaty obligations to defend Belgium against any aggressor. Accordingly, an ultimatum was delivered in Berlin to the effect that if all German troops were not withdrawn from Belgium soil immediately, a state of war would exist between Britain and Germany.

The given deadline came and passed. It became more and more obvious that the British ultimatum was being ignored. Britain and Germany, together with all their groupings were now at war with each other. August 4th 1914 would go down in history as the starting date of World War 1, otherwise known as the "Great War".

A small formation of troops, the British Expeditionary Force, landed on the Continent and took up positions in Belgium. These troops were all 'regulars' in the unit the Kaiser would describe as ".... that contemptible little army ..." . This description came to be regarded by members of that force, in effect, as a battle honour.

For the German army on the receiving end of the 'skill-at-arms' of their counterparts, the speed and accuracy of the British riflemen at Mons was such that they thought the B.E.F. was equipped with machine-guns. It was to be a Pyrrhic victory, however. The overwhelming enemy numbers meant that a fighting withdrawal into France had to be made in order to regroup.

Such was the situation in the late autumn of 1914. Something had to be done, and done quickly to bolster the small British army of the time, good as it was. Somehow, more men had to be persuaded to join the Colours.

Lord Kitchener, the Secretary of State for War, decided that a massive recruiting campaign had to be mounted, the slant of which would be based on patriotism and the "Big Bully" aspect of the war.

Was it not the case in the beginning that the much larger Austro-Hungarian Empire had attacked "brave little Serbia"? (For some reason, the assassination was not mentioned!) Then, as if that was not enough, Germany had invaded "brave little Belgium".

Soon, posters appeared everywhere stating quite bluntly "Britons! Your King and country need you! A call to arms etc. etc. ...." They went on to say that ten thousand men were urgently required in the grave National Emergency. Enlistment would be for three years, or until the war was over.

Others carried a likeness of Lord Kitchener himself with a similar message.

One society lady was heard to remark that whilst he was lacking in personality as a man, he made a fine poster! Be that as it may, recruiting centres the length and breadth of the British Isles were overwhelmed by the rush to respond to the call.

It so happened that as he made his way home from work at the local mill, Fred caught sight of one of these posters. Instead of going straight back to his lodgings as usual, he went to the Town Hall now being used as a recruiting office. Up the steps he went and crossed over to one of the tables where an official took the names and addresses of the volunteers who were then directed to a side room for the medical examination.

At this point, Fred was told in no uncertain terms to "Bugger off, 'shorty'!" The regulation, minimum height for acceptance was 5ft.3ins, but he was only 5ft.2ins. The fact that he was physically fit, tough as an old boot, and well built in proportion to his height made no difference. He was not tall enough!

With his latent patriotism rejected in such a harsh manner, he went back to his rooms. He would just have to stick to his day-to-day grind at the mill, and try to get over his disappointment.

Then, one day in December, he heard that some infantry regiments were accepting "Bantam" Battalions which were in the process of being raised by cities up and down the country. On enquiring, he found that the Lord Mayor and City Fathers of Ledford were recruiting for such a unit. It would be known as the 17th Battalion the Mid-Yorkshire Regiment, "The Ledford Bantams".

Units such as these were to be officially designated "Bantam" in recognition of the fact that they were made up of men who although physically fit, were nevertheless under the regulation height. Fred decided there and then that he filled the bill. He gave in his notice at the mill and set off for Ledford on his bicycle, a matter of some twenty miles or so there and back.

Having found the Town Hall, he joined the queue behind a youth who, even to Fred, looked far too young to be volunteering. When his turn came, the lad ingenuously gave his correct age, sixteen. The grizzled recruiting sergeant said "Sorry, lad, th'a's not old enough. Tek a walk rahnd t' gasworks over yonder ----- tha'll be much older when tha gets back 'ere!"

Fred was next and completed all the formalities. For better or for worse, he was in. As he turned away to join the other now-enlisted men, the young boy came back in and went straight up to the sergeant who had just rejected him.

"Age?" "Twenty-one". "Right, son. Sign here". The short walk had obviously worked wonders. Billy Cunliffe, a ploughboy from Wensleydale had been accepted.

All the day's intake were first addressed by the Lord Mayor of the city, and then given the day, time and place where they were to report. First parade would be at 0600hrs. (They would soon become used to telling the time of day in this manner).

Came the appointed day, Fred got out his trusty bicycle and set out for Ledford. As he had to cover ten miles or so to get there, with a fair selection of hills on the way, he left home at four o'clock in the morning, or rather, 0400hrs. Due to the lack of drill halls in the neighbourhood, the group of raw recruits who were to be known as "C" Company were to assemble at Armbeck cattle market.

Having duly reported in, Fred found that he was in No.4 Platoon. He was now known to officialdom as 17/541, Private F. Booth, 4 Platoon, "C" Company, 17th Mid-Yorkshire Regiment (The Ledford Bantams).

Their first duties were the dismantling of the pens in the market place and then the hosing away of all traces of the previous users of the premises. That done, they fell out for a smoke and a 'breather'. They were then addressed by their Company Commander, a Captain Yorke. They were told what their responsibilities would be. The list seemed to be endless.

They were then informed of their rights. By comparison, these were very few. They were reminded that they were effectively in for the duration of the war, no matter how long that might be.

As for uniforms, there were none as yet. Owing to the sudden and unexpected demand for them, the recruits would have to continue to wear their civilian clothes "for the time being".

Another shortage was that of billets. Put simply, there were none! Recruits would receive a victualling allowance and continue to live at home if they were local. If they were from further afield, then local private accommodation would be found for them. This would also be "for the time being".

How many more times would they hear that phrase over the coming months?

Then came the day when uniforms were issued for the first time. What should have been a momentous occasion turned out to be a definite flop! The uniforms (such as they were) turned out to be ex- Ledford Tramways outfits. The cap badges were in the form of the Ledford coat-of-arms. The similarity became even more apparent when it was found that the fixing pins for the badges fitted the holes in the front of the caps exactly. It was as if they had been made for each other! Then it was discovered that a very happy state of affairs existed. When the recruits boarded tramcars anywhere in town, they were automatically "accepted" as Tramways' staff, and allowed to travel without paying.

Following the issue of 'uniforms', rifles were produced. These were obviously Boer War salvage or deactivated museum exhibits, and for drill purposes only.

For the next three or four weeks, Fred cycled to Ledford every morning in time for the first parade at 0600hrs, despite all that the weather could throw at him. Then, duties over for the day, he would cycle all the way back home again, arriving late in the evening.

Finally, khaki uniforms were issued in place of the navy-blue ones they had been wearing. The city coat-of-arms were transferred to their new caps to continue as the badge of their unit. What had been a bunch of very raw recruits now assumed the appearance of the soldiers they had volunteered to become.

A combination of rigorous foot-drill, route marches, and hard physical exercise had changed a crowd of civilians into fledgling infantrymen. A very mixed bunch of men from all walks of life, and educated to very different levels, had, over the short space of time they had been together in the army, evolved into a single body capable of reacting as a unit.

Within the platoons of "C" Company, groups of men would find that they had an affinity for each other, and, as turned out to be the case in several instances, the weaknesses of one could be overcome by the strengths and skills of the others. Fred's immediate circle was one such group.

Nineteen years old, Fred had served his apprenticeship as a mechanic in a wool mill before enlisting.

Billy Cunliffe was the sixteen-year old ploughboy who was 'officially' twenty- one.

Bob Metcalfe was twenty-three. He had tried a variety of jobs since leaving school when he was twelve, but nothing seemed to suit him. As a result, he had drifted from town to town, and from village to village in the North of England. His approach to work was that he "would do 'owt' to eat".

Surprisingly, he seemed to have been cut out for army life, and took to it like a duck takes to water. He settled in very quickly. He was currently from Ledford.

Tom Gardner gave his age as twenty-five, but was definitely older. He said he was an 'estate worker', stating that as he moved about, his address would vary according to his location. He said he was from Ripon, or thereabouts when he enlisted.

Charlie Ackroyd was a labourer, nothing specific. He too would turn his hand to anything legal so long as it fed him. He gave his age as twenty-four, but again, this was doubtful. He also was from Ledford. His attitude to work was similar to that of Bob, but expressed slightly differently. So long as he didn't finish up in 'chokey', " owt that addled 'im brass was alreight by 'im"

William Sugden at twenty-two years of age had been a secretarial clerk in the office of a firm of solicitors. He was a bit of a weakling compared to the others but had nevertheless passed the physical examination. As the 'brains' of the bunch, he had immediately been nicknamed "Prof". He would be assisted by the others if and when necessary in anything requiring sheer muscle power, but he came into his own and stood out intellectually in the group when it came to understanding the King's Regulations or Company orders. He would help with letter writing if needed.

Chapter 2

December 1914 became January 1915. The Ledford Bantams were to move for the first time as a cohesive unit. Their destination was Ilkley and its moors. Boarding houses and hotels had been requisitioned for use as billets.

Round about midday, a long line of lorries and buses, (open and closed), rolled into the centre of the quiet spa town, and ground to a halt. The 17th Mid-Yorkshires got down, and proceeded to sort themselves out into companies and platoons. Individuals moved smartly to avoid becoming the target of abuse delivered in stentorian tones by the N.C.O.'s in charge.

As the bemused townsfolk watched in amazement tinged with shock, obscenities rent the air. What had confused the issue from the start had been the wide variety of vehicles used in the troop movement, and their arrival in Ilkley unannounced. As all the transport had had to be requisitioned as part of the war effort, the army had to make do with what was available.

Once order had been restored, the troops were assembled in the local church hall. This too had been requisitioned together with other buildings of similar size in the vicinity. As one officer was heard to remark, "You can't beat democracy provided everybody does what they're told!"

In the church hall, the billeting officer told off the various units to their allocated areas in the town or its outskirts. At this stage, the platoon commander would refer to the charts which indicated how many men were to be quartered at the addresses shown. By dint of what might be described as "fancy footwork", not to mention persuasion of a less than subtle nature, Fred's immediate group of six managed to organise things so that they were all billeted under one roof in a boarding house with three double rooms, situated on the Skipton Road just on the outskirts of town.

All the meals were to be taken in yet another hall about three hundred yards down the road from their quarters. This was equipped with full kitchen facilities which meant that all the food would be cooked on the premises, and so would be fresh and hot when eaten. It would not have to brought in in insulated containers.

As it was now late afternoon, the remaining time was given over to settling in. After they had eaten the evening meal, the town would have to reconnoitred, not so much from a military point of view, but more according to the needs of the ordinary, private soldier. Knowing the locations of the public houses was of prime importance. It was not just a case of knowing where they were, but more importantly, which were the best as regards the quality of the beer and the prices charged.

Fred and Billy would share a room as they had enlisted at the same time. Bob and Charlie finished up together as they came from similar backgrounds. That left Tom and William, as unlikely a pair of roommates as could be imagined. This happened by chance as they were the last to decide. All things considered, it was difficult to describe anything as strange or unusual in the current environment.

First parade from now on would be reporting for breakfast at 0600hrs. Our band of heroes found that as their rooms were the nearest to the cookhouse, they were always first in the queue. They got their food straight out of the kitchen the moment they arrived on the scene without having to wait for it. Not surprisingly they were always the first to finish, which gave them plenty of time to prepare for muster parade at 0800hrs.

After the roll had been called, they were marched to yet another commandeered building, this time, a warehouse. This had had to be emptied by the owner when faced with the dreaded Army requisition.

The premises could have been built for the purposes the Army had in mind for it.

Extending from the building proper was a solid stone wall about ten feet high topped with broken glass. This enclosed a large, cobblestoned yard of sufficient size as to comfortably take all the transport with room to spare. It had one lockable gate which opened onto the main road. This yard would be used as the "Vehicle Park".

The warehouse itself was formidably constructed of York stone, three storeys high, with iron bars across every window. It had an outside pulley-hoist system serving each floor through a delivery door set in the wall. At ground level in the front of the building were double doors which would allow vehicles to be driven inside for unloading or loading under cover. These exterior doors were fitted with massive bars and padlocks. Thus, anything within the building would be in a locked storehouse inside a locked yard.

It was to this edifice that the troops were marched.

On arrival, they were halted and told to stand easy. Then, by platoon, they entered the battalion store (which was what the warehouse had become during the previous week).

Once inside, they were issued with the necessary accoutrements of war. This was full equipment consisting of an array of straps, pouches, haversack and large back-pack. They were also given a modern rifle, and last but not least, a bayonet. This was eighteen inches of cold steel, not unlike a small sword which could be affixed to the muzzle-end of the rifle.

When C Company paraded past the quartermaster to receive their share of this largesse, they found that all the leather equipment had already been issued leaving them with fabric webbing items. Initially disappointed at not getting the 'traditional' kit, they realised how lucky they had actually been when the corporal issuing it pointed out to them that leather had to be polished whilst webbing only had to be scrubbed to keep it presentable. Not only was it easier to maintain, it would never leave polish marks on their uniforms.

Everybody's luck had run out by the time the rifles were issued. Straight out of storage, they were still in their wooden crates, and smothered in thick grease both inside and out!

Before leaving the stores, all the items just issued to them had to be stamped with the owner's regimental number.

Just over another mile of marching brought them to yet another hall. This one would be used for indoor instructions and lectures on infantry tactics, etc. Today, however, was to be spent getting the rifles into useable condition by getting rid of all that grease. For good measure, the new webbing 'Christmas tree' of straps and pouches also had to be scrubbed to an acceptable standard. In other words, it had to be immaculate.

When they arrived at their destination, they found that enough field kitchens had been set up in the yard to allow two to each platoon. The boilers were full of scalding hot water, whilst alongside each were five or six long-handled ladles, together with a similar number of metal 'funnels', the like of which they had never seen before.

The cone section of the funnel would hold about a pint and a half to two pints, whilst the outlet was configured as a tube some six inches in length and about a quarter of an inch in diameter. They were about to be introduced to the joys of 'boiling out' rifles!

After the bolt has been removed from the breech of the weapon, and with the rifle being held muzzle downwards over a bucket, the spout of the funnel is inserted into the chamber which normally takes the round. It is then a matter of pouring as much boiling water through the barrel as was necessary to flush out the grease or to soften the burnt cordite which fouls the bore after firing.

By the time that this had been accomplished, a fair amount of grease had been transferred to tunics and trousers which would now also have to be cleaned if punishment was to be avoided.

Eventually the stage was reached where the rifle could be 'pulled through'.

In the butt of the rifle behind a spring-loaded flap in the brass base-plate, there was a cavity which held not only a vial of thin oil and the 'pull-through', but also a small roll of flannelette. This was the 'four by two', these being the dimensions of the piece to be torn off, expressed in inches and as marked on the roll. The 'pull-through' was a length of strong cord with a cylindrical brass weight at one end, its diameter being such as to allow it to pass through the barrel of the rifle. At the other end of the cord, there was a loop into which a folded piece of fabric could be inserted.

A little oil was then dripped onto the material which was then folded lengthways, twice, then passed halfway through the loop before the weight was inserted in the chamber of the rifle. When it emerged at the muzzle, it was seized and dragged though the barrel by means of the cord. With the butt resting on the ground, both hands were needed for the task – one to hold the rifle round the stock just behind the foresight, the other hand having the cord wrapped round it to haul the oiled wad through the weapon.

This ritual, in time, would become as automatic as breathing. "Clean, bright, and slightly oiled" would be the mantra to accompany the action.

As the Army put it, the rifle was the soldier's personal weapon, his best friend, to be cared for and kept clean as if his life depended on it BECAUSE ONE DAY, IT WOULD!

The serial number of the rifle also had to be memorised.

So, with rifles and equipment cleaned, once the evening meal had been eaten, the rest of the day was theirs. That is, after boots and brasses had been polished. Then, of course, there was the not inconsiderable task of getting the rifle grease out of their uniforms.

This was easily done. Fred, having worked in a woollen mill was used to this kind of situation. He had been down to the transport lines to see one of the drivers he knew by sight. For the princely sum of a packet of ten 'Woodbine' cigarettes, he 'bought' a couple of pints of petrol which they siphoned out of the tank of one of the lorries. This made short work of getting the uniforms back to presentability.

When everyone in Fred's billet had cleaned their uniforms, Tom took the remaining petrol down the road to the next billet where he sold it for TWENTY cigarettes.

From that time on, the days were more than filled with rifle drill and bayonet practice, as well as field craft and infantry manoeuvres out on the open moorland.

Then, one day, twenty rounds of ammunition were issued to each of them. They were to actually fire their SMLE rifles for the first time. (They would learn that the initials stood for Short Magazine Lee Enfield, and that the calibre was 0·303 inches).

Firing ranges had been constructed on the top of Otley Chevin, a heather-covered plateau which was a local beauty spot. In peacetime, it had been a favourite location for picnics and summer walks for families from miles around. Needless to say, it had been cordoned off "for the time being".

The first firing practice was five rounds at five hundred yards range. This was to let the first-time users of the rifle get to know the feel of it and its characteristics. One such was the 'kick' it produced when fired. This exercise would produce the Ledford

Bantams' first casualty, a broken collarbone, sustained by one private who could not have been paying attention to the instructor.

The drill was to clamp the thing to the shoulder as tightly as possible, then to grip it even tighter, as the trigger was squeezed (not pulled!). It still gave one hell of a kick but nothing like the one the rifleman would get if he merely rested the butt against his shoulder.

They would learn that this kick could be used to extract the bayonet from a body if the bayonet had jammed in the victim's ribs, for example. In this instance, the rifle would be held away from the rifleman's body and allowed to move backwards as a round was fired into the corpse. This, apparently, worked every time.

It was during field craft training and manoeuvres across the open countryside that Tom's skills in this area, not to mention his uncanny accuracy with his rifle became apparent. Captain Yorke on hearing this sent for Tom and asked why this should be so. When asked about his peacetime occupation, he said he was an 'estate worker'. When asked specifically what he did in this capacity, Tom said that he was a sort of gamekeeper.

He was immediately promoted to the rank of Corporal (acting, unpaid) and given responsibility for the field craft, together with some of the musketry training. As Capt. Yorke was to say later, Gardner knew more about field craft than the instructors, and was as good a shot, if not better, than anybody on the training staff.

What could have been a decisive element had now been introduced into the group, but it did not turn out that way. As Billy remarked "Wi' 'is tapes,'e's no wuss nor 'e were afore 'e got'em. 'e just 'as more to do now but 'e gets no more brass for doin' it! If ony yan 'as to 'ev 'em, it might 'as well be yan o' oor lot!"

A few days later, the Ledfords took their second casualty. This time, it was the commanding officer of 4 Platoon, Lt. Brydon. It was a simple accident which unfortunately resulted in a broken ankle for him.

When C Company were advancing across the moors in 'artillery formation', he had stood on a clump of heather which just happened to be concealing a gap between two rocks. When he fell forward, as his foot was jammed in the gap, something had to give. It did. Unfortunately it was his ankle.

Forty eight hours later, his replacement arrived. This was a Lt. Richardson. He had been a peacetime volunteer in the Green Howards. Before mobilisation, he had been a reporter with the Yorkshire Post. His particular area of expertise was court work, both local and county.

Although living in Harrogate, his work took him as far afield as was necessary, particularly if a 'juicy' case was to be covered. During the course of his travels, he had come across Corporal Gardner (as he now was).

One night in the officers' mess, he remarked that he was surprised to find a convicted poacher in a position of authority. Not unnaturally, eyebrows were raised, and questions asked as to the identity of the felon.

Next day, Tom was required to report to Capt. Yorke who immediately demanded the truth " --- and no more lies ---". Tom replied, politely, that what he had told him had been the truth. What he had told Capt. Yorke had been enough to answer the questions which had been put to him. He had not volunteered any information he had not been asked for. "Yes, he was an estate 'worker', sort of – he worked his way from one end of an estate to the other. Yes, he was a gamekeeper, but not, perhaps, in its usual sense. When he shot game, he kept it. It was either that or starve."

The outcome was that Tom kept his stripes, but was warned that he must answer all questions fully in future when asked. If he stepped out of line just once more, he would wonder what had hit him!

This exchange would keep Capt. Yorke in drinks in any officers' mess for the rest of his army career. It was now very obvious why Tom was so skilled in the field, and such a good shot.

Chapter 3

By now, it was the beginning of June, and winter was well past. The Bantams had survived the worst conditions imaginable during their training on the bleak, open moorland. As a result, they were hardier and tougher. To Billy, in his experience it was no different from any other winter in the dales.

All the spare fat --- and there had been precious little of that to start with --- had been burned off to be replaced by good, solid muscle. They were bursting with energy just waiting to be used.

They were now on forty eight hours stand-by for the move to join what was to be their Division in the army proper. They were to join the 35th (Bantam) Division at present in camp at Colsterdale near Masham.

All their transport had by now, been repainted in a uniform, khaki drab. The regimental titles and insignia had been added. For good measure, all the vehicles were emblazoned with the divisional symbol. This was a fighting cock, in white, on a scarlet diamond. This badge in embroidered cloth was now proudly carried by all ranks on the upper arms of both sleeves of their tunics just below the regimental titles. The Bantams would now be immediately recognisable wherever they went.

In the days prior to the move, there had been much discussion amongst the officers as to the best route to Masham. There were those who favoured the shortest, more direct road. This would take the column of lorries up Wharfedale to Hubberholme. Here they would take a narrow road over a series of steep climbs to come into Wensleydale at Aysgarth.

Those who knew this part of the world argued strongly against this route. Apart from the steep climbs which would be encountered, there were tight bends to be negotiated on these hills. There was also the fact that as yet, the roads in the upper reaches of the dales had not been tarred. Motor vehicles using these roads could be faced with loose gravel on the bends, a situation which could be very risky if a driver was not familiar with the area or with his heavily loaded lorry

It was eventually decided by a majority vote that the convoy would go down Wharfedale to Pool, then turn northwards on to the Harrogate road. It should then be a straightforward run to Masham once they had reached Ripon..

All went well with Colsterdale being reached without mishap in the late afternoon. As newcomers to the camp, they were in bell tents, all the huts having been allocated to earlier arrivals. This would prove no hardship as it was now summer. Having established themselves in the camp, they now took stock of things.

The 17th Mid-Yorkshires (The Ledford Bantams) were part and parcel of the 35th (Bantam) Division which in itself, was part of 106 Brigade.

Training would now be continued but at a much more urgent pace. Whilst in Ilkley, the 17th Mid-Yorkshires had come to the conclusion that they had learned quickly, and well. As far as they were concerned, there was little else they needed to know. They would soon discover to their dismay that all they had mastered were just the basic elements with which a trained soldier had to be proficient. At least, they could be thankful that they did not have to start from scratch.

Every aspect of training was now intensified. More and more field exercises involving much larger bodies of troops were now the thing. Route marches were increased in distance, now to be endured whilst carrying full kit, a total of about sixty five pounds weight. All this was during the full heat of high summer.

None of Fred's group dropped out, all struggling on, helping each other as necessary. All the time they were suffering under the mounting pressure of training, they were acquiring a standard of fitness which would stand them in good stead during the terrible times which would be on them all too soon. As yet, they were blissfully ignorant of what Fate had in store for them. But make no mistake, a terrible price was to be exacted.

Chapter 4

With the arrival of August, the Division moved at short notice to Salisbury Plain. The move was mainly made by lorry and train, and also by good old-fashioned footslogging. They *were* infantry when all was said and done! The Divisional stores went by train.

Once again the tempo and pressure of training increased. Yet again the emphasis was on stamina and physical fitness. More bayonet-fighting techniques were drummed into them. Skill-at-arms became more and more a priority. Selected individuals were introduced to the Lewis light machine-gun. They practised with it every spare moment of the day until they could change magazines, strip it down and reassemble it in total darkness. Clearing 'stoppages' became as easy as blowing their noses.

Others became 'bombers'. They would be trained to a higher level in the use and application of the Mills '36' grenade.

The yardstick for the selection of potential bombers was whether the man had played cricket. The theory was that as the grenade was roughly the same size and weight of a cricket ball, the handling and throwing of the missile would be second nature to cricketers. This worked reasonably well once the initial distrust of the device had been overcome.

It is an essential facet in the instilling of confidence in the man that he should fuse his own grenades. To do this, the base plug is unscrewed to give access to the cavity into which the fuse and detonator assembly are to be inserted. Until it has been fused, the grenade is inert, dead. It is just a casing containing high explosive, but with no means of firing it. Once the fuse has been inserted, it is a totally different matter.

An experienced bomber can be spotted the moment he picks up the inert grenade. Before he even touches the base plug, he will address himself to the split pin which will be withdrawn by means of the ring attached to it when the bomb is about to be thrown. The open ends of this pin protrude about a quarter of an inch through the lugs which locate the safety lever.

When this pin is pulled out prior to throwing, the grenade is held so that the lever is against the palm of the throwing hand and so will fly off as the bomb is thrown. This releases the spring-loaded plunger which smashes down onto the percussion cap on the end of the fuse connected to the detonator which is fired four seconds later.

The experienced man will spread the open ends of the pin so that a little more effort will be needed to withdraw it. This is to ensure that whilst the pin can still be pulled when circumstances require, there will be little or no chance of it being accidentally dislodged if the ring snags on equipment, for instance.

Having made the bomb secure against mishaps, only then is the plug unscrewed. The fuse assembly is then very carefully picked up. In shape, it is akin to a letter 'J' with only one comparatively safe place to take hold of it. That place is halfway round the 'hook' of the bend. Even then, it is a case of not wasting time but of getting it in place as quickly as possible.

If the fuse is held by the percussion cap at the short end, or by the detonator at the end of the longer, straight section, the heat of the hand could initiate an explosion, with the hand being taken off in the process.

As will be appreciated, the '36' can be a nasty little brute if handled carelessly, but equally, it is a useful friend in tight situations.

Although neither Charlie or Bob had ever played cricket in their lives, the shoulder and upper body strength they possessed as a result of years of labouring made them ideal bombers. The missiles were lost in their hands, and were thrown by them over greater distances than anyone else.

Thirty to forty yards was the distance achieved by average throwers, but these two could put another seven or eight on top of that. Apart from their physical strength, both men were so lacking in imagination as to be almost phlegmatic, All in all, an ideal combination for trainee bombers.

Whilst on Salisbury Plain, Charlie would win the Divisional grenade-throwing contest narrowly beating his pal Bob into second place.

It was whilst the Ledford Bantams were on the Plain that the regiment was taken over by the War Office. It would no longer be funded and supplied at the expense of Ledford and district. The city coat-of-arms was withdrawn and replaced by the white rose of the Mid-Yorkshire Regiment. Although they had, until now been nominally the 17th Battalion of that lot, they were now obviously so.

They had arrived at last! They were now fully and correctly designated, and trained to as high a standard as possible without having been involved in actual combat.

Or so they thought!

Fred had rated as 'rifleman/marksman'. Bob and Charlie were not surprisingly, 'bombers'. Tom still had his stripes but they were now substantive, and paid. He was also a 'marksman'. Billy, whilst not attaining any trade qualification apart from basic 'rifleman', was, however competent to deal with any aspect of the infantryman's calling. William also qualified as 'marksman'.

To mark their skill with their rifles, Fred, Tom and William now wore on the left sleeves of their tunics, just above the cuff, the 'marksman' emblem in the form of crossed rifles, in brass.

The 'bombers' now carried the insignia of their trade in the form of a 'B' within a laurel wreath. This was an embroidered badge in off-white on a khaki ground. This also was worn on the left sleeve but above the elbow just below the Divisional insignia. In addition to adding character to otherwise dull tunics, these proficiency badges had a much more useful effect. This was the adding of a few coppers to their meagre pay.

The Ledford Lads as they were now officially known were indistinguishable from the thousands of soldiers who swarmed across Salisbury Plain. That is, apart from their size. But that was why they were "Bantams", and proud of the title.

One day, Daily Orders required them to parade outside the quartermaster's stores where they would be issued with an item of equipment that was just coming into use on the Western front. This was the steel helmet, which the troops had christened the 'battle bowler', or 'tin hat'.

On being issued with it, they were amused to be told to report to one of the training huts to receive instructions on how it should be worn. Surely the thing could only be plonked on the head and the strap hooked under the chin. How else could it be worn? Daft as the order seemed at first, they were to learn that the helmet was not to be worn in that manner, and for a very good reason.

That style of wearing had been the original intention when it was designed, but the bitter experience of the first troops to do so at the Front had shown that the blast from shells exploding near the wearer had, on occasion, gone under the front of the helmet, and in so doing, had violently yanked it upwards and backwards. This had, like as not, broken the neck of the man it was supposed to protect.

The new line of thinking was that the helmet be worn tilted slightly forward onto the forehead whilst the so-called 'chin-strap' was worn behind the head under the bulge of the skull. Any blast should lift the helmet clear of the head without doing any damage to the wearer. That was the theory as yet to be proved (or disproved) in action. At least, it sounded plausible.

They were also told that the fit of the headgear to the wearer's head could be adjusted by means of the 'head cradle' inside it. The fit should be tight enough to hold the helmet in place, but not so as to be uncomfortable.

As they were absorbing all this information, the Lads began to wonder why the helmets were being issued at all. There had been no suggestion or even any rumour of an imminent move to France. Why too was there an insistence on safety if the helmet was worn correctly? Then there had been this emphasis on "--- the significant reduction in head wounds from shell splinters since the protective head gear had been issued ----".

Two days passed in an agony of suspense, aggravated not only by the absence of any definite information, but more so by the increasingly wild and inaccurate guesses now flying round the camp. Finally, all was made clear. The next training exercise would be as near possible as it could be to the real thing without involving any real fighting.

An 'Infantry advance on a battalion front' was to be practised, supported by an artillery barrage. The novices would also experience for the first time live, small arms fire in very close proximity to them.

Machine-guns operated by skilled marksmen would be set up on one side boundary and aimed across the line of advance. These guns would lay down a carpet of fire in front of the troops, the bullets striking the ground about twenty feet in front of them. They would be firing on 'fixed lines', and traversing so as to keep pace with, but in front of the advancing troops until the rounds were striking the spot which had been designated as the enemy position.

At this stage, the guns would lift so as to be firing about ten feet above the ground, then swing round so as to be firing over the heads of the trainees who would now experience the whizz and crack of live rounds passing close by them!

Meanwhile, artillery would be maintaining a standing barrage on the target zone.

At a given moment, this would also lift but to a point beyond the 'enemy strongpoint'. So, the machine-gun fire must not be overtaken, nor must anyone raise himself too high when walls had to be crossed.

In order to simulate incoming enemy shells, observers would explode by wireless signals, packs of guncotton previously buried at random across the training ground. The 'enemy' explosions would be close enough to the advancing troops so as to cause concern, but not so close or violent as to injure them. This always presupposed that the advance progressed at a constant, regular rate. These simulated shell bursts would take place both in front of and behind the line of advance.

It was at this stage of the lecture that the colonel in charge of proceedings introduced the notion of 'an acceptable level of casualties'. Some genius in 'cloud-cuckoo land' had decreed that any casualties sustained during the course of a 'live-fire' exercise were tolerable up a level of five per cent of the troops involved. Provided that no one was killed, then any enquiry would be a limited, local affair. Above that, or for any deaths, it would be a full-blown inquest.

So, with that cheery thought in mind, the Lads set out a first light the next morning.

At first, the day went well for all concerned, not the least for those doing the advancing. There was the expected, usual crop of minor accidents such as bruises, cuts, sprains and so on, but there were no mishaps caused by the live fire or the explosions --- well, not at first ---.

As the day wore on, with the repeating of the exercise, fatigue set in, and as tempers became frayed, the rate of advance became erratic. Some rushed forward, some lagged behind. The inevitable result was mistiming in the firing of the buried charges.

Things started to go awry when a burst of machine-gun fire struck the face of a half-buried boulder. The resulting ricochets whizzed past the heads of the advancing warriors much closer than had been intended, and in doing so, caused a mild panic. The dash forward coincided with the firing of a charge which exploded just as a man was about to step on it. He tripped up in alarm, and as he fell, lost his grip on his rifle. This flew to one side and struck the man who was slightly ahead of the faller. As all rifles had bayonets fixed, this soldier was speared through the calf.

Two others were to receive minor flesh wounds from errant shell splinters.

The Ledfords came through this baptism of fire unscathed.

At the conclusion of the exercise, there had only been these three casualties. As this figure was well below the magic five per cent, and no one had been killed, it was deemed to be acceptable. Whilst 'acceptable' to those running the exercise, it is unlikely that the recipients of the wounds found them to be so.

The following day, gas masks were issued to all and sundry. These were not the crude affairs consisting of goggles, nose clips and mouth pads which had been rushed out to the trenches following the first gas attack at St. Julien in Belgian Flanders earlier in the year. The ones now being issued were an improvement on these, but only just. This type was the 'hypo' smoke helmet, which despite its name gave better protection (but not much) from gas than before.

It consisted of a hood of cotton and flannel impregnated with chemicals. In its front was a celluloid window to allow forward vision. When not in use, it was carried in a canvas pouch worn on the body along with all the other paraphernalia the infantryman had to carry when going into action. When in use, with the hood covering the head, the skirt of the device was tucked in to the collar of the tunic.

It was a crude arrangement and did afford some protection, but not totally. The strong point in its favour was that it gave confidence to the wearer, albeit to some extent, false confidence.

Having donned the hoods, 'C' Company marched to a hut which had been dubbed "The Gasworks". This was a windowless construction with only two doors, one in each end of what was in effect, a long corridor. This must have been designed with a specific purpose in mind. What this was, they were now about to discover.

By section, each platoon entered the building. Inside, they were halted and the lights switched on. All they could see through the misting-up eyepiece was a swirling, greyish mist. After a couple of minutes of breathing 'normally' (the instructor's term!) through the mask, they were told to lift one edge of the its skirt out of their tunics. Immediately everyone started to cough and choke whilst their eyes watered copiously. Everybody was affected, apart from the instructor who left his mask in place, untouched.

The grey mist was smoke from a smoke canister with a bit of tear gas mixed in for good measure. This was to show that the masks did work.

The exit door at the far end was now opened whereupon the victims rushed out in to the fresh air, tearing the hoods from their heads as they went.

No time was wasted in allowing them to recover from the experience. There was a war on, and it would not wait. Off they went, this time at the double. Once again there was an official reason for this ---- the harder they had to breathe, the sooner the smoke would be out of their lungs.

Soon they were at another training field, as yet unvisited. This was where they would learn the art of trench construction and the correct use of sandbags. Having dug the trench and sandbagged it, they would learn how to establish a barbed-wire entanglement in front of it. No breaks would be allowed for any reason, not even for meals, until the job had been finished to the total satisfaction of the instructors who did, of course, take breaks from time to time. It was very much case of "Do as I say, not as I do. This training is for your benefit, not mine!"

Digging the trench was no problem for the ex-miners, the labourers, or the farm lads, although it was somewhat hard going for the 'townies'. Fred and his pals worked together and had their length of trench finished in good time, thus getting a bit of 'stand-easy' time whilst waiting for the rest to finish.

Then came the sandbags. Each one had to be three-quarters full, not totally filled, thus allowing for the neck of the bag to be tied. The slack fill also allowed for the bag to be moulded into shape when placed in position.

The correct method of laying the bags was demonstrated. After putting one in place, it was then hammered with the back of the shovel. This was why a slack fill was essential. The contents of the bag could move under this treatment, becoming almost solid when correctly laid. The end result was a firm, stable construction which would raise the front of the trench and continue the wall upwards to the required height, It would also be capable of taking the weight of a moving soldier leaving the trench when going out on patrol. The trainees were then shown how to produce the correct degree of slope, the 'batter', at the back and front of the parapet needed to give it stability.

What was equally important was that a properly built parapet would stop and hold enemy bullets. Uncovered, bare earth would allow ricochets.

Then it was time for the barbed wire.

In the early days of the war, wire had been carried on wooden stakes which had had to be hammered into the ground. The noise this made had advertised the presence of the wiring parties to the enemy, and indicated the location where they were working.

Subsequently, screw pickets had been introduced which did not need driving into the ground. The new supports were made of steel rod, one end of which was like a giant corkscrew. Along the main length, loops had been formed to carry the wire. These supports were literally screwed into the earth by means of a bar through one of the loops. In practice, the pickets could be set up reasonably quietly. It was when the wire took charge that things became noisier. The noise took the form of choice obscenities and oaths delivered with feeling in flat, Yorkshire accents.

Bearing in mind its purpose, the wire had to be tough, unyielding and able to stand up to abuse -- physical, that is --- it was getting plenty of the verbal variety! Come to think of it, its character was not unlike that of the typical "Tyke", a Yorkshireman.

As if that was not enough, the wire carried vicious barbs at regular intervals. Despite the leather gauntlets which had been issued to each man, it was still a hell of a job getting the stuff unwound. It would insist on retaining the curvature of that accursed coil. Then it just refused to go through the loops of the pickets. When that had been managed, it still had to be pulled tight!

And that was only the first run, a single wire.

The next, higher length was the mixture as before, but much worse. There now was a lower run of wire on which the next and subsequent runs would inevitably become snagged.

The instructor, whilst not being totally satisfied, was at least half human. Although he criticised the 'tangle', he did not require it to be rebuilt. As they had discovered, barbed wire was bastard stuff to handle, even when there was no one shooting at you! This last point had, until now, been completely overlooked by all on the wiring exercise.

As it was now well into the evening, the cookhouse was the next port of call where a cold meal was waiting for them. They had missed lunch, and were about three hours late for tea. Whilst standing in line for their food, the sorry-looking bunch inspected the rips in their uniforms. These would have to be repaired before they could turn in for the night. Then there was the small matter of the bloodstains round the damage springing from the cuts and gashes inflicted by the wire.

At last they had been fed, all repairs had been effected and kit cleaned. They were now ready for tomorrow, and whatever pain and suffering was in store for them.

Came the dawn and with breakfast over, they were told that the day's training schedule as posted in Daily Orders had been cancelled for the day. They were to do another battalion advance, again with artillery support, but this time, under cover of 'gas'. Respirators would be worn. That was why they had been issued. Smoke would be used instead of the genuine article. They would get more than enough of the real stuff at the Front.

Gunners and guns had been standing by for just such a day as this when the weather conditions would be just right – overcast and with some mist. In addition, a slight breeze was blowing from the 'start line' in the general direction of the advance. The smoke screen would be held in the mist without dispersing too quickly, and carried forward on the breeze.

As the observers would not be able to make out the exact whereabouts of the troops without being in amongst them, there would be no firing of hidden charges. The machine-gun fire on fixed lines would still be used, however, but this time, it would strike about twice as far ahead of them than it had done in the earlier exercise. The switch to overhead firing when it came would still be to about ten feet above their heads. On this occasion, as they could not be seen clearly, if at all, it would take place after a set time had elapsed, when the guns could be expected to be firing on the target area.

The field guns were also laid to fire further forward ahead than would have been the case with unrestricted visibility. They too would advance their fire after an elapsed time calculated so that the exploding shells should be well ahead of the advancing infantry. It too would cease after a pre-determined period. In theory at least, shells and bullets would be kept well head of the infantry.

The 17th Mid-Yorkshires formed up for the start. The assorted gunfire commenced, whistles sounded and they were on the move. Into the murk they went, stumbling and tripping over tussocks of grass and the exposed roots of shrubs and bushes. If anyone was unlucky, --- and most were ---, they would put a foot in one of the many miniature craters left by the charges exploded during previous exercises. As these obstacles were invisible until encountered, surprise was total. The victim fell full length, picked himself up and carried on until he did it again. The really unlucky ones broke or twisted wrists or ankles.

At last, and not before time, the trial was over. Once again, the casualty rate was minimal in official terms, and so was 'acceptable.

By now, it was January, 1916, and the depths of winter. Route marches of varying distances and difficulties were still a regular feature of the training routine. Physical exercises involving the use of Indian clubs were endured, with the men stripped to the waist in the snow and frost which gripped Salisbury Plain. Other testing drills devised by staff officers ensconced in heated buildings were also imposed on the long-suffering squaddies in the dreadful weather conditions.

As these invariably involved the use of the rifle, it was vital to ensure that snow and ice, not to mention mud, was kept out of the breech and muzzle of the weapon. Spare puttees which had been 'acquired' were cut into suitable lengths and bound round the trigger and bolt area. As Fred had damaged a thumb when on the wiring stunt, he had been issued with two leather thumb stalls, one of which he was wearing. The spare made an ideal cover for the muzzle. Slipped over the end, and with the tapes tied round the stock just behind the foresight, it solved the problem very nicely.

Chapter 5

January was almost at an end when orders showed that the expected move to France was imminent. They were now on a moment's notice stand-by. Each man checked, and double-checked his equipment against the day that they would be off. This turned out to be the 31st of January, with Southampton being the port of embarkation. They would set foot in France at Le Havre the following day.

With the midday meal swallowed, 106 Brigade started to move, assembling by regiment, at first on the parade ground, and then, as that filled up, on the surrounding grassland.

The troops would be taken by road the dozen or so miles to Salisbury where trains would be waiting. They would go there either by lorry or by charabancs provided by the local coach and haulage company.

For some reason, the Ledfords were amongst the first to move out. They drew the short straw, being allocated lorries as their means of transport. The journey was not the most comfortable, their vehicles having leaf springs which felt as if they had been designed to cope with much heavier loads than a platoon of troops, even with full equipment. On solid tyres, grinding along at about twenty miles an hour over badly surfaced roads replete with potholes, the journey seemed to last forever.

But arrive they did, and dismounted at the railway station on legs wracked with cramp. Each unit filed onto the trains, which when full, pulled out and headed for Southampton. As one full train pulled out, another one took its place, whereupon the whole procedure started all over again.

Whilst the troop movement was taking place, the divisional stores and *matériel* were loaded onto the lorries which were to be driven directly to the port for shipment to France.

On leaving the trains, the troops assembled on the open quayside opposite the ex-passenger ferries which would take them across the English Channel to the Continent. These were no longer resplendent in their peacetime company liveries, but were now a dull, Admiralty blue-grey colour overall.

As the soldiers waited, a chilly, dank mixture of drizzle and sea mist drifted in from the Solent. Soon the quay was solid with troops standing there in the open, slowly but surely becoming soaked to the skin.

It was while the Lads were standing there in abject misery, with the rain dripping from their caps and seeping down their necks, they were to get an indication of the quality of the officer they had as their platoon commander.

He had noticed that although the rank and file were out in the appalling weather, all the officers (apart from himself) were nowhere to be seen. On investigating, he found them all to be under cover, tucking in to a meal which had been laid on for them by the Port Movement Officer. On enquiring what arrangements had been made to feed the men, he was informed that there were far too many for that, and also, as the Port Canteen would not be able to cope with the numbers involved, that would be closed as well.

When asked when embarkation would commence so as to get the men under cover, he was told "In due course!" The fact that the ferries were in place, moored alongside the dock-wall with the gangplanks already in place was not the concern of Lt, Richardson. "Boarding would take place at the scheduled time, and not before." When asked when that would be, the P.M.O. refused to divulge what he described as "vital information". "Didn't the Lieutenant know there war on?"

Seeing that nothing was to be gained by flogging what was obviously a very dead horse, Lt. Richardson left the cosy warmth of the office and returned to 4 Platoon where he took up his position at their front. A little later, he produced a packet of twenty cigarettes. Going up to his sergeant, he told him to share them out amongst the men, adding "Smokers among you will share one between two."

A spare brigadier gazing out into the murk after his post-prandial brandy saw what was going on. His orderly was immediately despatched into the gloom of the night with orders to tell "that officer" to report to the brigadier immediately. The orderly was on the point of asking "Which officer?" when he realised that there was only ONE officer outside on the quay, Lt. Richardson.

Lt. Richardson reported as ordered and was asked what he was doing outside when he could be inside, out of the weather. He replied that as an officer, his first responsibility was for the welfare of the men under his command before he saw to his own comfort. He would not leave his platoon to endure the conditions which prevailed outside, especially when no arrangement had been made to cater for any of the men, never mind 4 Platoon.

He would not leave his platoon to suffer while he filled his belly in a cosy mess hall. He would therefore put up with what the elements (and the Army) chose to inflict on his platoon, and would suffer it with them. And, with a smart salute, and an equally smart 'about turn', he left the office and returned to the misery outside.

Eventually, embarkation commenced at 0500hrs. It was now February 1st, and the middle of winter. After five or six hours standing in the open, soaked to the skin and frozen stiff, not to mention being battered by squally showers of sleet and snow, the men could barely move when the time came to do so.

The ship which was to take them across to France was "La Marguerite". Until taken over by the Royal Navy in 1915, she had worked between Llandudno and her home port of Liverpool. She had a gross tonnage of 1,554 and was a side-wheel paddle-steamer with twin funnels and could do twenty knots. Built in Glasgow in 1894, she was licensed to carry 2,077 passengers, (in peacetime, that is!)

She had originally been built for a new passenger service between London and Boulogne, but had been found to be too large for the City stretches of the Thames. When the departure point was moved to Tilbury with a call at Margate, the service was scrapped. Although it had been a popular excursion, it was not profitable.

Now, after operating off the north coast of Wales, she was back to visiting France. She would carry over 360,000 troops covering some 52,000 miles doing so before resuming her peacetime role in 1919.

This, then, was the ship which was to carry them across the Channel to the conflict which was tearing Europe apart.

They hobbled and stumbled across the cobbled quay and staggered up the brow, or 'gangplank' to landlubbers like the Lads who had never even seen the sea before in their lives, let alone sailed on it.

As each man stepped aboard, a mug of hot tea was thrust into his hands together with a doorstep-sized bacon sandwich. These had been produced by the Navy in time to give to the troops as they embarked. Whereas the Army hierarchy had not thought it necessary for the ordinary footslogger to know how long he was to be kept unfed and exposed to the elements, the 'matelots' had known for some time precisely when loading would begin. Hence the exact timing of the 'char and wads'. Although all the lower ranks of the Senior Service considered that they were 'senior' in all respects, the manner in which the rank and file of the army had been treated was not on! Somehow, enough mugs and supplies had been found to enable all the troops to be fed to some extent.

When, at last, everybody and everything was on board, mooring lines were cast off, and the troopship (which the ferry now was) moved slowly away from the dock-wall, down the Solent and into the open sea, (the English Channel) where they would meet their first test. It would be the first time that many of them had ever seen the sea let alone sail on it. Would they suffer from seasickness, always assuming that they knew that this affliction existed? Would they succumb to the dreaded *"mal dee mare"* as the show-offs insisted on calling it?

They were to be lucky once again and were blessed with a flat calm for the crossing. Only the odd few unfortunates here and there would be afflicted. These could be referred to as 'first phase sufferers'. The 'second phase' were those jammed anywhere within range of those who were actually sick. Friendships came under severe strain on several occasions.

The Needles were a momentary source of interest, but only to those who could see them.

Then came cries announcing that the French coast had been sighted.

They entered the estuary of the river, the Seine, and the port of Le Havre lay in front of them. Mooring was attended to with swift efficiency, the gangplank put in place and disembarkation commenced It was now mid-morning. The moment their boots struck dry land, they would be in France. The big adventure was about to begin!

Part Two
"Innocents Abroad"

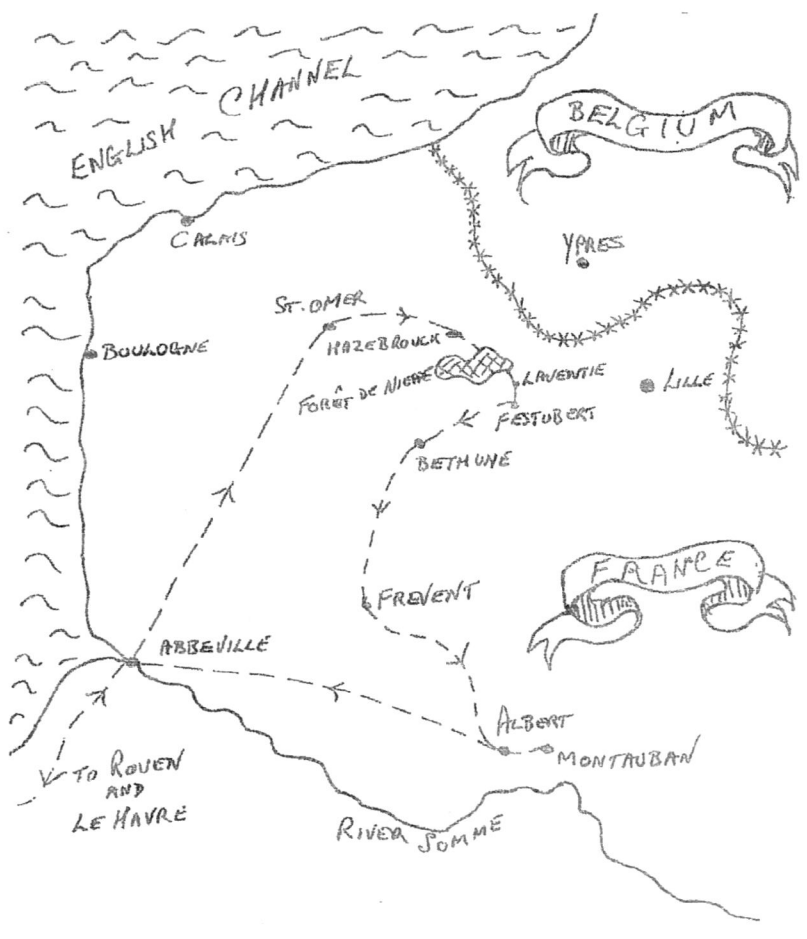

*Fred's Travels in France
February, 1916 – August, 1916*

Chapter 6

As the troops disembarked, the individual units were directed to the part of the quay which had been allocated to them as their assembly area. This operation was being supervised by a rather flustered, very young second lieutenant. Having established groups up and down the cobbled waterfront, he would dash back and move them to a totally different location. This happened not just once, but on several occasions.

After the Ledford Bantams had been moved yet again, Charlie started to bleat like a sheep. In no time at all, it had been taken up by the rest of "C" Company, and soon by all the troops ashore. Charlie was heard to remark "It's a good job we did our training in a cattle market!" When he described the Movement Officer as running around like a headless chicken, William pulled him up sharply, suggesting that his last comment should be rephrased. When Charlie asked why, his attention was drawn to their Divisional emblem, the Fighting Cock. Whilst not actually superstitious, William thought it might be wiser not to push their luck!

By now, chaos reigned supreme. The young officer had completely lost control, and was well out of his depth. He was bright red in the face with embarrassment, and looked as if at any moment soon, he would stamp his foot in frustration, and burst into tears.

Officers now took back control of their units, ordering the men to stand fast and not to move unless given direct orders to do so by one of their own seniors. The Movement Officer was then told that this would be the position until the chaos had been sorted out in order to prevent the current shambles getting any worse.

Individuals stood easy, or sat on the ground as fancy took them. Captain Yorke then instructed platoon commanders to remain with their men whilst he went for a look round. At the same time, he asked if any man spoke French.

William Sugden did, as it happened. So the two of them headed for the open doors of one of the port's transit sheds and went inside. There they were greeted by the smell of cooking and the sight of scrubbed, deal tables of army origin. Venturing deeper into the building, they came across army cooks hard at work.

Further investigation disclosed an agitated catering officer who looked at his watch at frequent intervals. He could not understand the delay in getting the first lot of troops in to the sheds, fed and out again so that the next lot could come in. Apparently troop movements were to continue practically all day with the catering staff working without any breaks so as to provide all newcomers with a hot meal.

"Right" said Capt. Yorke. "The first hundred will be in as soon as I can get back to them and give the order."

Other officers on seeing what was happening followed suit, ignoring the protests of Port officialdom. Each platoon provided a volunteer to guard packs and other equipment which was left stacked on the quay. Rifles were 'piled' by means of the swivels located underneath the weapon just behind the muzzle. These interlocked to produce a pyramidical stack of rifles with their muzzles pointing upwards and their butts resting on the ground. The volunteer would have his meal brought out to him, with the promise of 'seconds' if he wanted more. Charlie volunteered, and, on getting his plateful, started to wolf it down

Just then, he realised that a French railway worker who had been wandering suspiciously close to some of the baggage was now no longer in sight. Charlie stood up to see where he had got to and found him opening "D" Company packs. Charlie went for him.

When the Frenchman stood up, he was a good head and shoulders taller than Charlie. This was not really surprising, Charlie being a Bantam.

This disparity in height seemed to amuse the Frenchman who laughed, knocked the Yorkshireman's cap to the ground, then spat full in his face. Whilst noticing Charlie's size, he had overlooked the fact that he was squarely and solidly built. Nor could he have known the Bantam's background. He had been brought up in back-to-back slum tenements where it was very much a case of the survival of the fittest, or the quickest. Charlie was more at home fighting dirty than trying to keep to the rules. He probably never knew that any rules existed in the first place.

His very harsh, formative years had been followed by a life of labouring, On top of all that, the months of hard training had, if anything, increased his toughness. Did he but know it, the Frenchman had picked on the wrong man.

Wiping the spittle from his eyes, Charlie saw that "Mongsewer Froggy" was wearing *espadrilles,* although he did not know they were called that. What he did see was that they were rope-soled canvas shoes. Charlie of course was wearing his ammunition boots which had just been newly studded before he left England. To his mind, this was the ideal combination.

Stepping inside the wild swing which came his way, he performed his best parade-ground halt.

"Right thigh and sole of boot parallel to the ground, shin vertical, the foot is then brought smartly to the ground to make as much noise as possible when the sole of the boot strikes the ground". That was how the drill manual required it to be done.

On this occasion, there was no noise of the boot striking the ground because it didn't. As the Frenchman's foot was directly underneath, *he* made the noise as he screamed in agony with a crushed foot.

As he lurched forward to cradle his mangled foot, he leaned over the top of Charlie's head. This was too good an opportunity to be missed! Charlie sprang up and slammed the top of his head against the underside of his adversary's jaw with a crack which could be heard across the docks. The man went down as if pole-axed. Having checked the would-be thief's pockets and removing anything which might have come from army baggage, Charlie tipped him off the jetty. As he did so, Capt. Yorke dashed up and demanded to know what was going on. Charlie said that when he had caught the Frenchman going through the baggage, he had been attacked by the Frenchman when he had challenged him.

As he explained "Don't thee fret thissen, sir. 'E knocked mi 'at off, then gobbed in mi face. Ah don't tek kindly to that even from an Englishman. An' 'e's a furriner!"

"But why push him into the river where he might drown?"

"Ah wur just tidyin' up. Onyway, ah knew 'e wor awreight, ah didn't 'av to luk. 'E fell in a bo-at. Ah know 'e did. Ah 'eeard 'im 'it it!"

It was at this point that the conversation languished. There was not much more that could be usefully added. Apart from that, Capt. Yorke was having a struggle to keep a straight face.

After everyone had eaten, William's command of French came into play. As the ferry had been making its way into the harbour, Cpt. Yorke had spotted an impressive array of chimneys. As they were carrying smoke up into the atmosphere, then the furnaces beneath them must be working. That meant heat, and plenty of it. Heat was necessary to dry the troops' wet clothing if something could be arranged. Someone who could speak French was obviously required for the initial enquiries and negotiations.

Off they went and entered the factory through the first door they came to. As far as the factory manager was concerned, of course they could come in to dry out, but not all at once. Provided that only small, manageable groups came in at any time, they were more than welcome.

As "C" Company had arranged things, they were the first to avail themselves of the heat in front of the furnaces in the boiler-room. With their soaking uniforms off and held out to the heat, their underclothes dried out on the wearers. With a good meal inside them, and now dry and comfortable as they went to board the train, the Lads were now ready for the next stage of their journey to the Front.

They found that they were not to be in passenger carriages on the train but had been put in railway vans. Not exactly the height of luxury, these were stencilled "*10 chevaux, 40 hommes*". For the benefit of the non-linguists, William told them that this meant "10 horses, 40 men". It was quite obvious that the previous occupants had been horses.

Boarding was delayed until brooms had been 'borrowed' from the railway workers who should have cleaned out the trucks, but who had been too busy watching what was going on elsewhere to do the work they had been paid for. With the vans swept out, as they were still none too sweet, the doors on both sides were left open for the journey.

The train started, then after about a mile, shuddered to a halt. It did this again a little later. This was to be the pattern for the rest of the day, although the periods when the train was actually moving gradually became longer.

At one stage when the train was at a standstill, a hail of stones rattled around inside the van. One of them hit Charlie who by now was beginning to think that the French did not like him. A crowd of youngsters would throw the stones and then retreat on their bicycles. They moved in close when the train moved off, keeping pace with the open van as they followed the road which ran between the railway line and a wide, deep, overflowing drainage ditch. They shouted what presumably was abuse as they did so.

Charlie was nothing if not observant. Up ahead, he had seen that level-crossing gates were set against the train. It would have to stop. The stretch of road the youngsters were now on was dead straight without any side-roads or paths joining it. Just ahead and blocking the road was a herd of cows. With the railway on one side, and the ditch on the other, the youths were trapped.

Charlie was out in a flash and grabbed the lad who had hit him with the stone. While he was giving him a good working-over, Charlie kept the others at bay by vigorous use of his boots. If it had been needed, there would have been plenty of help available from the others in the railway van. However, none was required as he was doing a good job on his own.

Just then, the train whistle sounded signalling imminent departure. So, as a farewell gesture Charlie tossed the lad into the foul-smelling stagnant water in the ditch. His bicycle followed a moment later. Honour satisfied, Charlie climbed back on into the van just as it started to move.

The night was spent in a warehouse just outside Abbeville which had been commandeered in the early stages of the war for just such a purpose as this. Camp kitchens had been established on the premises and cooking was in full swing. Savoury smells filled the air.

Later on when they had eaten, as they casually chatted about the day's events, William mentioned the two unfriendly acts which had been directed against them. He raised the question of the so-called *Entente Cordiale,* the Friendship Agreement which Britain and France had both signed in 1904.

Cpt. Yorke agreed that it did not seem to be working too well in the part of France they were in, particularly as far as the locals were concerned. He went on to remind everyone that France, not Germany, had been our traditional enemy since 1066 when William of Normandy had invaded England. Since then, our two countries had fought each other over the centuries until the Battle of Waterloo in 1815. All in all, we had been at war with each other for the best part of 800 years. Ingrained traditions so long established do not just vanish overnight.

Wearing great-coats, and with the doors firmly closed, the men were reasonably warm in the building. The floors were not very welcoming as beds, but following the totally sleepless night they had spent standing soaked to the skin, they were past caring. The moment they lay down, they became unconscious.

Reveillé next morning was at 0400hrs. A quick 'lick and a promise' passed for washing, followed by a token shave if anyone in authority was watching.

Breakfast was already prepared and waiting for them. Porridge (if wanted), two fried eggs and a couple of rashers of bacon followed by a thick slice of bread, a chunk of butter, and a dollop of plum and apple jam. How they would come to hate that jam before much longer!

It was here that they learned how to cope with a combination of new bread and hard butter. Butter in this condition is impossible to spread. If an attempt is made, all that happens is that it tears a hole in the bread. The more one tries, the bigger the hole becomes until eventually, the precious butter falls through, and ends up on the floor. This is not very good if the floor is that of a barn which has previously housed cattle.

No. The most practical solution is to first spread the jam on the bread, and then to chip the hard butter onto the jam. As it all ends up in the stomach, it does not really matter in which order it arrives there.

Muster parade and roll call followed. All present and correct ----- as was to be expected at this stage of the adventure.

On board the train once more, it was pretty much the same as yesterday --- start, crawl along for a while, and then stop. A little, later, start up, crawl along for a while, and then stop again. So it went on till it just about drove them out of their minds.

Then, early in the afternoon, St.Omer was reached. As this was as far as the train was to take them, the men left the vans with feelings of relief. Somebody asked about the mid-day meal they had missed. When and where would it be available? Talk about "Innocents abroad". "They were soldiers going to war. They were not holiday-makers on a Cook's Tour! They would be fed when they got to camp, and not before!"

As they waited on the station platform, they thought they could hear the rumble of thunder. This was strange as the sky was a crisp, clear blue without a cloud to be seen anywhere. Then it dawned on them. What they could hear was the noise of artillery in the distance. They were not all that far from the Front.

Leaving the station, they crossed the footbridge over the canal, and turned left down a gently sloping road, heading in an easterly direction. At the foot of the hill, they passed the local *caserne* or town barracks on the right-hand side of the road.

They were now making for Hazebrouck, about ten or eleven miles away. This was when they first made their acquaintance with the *pavé*, the cobbled roads of northern France and Belgium. It would not be the last by any means.

Three and a half hours later, having reached the town they were making for, they turned off onto an even smaller road than the one they had just left. Following the bank of yet another canal, it headed somewhat more to the south than had been the case when they left St. Omer. A further six miles saw them entering the *Forêt de Nieppe* where they left the road and turned off amongst the trees. Ahead of them, they could see lines of wooden huts. These were to be their first real quarters in France.

Once their huts had been allocated to them, the next priority was a meal, and were they ready for it! Then followed the lengthy process of cleaning kit, uniforms and themselves. This was badly needed. Tomorrow was another day and would soon be on them. In the Army, what had happened today would be no excuse for scruffiness on tomorrow's parades.

The day over at last, they turned in to sleep the sleep of the dead. They were so exhausted, they gave no thought for the morrow, and what it might bring.

Next day turned out to be what the Army euphemistically refers to as a 'rest day'. It was spent getting fully organised in camp, and then unloading the lorries which had arrived sometime during the night bringing their stores from England. All the provisions and equipment had to be manhandled into the empty store sheds and armouries.

After the midday meal had been taken, Lt. Richardson instructed 4 Platoon to get cleaned up after they had completed the day's work required of them, and to report to the cookhouse for the early tea at 1600 hrs. he had arranged for them. They were then to assemble at the camp gates without equipment, but wearing belts and uniform for a short march to 'stretch their legs', (not that they needed stretching).

The march would be about six miles in all, the outward 'leg' finishing very conveniently at an *estaminet* (or inn) which he had spotted just before they arrived at the camp. They would visit this establishment in order to 'practise speaking French'.

Just before leaving England, every man had been given a copy of " Hugo's Imitated Pronunciation of the French Language". This was a booklet listing useful English phrases printed down the left-hand side of the page, with opposite, the French equivalent together with its pronunciation written as English sounds. The meanings were also given. It may seem complicated, but in practice, it worked.

They would have until 2100hrs. to try the system. By then, it would be time to return to camp. They were to be on their best behaviour, with no signs of drunkenness. If anyone overindulged, he would be for the 'high jump'.

On arrival they went into what seemed to be quite a respectable establishment, and not at all like some they would come across in the future. Billy, who had taken the lieutenant's words literally was itching to try his luck at speaking French and said he would order a meal, provided no one was too fussy about what he wanted.

Nothing daunted, he started. Waving his arms around the table to include all six of them, he asked for "*Burf 'n' pom dterr*". Another inclusive wave of his hand was followed by the word "*Vang*". (He still had to find the page dealing with numbers.) He had also decided that as they were In France, he'd try the wine. He was overjoyed when, despite his north Yorkshire accent, not only did they get it, they got the meat and potatoes he had ordered, as well.

After he had finished eating, Billy was asked what he thought of the meal.

"It were awreight Ah reckon. 'T meat were tasty enough but not like t'stuff we get at 'ome!" (Did he but know it, he had eaten horsemeat for the first time in his life. He would eat more whilst he was in France).

"As for t'wine, 'A've put better stuff on mi meat and taties. What 'A really could do wi' is a pint or two of good Yorkshire ale --- that'd set me up for't war!"

William, although fluent in the language, had decided to keep quiet and let his mates press on with their attempts to get to grips with the language rather than appear a 'know-all' and do all the ordering. He would, of course, help out if any problems arose, but more importantly, he would make sure they were not overcharged. He would help those interested in the language, and would be available, officially, when an interpreter was needed.

2100hrs. arrived all too soon, but as all legs had been well and truly stretched, it was time resume the march, this time back towards their camp. General opinion had it that six miles marching was just about right for this kind of exercise after a hard day's work.

Chapter 7

At last came the day for which they had trained so assiduously ---- they were going into the front line! This was to be for a period of battle instruction, but this time, it would be the real thing. This would mean that the manning of a section of the trench would be doubled by putting the raw newcomers alongside experienced men who were already there. Their tutors were to be the Welsh Fusiliers. Before going out into the as yet unknown, the Ledford Bantams assembled to be told just what would be involved and the form that the instructing would take.

They were addressed by a battered-looking officer who had recently been promoted from the ranks after several officers from his battalion had been killed recently in fierce fighting. His concluding remarks were "All that I have told you can be boiled down to 'Keep your rifles clean, keep spread out, and keep your heads down'. Mind you, with you lot, that last bit won't be difficult!"

It would seem that over the next few weeks, they would be involved in a mad kind of Musical Chairs ----- or perhaps Blind Man's Bluff would be a more accurate description.

A series of staggered, overlapping reliefs had been devised by Divisional Command for troops in the line. This allowed for three days 'IN' the line followed by three days 'OUT' so that 'green' troops were never in the trenches without the stiffening of battle-hardened veterans.

The scheme was such that old-stagers took over during one night, followed by the novices the next. Then, two nights later, the veterans would be replaced by another group of experts. The night after that, it would be the turn of the now not-so-green tyros.

It would continue in this manner until the erstwhile newcomers were assumed to have become inured to existence in the ditches which the 'brass-hats' would insist on describing as 'trenches'. With hindsight that is, if the troops which actually did the fighting lived long enough to have any, they would think of it in terms of 'survival'.

So, having had the theory, admittedly from someone who had obviously learned the hard way, it was now time for the men to put it into practice.

Immediately after the evening meal which some would-be comedian just had to refer to as 'The Last Supper', the Lads paraded wearing steel helmets, full equipment and with rifles slung. At the gate, they set out in a vaguely south-easterly direction towards their appointment with Destiny. This was to be near Neuve Chapelle not far from Festubert, about ten miles from camp. The journey would be made under the cover of darkness to avoid being seen by the very efficient German artillery 'spotters'. Their route at first took them along what were little more than rural cart tracks but which were easier on the feet than the cobbles of the bigger roads.

On they trudged into the night. In addition to their personal kit and the ration bag issued to each man as they left camp, they were being used as a carrying party to take much-needed supplies up to the trenches. Coils of barbed wire were amongst the stores to be taken up there.

Quick as a flash, Fred and his bunch volunteered to carry water cans. Two square tins, each holding three gallons were slung on carrying poles between two men walking one behind the other. An awkward load perhaps, but one which was totally lacking in the viciousness of coils of barbed wire which was one of the alternative loads.

After five miles or so, it started to rain, and how it rained. It made a loud drumming noise as it bounced off the tops of the tins. The roads which up to now had been firm and reasonable going now deteriorated rapidly into mud which came well over the tops of boots. The further they went, the worse it became.

As if the weather was not enough, they were now struggling across an area which had very recently been the scene of fierce fighting. As they stumbled through the shattered ruins of what had been a large village, their way was illuminated from time to time by the light of star-shells. Someone was expecting visitors!

An idle thought passed through Fred's mind: "Are we going to see them, or are they coming to see us? If they are coming to us, will we be set up before they arrive?" Philosophically, he decided that as there was nothing he could do about it, there was no point in worrying.

He then started to take an interest in the countryside around him. At the edge of the ruined village, he could see the remains of the local agricultural engineers' workshop. With the roof off and most of the walls down, the machinery now exposed to the elements showed it to have been well-equipped and up-to-date. If he got the chance, he would have a look round some time.

As they struggled onwards, ever nearer to the bursting flares, the rain stopped. A weak and watery moon broke through the thin cloud cover. At the same time, the wind dropped to a fitful breeze. It was at that moment that they noticed a peculiar, nauseating smell. Not only hard to identify, it was harder still to describe. It was the smell of the battlefield, the unmistakable smell of the trenches.

All round as far as they could see, the earth had been viciously mutilated by a multitude of shells. It was a nightmare of craters ---- new craters, old craters, craters overlapping other craters. It was as if the very ground itself had succumbed to a virulent attack of smallpox.

By the pale light of the moon, they saw that the newer ones had very little water in them while the others were filled to varying depths. The older ones had a frothy scum on the liquid which could hardly be described as 'water'. Scattered indiscriminately amongst these holes were the corpses, the dead bodies. Some were half in, half out of the craters.

As they got nearer, they saw in horror that not all the bodies were complete. And, if they thought about it, --- and it was difficult not to, --- then there must be bodies concealed by the liquid in the shell holes.

What they could smell was the stink of death in all its worst aspects. The miasma was a compound of the vile, sickly-sweet smell of flesh in all stages of putrefaction. Lingering traces of poison gas, fumes from the explosions of countless shells, the fermentation products of whatever horrors were hidden in the depths of the flooded carters, all were superimposed on the all-pervading stench of earth and clay now in a permanently waterlogged state. Truly a cocktail for the damned.

While they were retching and struggling to control their nausea, a figure popped up out of a length of collapsed and abandoned trench leading off the track they were now on. Underneath the mud and filth with which he was so liberally coated was a Welsh Fusilier. This was their guide who would take them to the unit which was to instruct them in the niceties of trench warfare.

They were, he said tersely, to follow him, and to keep to the track he was on. They were to keep quiet and not 'muck about'. If they got shot, that was their hard luck, but he was buggered if he wanted them to get <u>him </u>shot! The fact that there were officers present did not seem to worry him at all, although at one point, he did add a rather belated 'sir'.

On they squelched until a place was reached where a junction point for three trenches had been heavily shelled. The guide remarked that as Jerry had the spot registered, " -- we don't hang around!"

To the Lads whose stomachs were by now tied up in knots, he seemed to take ages before deciding in which direction to head, and as to where he could find the entrance to the trench he needed. Suddenly, he bent down, then straightened up with the end of what they would come to recognise as the white cotton marking tape that the sappers used. Having frequently been a guide, he had taken steps to make sure that he could find his way back into the correct communications trench. What he had been looking for was the hilt of an old bayonet with which he spiked the tape to the ground. An incoming shell had all but buried it.

Now, with this tape running through his fingers, he set out with the newcomers crowding his heels. At one stage, he stopped and told them spread out in order to reduce casualties if they should happen to come under shellfire, but not so far as to lose touch with the man in front.

On this occasion, they were lucky, continuing the slog through the mud until their next staging point was reached. This was a second line of trenches where they were taken off into a line of earthworks which were no longer used as part of the main defences. It was utilised for stores, or as the handing-over point when the changeover of troops took place.

Here, the Fusiliers' R.S.M. materialised. His welcoming homily went along these lines. "Well, you've got here. Let's hope you live to go back! So how do you do that? You listen to me for a start."

Just at that moment, a star-shell exploded overhead. At this, the R.S.M. broke into song. He had a fine tenor voice, so typical of the type to be found in a Welsh, male voice choir. "Twinkle, twinkle little star, how I wonder what you are!"

"But Mr. Jerry sniper thinks "Voz them twinkles fire-flies? Nein. Dem voz 'Tommies'." Bang! One 'Tommy' less".

"The twinkle is not from that flare up there, it is from you lot down here. No ---- I am not joking! On the parade square, you will have all your brasses so highly polished you can see your face in them. Out here, if you want to make me happy, they can be as black as the ace of spades and as dull as ditch-water. So get some mud on anything that shines, then you might have half a chance of living a bit longer".

"Which reminds me. Your helmets --- cover them with sandbag sacking. Why? A wet helmet will also reflect light, even weak moonlight, so get them off your heads until you have done that. No! Don't put your caps back on, they need fixing as well. Take the wire stretcher ring out of the top and throw it away. Then screw the cap into a ball before putting on again. What you will have done is destroyed two shapes which do not occur naturally. So, if you should accidentally show your head above the parapet, you might just get away with it, if you're lucky!"

"All that lot applies equally to all of you. This bit is for the officers among you.

The cut of the uniform you are wearing at the moment is a dead 'give-away' marking you out immediately as officers. So does your 'Sam Browne' belt. Leave them back in camp. As soon as possible, get yourself an ordinary private soldier's uniform and mark your 'pips' on the shoulder straps so that they can be seen by anyone nearby, but not from a distance. The light-coloured rank markings on your cuffs can be seen for quite a distance. Keep your pistol if you must, but don't carry it openly. Get yourself a rifle, there's plenty lying around. As you are at the moment, you are prime 'sniper-bait'. Until these measures were adopted, a hell of a lot of good officers were killed, not to mention some duffers who were no great loss. All regiments do this in the trenches nowadays, so you won't be by yourselves".

"Another thing --- you'll see that some of my lads, the ones who prefer their greatcoats to cape/groundsheets have cut them off at about knee level. We all know what King's Regulations have to say regarding Government property. Out here, that's the least you should be worrying about. If left at its full length, the skirt would soak so much water and mud that the coat would weigh a ton. The weight saved by shortening the coat could make all the difference when getting back on your feet if you fall, or have to dive for cover whilst wearing it."

"And now for my final point --- harking back to the star-shells, when one goes up, freeze! Do not move until it has gone out. Despite what you might think, you will be less obvious if you stand still".

"You will now go into the front line, a few at a time, and will spread out amongst my lads. Do as you're told, immediately and without arguing. They all know what they are doing otherwise they wouldn't be still with us. Do as you're told without question and you might last all of a week!"

"You will see that we have breastwork of sandbags on the parapet. That is because all the ditches and land drainage has been destroyed by the all this shelling. Jerry has built his trenches half-way up the hill in front of us. Any water will drain down from him into our positions. He will be dry, or at least, drier than we are. We, being at the bottom of the slope are permanently flooded. Jerry can also see in to some sections of our ditch. All right then, 'trench', but you will find that 'ditch' is a more accurate description. When we tried to dig deeper, we soon found that we were up to our waists and above in water. You buggers would have drowned!" (This was once again a reference to the size of the Bantams.)

"For any marksmen among you, there are four or five Jerry snipers working us over. See if you can even the odds."

"Right, now, into the front line. Good luck to all of you. Believe-you-me, you'll need it! Oh yes, before I forget --- Welcome to Flanders!"

As the Lads waded into the trench, they were settled in amongst the "Taffs" already in residence. As advised, helmets were not now being worn but dangled from their belts. The caps they now sported instead had been bashed about to such an extent that if one had been dropped in a cow pasture, it would have been hard to find. Cap badges and brass buckles were now difficult to make out under the generous amount of mud which had been applied to them. As they passed him, the R.S.M. beamed his approval at his latest batch of new pupils.

And so were the Ledford Lads introduced to the Front Line, the Western Front, of which they had heard so much, but as yet, knew so little. They would have to learn, and learn quickly if they were to have any chance at all of surviving.

Chapter 8

By the time the Lads had taken up their positions, it was the period known as 'false dawn', just before daybreak proper. It is the time of day when the human spirit is at its lowest ebb. Your imagination works overtime, your eyes betray you, 'Stand to!' was always at this time, as well as at dusk, in anticipation of any nastiness on the part of the enemy.

By now, the Bantams had settled in to their posts to the accompaniment of all the by-now, well-worn jokes on account of their size, or rather, lack of it. There were the usual references to "Ducks' disease", and the enquiries as to how long the seats of their trousers lasted with them always dragging on the ground. The 'Bantams' had learned early on that this sort of thing would be normal, and that it was best to take it in good spirit as part of the game.

After the time they had now been in the army, they were ready for this, and had a stock of suitable replies in readiness. Now, on occasions such as this, they gave as good as they got. The fusiliers were told that they, the "Banties", did not need to dig trenches as deep as other troops. They could take cover in much shallower holes. They needed less cover than the others. In other words, with Bantams, there wasn't as much to aim at. The point was taken and the jokes died away.

An hour and a half passed, and it was now broad daylight. Everyone 'stood down' apart from the duty sentries dotted up and down the line. The rest relaxed as much as was possible in the circumstances. That is, until there was sudden, single shot from the enemy trenches. The Ledfords had taken their first fatality.

A member of 5 Platoon had decided that as it was quiet, he would have a look at 'No-man's Land'. He had remembered what he had been told about not looking over the top of the breastworks, so had found a spot where there was slight dip. Although the victim had not raised his head higher than the sandbags on either side of this spot, the movement must have been spotted by a sniper. One shot, and that was all it took. 'Curtains' for one newcomer who now had a bullet between his eyes. They were horrified. All that they had been warned about had been demonstrated so violently in front of them.

They were no longer 'playing' soldiers, in training, with an officially accepted casualty rate of 5%. The rate had suddenly gone up to the maximum that Jerry could inflict on them. What was more to the point, he had just shown how good he was at it.

Paybook, personal papers, and the red identification disc, were them removed from the body. The green one was left on it. With the contents of his pockets removed for return to the next-of-kin, the dead man was lifted over the parados and gently rolled onto the wasteland behind the trench.

As he dealt with this, the R.S.M. was heard to remark, "He can't stay in here with us, we are crowded enough as it is. Anyway, he's past caring now".

At this point, Tom asked if he could spend a little time with 5 Platoon as he thought he had a good idea where the enemy sniper might have hidden himself. Permission given, Tom was next seen making a hole between two layers of sandbags in the parapet, just big enough to take his rifle muzzle, with a little extra to allow him to aim it. It would enable him to see, but without been seen himself. Apart from its working parts and the sights, the rest of the weapon was smeared with mud.

When the peephole was ready, one of the others hung Tom's cap on a bayonet, and tentatively moved into partial view in the dip which had been featured so dramatically just a short time earlier. Sure enough, as expected, an enemy round just missed the cap which was hastily brought down as if in panic. Tom said quietly "Good. Ah knows where 'e is. Gi' 'im ten minutes, then ah'll get 'im. Mustn't let 'im get too settled".

As that time went by, Tom readied himself for the one shot he would get.

The cap was again cautiously raised, and moved slowly as if the wearer was checking his front. There was crack from the opposite lines and the cap flew off the bayonet. When it landed, there was neat hole through the front, just missing the cap badge.

Tom's shot came as an echo to that of the enemy. He, and those who were watching through 'trench periscopes' saw in the enemy lines what must have been the sniper jerk into view, throwing his arms above his head as he did so. He fell forward across his parapet and lay there, motionless.

At that, Tom picked up his kit, said "Cheerio" and returned to 4 Platoon. Apart from that one word, he said nothing. When he got back to his immediate circle of friends, he was asked what it felt like to kill a man, even though he was the enemy.

It was rather surprising to hear that Tom had had no qualms at all, no feelings of any kind. If anything, he was numb inside. The shock of the sudden, violent death suffered by one who had been around since the early days and with whom he had drunk and played cards had destroyed any emotions he might have had at the thought of what he had just done. But that sort of thing was what they were all here for, whether they liked it or not.

Overall, amongst the others who had not had to do that as yet, there was a feeling that that was what Jerry would get if " 'e mucked abaht wi' Tykes, especially if they were Ledfords!"

While all this had been going on, the Welsh R.S.M. had said a prayer over the dead Yorkshire boy. It seemed that the warrant officer had, in earlier days, been in the Church until, as he put it, he had 'strayed'. He had taken refuge in the army.

As it was now full daylight, breakfast was taken from what they had in their ration bags, and washed down with what the Fusiliers referred to as 'gunfire'. This was their name for tea brewed so strong and sweet that a spoon could be floated on it. At least, that was, apparently, their intention when it was being made. One day they intended to achieve that feat if they could! It was drunk as hot as could be managed when the often crude means of heating the water were considered.

It was only after the first mouthful of the concoction had been tasted that the drinker discovered just how revolting it was. Apart from the overpowering, bitter taste of tannin, the water which had been carried so laboriously for many a weary mile did nothing for it. In itself, it was thoroughly disgusting. Stored in heavily chlorinated tanks behind the lines, it had been filled into cans which had previously been used for the petrol supplied to the lorries and staff cars with which the rear areas now swarmed. As these cans became empty, they were to be scalded out and stored for use in carrying water up to the trenches. There was no denying the fact that they had been stored, but there was a great deal of room for questioning the efficiency with which they had been scalded out, if at all.

The vile brew was strong enough to rot socks (figuratively speaking), and had a foul taste of chlorine and petrol. The best that could be said for it was that it was hot, if the men were lucky to get it in time.

The rum ration was now issued. The official reason for this was that it would restore warmth to the body after the chill of the night, and cheer them up. The unofficial reason which was widely held was that it was to get rid of the taste of the tea.

The novices were now introduced to what was an inexplicable feature of the war in the trenches in many sectors.

The first hour of daylight, was always the time when the first meal of the day was taken, no matter what the nationality of the troops in the line. It was as if by unwritten agreement that this period was sacrosanct. Meals could be prepared and eaten during this first hour without being disturbed by anyone being belligerent, and acting as if there was a war on.

After this quiet period, it was business as usual, and the morning 'hate' would begin. This was the trench troglodytes' name for the swapping by both sides of a variety of explosive devices of varying degrees of unpleasantness.

The lads would soon learn to recognise the more unusual offerings of their opponents. They would also discover that a lot of their casualties would be caused by British shells falling short of their intended targets, or bursting prematurely while passing overhead. Whatever the cause, the victims were still either wounded or killed.

This, then, was their first full day in the trenches. This was the start of the 'blooding' process. (No matter what it was, or what was happening, the British 'Tommy' would have selection of words or phrases suitable for the occasion. If not, he would invent some. Some might even be polite!)

As for their immediate surroundings, the best way to describe them would be to say that they were standing in an open sewer. But that would doing an injustice to a good, honest, open sewer. Surface water was continuously draining down into their trenches from those of the enemy, together with what he chose to dump in it. It either flowed amongst the debris and carnage of no-man's-land picking up the fluids from the putrefaction with which the ground was covered, or seeped through the soil to emerge via their trench walls. To add to the misery, an equally sickening mixture drained in from the charnel house behind their own lines. This was where they would have to survive for the next three days and nights. Having taken note of all this, they now had to find out how to deal with what the Army refers to as 'Good House-keeping'.

R.S.M. Griffiths (who seemed to run the show in this section of the Line) summed it up quite simply. "There isn't any! Make sure the working parts of your weapons are kept cleaned and oiled. That matters above all else. There is no washing or shaving. As all the water has to be carried in, there is none to waste on such luxuries. What about bodily functions? As you will have noticed, there are no latrines. It is impossible to dig a pit when there is over two feet of water in the trench. So, pee in the water. What you will add is bound to be of better quality than what is there already. If not, then you should be in hospital, or already dead. As regards the other, save your jam or bully-beef tins for when the need is upon you. Use them, then chuck them out over the back of the trench as far as you can. Think of it as 'grenade' practice. There is an art in using empty tins in this manner --- you just have to be wary of the jagged edges!"

He then went on to tell them that prolonged immersion of the feet in filthy liquid such as the stuff they were now standing in could lead to 'trench foot', or foot rot. Some genius had decreed that anyone who succumbed to this condition would be charged with 'neglect of the person' or some such nonsense. The official method of preventing this was a daily application of whale oil.

Right on cue, a fusilier corporal produced a small drum of the stuff, and issued a portion to all the troops.

The best method of applying the evil-smelling muck was now demonstrated.

Puttees, boots and socks had, perforce, to be removed to bare the foot. As there was nowhere to sit, only one foot at a time could be done. A bayonet driven into the trench wall held the clothing from the foot being anointed. Oil was worked well in, between the toes and over the foot generally. At this stage, if balance had not been lost, the sock was placed in the boot, and the balance of the first foot's oil poured in. When the sock had been soaked in oil, it was replaced on the foot which was then returned to the boot which still contained any surplus oil. In this way, that foot was now well and truly plastered with the stuff. After rewinding the puttee, the other foot was dealt with in a similar manner.

As the R.S.M. remarked, "We must be a right lot of mixed-up sinners! Whereas the Good Book talks about anointing the heads of the righteous with oil, we are anointing the other end. Doesn't say much for us, then!"

So, the situation the Lads now found themselves in could be summed up as living in squalor whilst trying to stop their feet rotting off! Not quite the war they had envisaged when enlisting, but, as the saying goes "If you can't take a joke, you shouldn't have joined!" Some joke this --- nobody was laughing.

As they looked about them, they saw that practically every Welshman had some form of club. These ranged from cut-down pickaxe handles --- the thick end which would have carried the blade --- through to much more elaborate modifications on this basic theme. There was the simple cudgel with a six-inch nail sticking through the business end. Crude and simple, but effective they were assured. The *de luxe* version had barbed wire wrapped round the head as well.

The reason for these home-made weapons was that on trench raids and fighting patrols, rifles were too cumbersome for the close-quarter fighting these activities provoked. The fighting was too sudden to bring a rifle into action even without a fixed bayonet. Rifles were also liable to snag on the barbed wire thus drawing enemy fire onto the party.

Just then, Jerry sent over his first daily offering of assorted ironmongery. He always seemed to know when raw troops had come into the line and had evolved his own welcome for them. To this end, he mixed what he had available.

First would come the 'minnies'. (This was the troops' pet name for the *minenwerfer.*). These were enormous mortar bombs which were very ungainly in flight. The noise when the mortar was fired was hard to detect, but if the wind was in the right direction, it was often possible to hear the German mortar captain's whistle as he blew it to warn his team that he was about to fire the device.

There was also another type of mortar bomb which looked like an overgrown toffee-apple. This had a circular explosive head about the size of a football, mounted on a shaft some two feet long. This shaft was inserted in the barrel of the mortar for firing. It turned over lazily in flight, making a "whoff, whoff, whoff" noise as it did so. Again, it was easily seen when it was on its way.

Another slow-motion offering was the 'Jack Johnson', a heavy shell which exploded in a cloud of dense, black smoke. (J.J. was the negro heavyweight boxer of the time, hence the nickname). It was also referred to as a 'coal-box'. When the artillery piece was fired, it produced a dull thud which was readily heard by those on the receiving end.

The other weapon frequently used in combination with these was the 'whizz- bang', so-called because the noise it made in flight was heard virtually at the same time as it exploded on arrival.

The scheme was to lob one or two 'minnies' towards the British lines, together with a few 'Jack Johnsons' for good measure. The immediate reaction of inexperienced troops was to move to either side, away from where the slow- moving objects could be expected to land. After all, why wait for trouble when they could get out of the way before it landed?

But this was where enemy cunning came into play. Troops moving into the bays on either side of the anticipated impact area would mean an increased number of men in those bays. So, guess where the whizz-bangs would land?

As soon as the men realised what was happening, and that their chances of survival were just as good in their own bit of trench, it became very much a case of staying put, enduring it where they were, and hoping that it was not their turn to be unlucky.

All bar a sentry would, if they got down on the floor of the trench, escape the blast and splinters from explosions in front or behind them. If a shell or mortar bomb was actually lobbed directly into your bay, there was nothing you could do about it.

As for the lucky lad on sentry-go, he was there in case the Huns chose to use the barrage as cover for an assault on the British positions. He could see the slow stuff coming and duck below the parapet at the last moment. With a whizz-bang, he wouldn't know anything about it.

The only snag was that the trenches occupied by the Ledfords were half-flooded with liquid filth. So they could choose from at least three ways of dying. They could duck right down and risk death by drowning. If they did not drown, they might die of poisoning from what they swallowed. The other alternative was to stay upright and risk death by shellfire. This last choice had the benefit of at least being a reasonably clean way out. Not much of a choice, but all there was in the circumstances.

All they could do was to press as close to the breastwork as possible and work on the principle that what they couldn't see might not hurt them. Whatever they did, they just could not win. Pressed up against the front trench wall, a 'minnie' exploding just in front of them would slam sandbags back at them with some considerable force. If it exploded behind them, they would be slammed against the bags!

The first day wore on, slowly, and it was soon time for the second meal of the day. This would be 'bully beef' (remembering to save the tin, of course) followed by hard tack biscuits plastered with plum and apple jam. There was no butter, but then, they were not at the Ritz.

Then, after another long period of boredom, it was time for the evening meal. This time it was McConachie's meat and vegetables from another tin. This was eaten cold as there was no means of heating it. For a change, it was followed by apple and plum jam on hard tack biscuits.

Time crawled past, daylight dwindled into dusk then it was 'stand-to' time again. Then, this critical period over with no alarms, and all quiet, they stood down.

Throughout the night, from time to time, flares and star-shells lit up the sky. Nothing moved. Occasionally the single crack of a rifle would be followed by bursts of machine-gun fire. Nerves must be on edge somewhere, and imagination running riot.

Then, shortly after midnight, something rattled the tins which both sides hung on the wire to warn of intruders. Immediately, all hell was let loose. Bantams and Fusiliers alike blazed away at the area the noise had come from. Jerry did the same. Up went a British flare followed by several from across the way. There was nothing to be seen anywhere. It must have been a false alarm, probably due to some animal making its way through the wire.

When the firing had died down, immediate thoughts were as to how to clean the rifles and getting rid of the burnt cordite now fouling their barrels. There was no question of boiling-out as in training, there was no way of doing that in the trenches.

They soon found the answer when the fusiliers removed the bolts from their rifles, and opened the front of their trousers. They then urinated into the barrel through the cartridge chamber exposed by the removal of the bolt, followed by the normal pulling through. It seemed that this was effective enough in an emergency.

There would be no complaints about the false alarm disturbing anyone's slumbers as it had been far too cold to sleep in any case. When dawn finally broke, the liquid in which everyone was standing up to the knees or above had a thin covering of ice on it.

The next day was exactly the same as the previous one with exactly the same rations.

The Bantams' second night in the Line was when the Welsh Fusiliers were relieved by others from that regiment. R.S.M. Griffiths went out for well-earned rest.

The moment they stood down at dusk, the fusiliers collected their bits and pieces, and waited in readiness for the relieving companies. Meanwhile, one of the outgoing men went down to the rendezvous point where the Ledfords had been met all that time ago. In fact, only thirty-six hours had gone by.

Sometime later, the guide reported to his C.O. that the fresh troops were gathered in the stores sap just off the second line. They were waiting to let the 'old guard' pass before moving in to take up their positions. This way, congestion would be avoided and the changeover effected with the minimum of fuss.

For the Ledfords, the high points of the day were, of course, the issue of the rum (naturally), and the foot-anointing ritual. They were getting used to the rank smell of the oil. After all, it was just another stink to add to the atmosphere they existed in nowadays. But tomorrow would be different. They were to be relieved by other companies from their battalion. The move could not come too soon

The evening dragged past, and eventually the evening stand-to was on them again. By now, their days had settled into periods of boring inactivity linking the stand-to phases at dusk and dawn.

At the end of another tedious day, they moved out to the sap to let their reliefs take over the vacated positions. The usual pleasantries were exchanged, then they were on their way back to the nearest they would get to civilisation for some time.

Back along the communication trench they went, dragging their weary bodies through the muck until at last, the junction was reached. This was where they were in danger of being seen by the enemy. So, extreme caution was needed. Even during the night when visibility was poor, the odd shell or two would be sent over to keep people on their toes.

Over the junction they went, a half section at a time. Just as the last group were making the hazardous crossing, a star-shell caught them out in the open. Immediately, a salvo of shells straddled the spot. Once again, the enemy had done his homework. His artillery had registered all spots for potential targets, and so was capable of immediate response if a target of opportunity presented itself as on this occasion.

The corporal bringing up the rear and the last two men were killed outright. Some of those remaining found when they had picked themselves up that they had suffered wounds ranging from an assortment of cuts to a head wound and a broken arm. When 'field dressings' had been applied, those injured carried on back to camp as 'walking wounded'.

Fred passed the shattered machine-shop without even noticing it. From here onwards, it was a matter of following roads they had taken on their outward slog to the trenches, but this time, in the opposite direction.

Finally, they were there, back in camp. They could now walk, not wade, without crouching, and, joy of joys, there would be a hot meal waiting for them. They would have real food for a change. But first, they had to scrape the mud off each other.

This was done by careful use of the bayonet until as much as possible had been removed. Then, and only then were they allowed into the warmth of the cookhouse to savour the succulent aromas wafting across to them from the dixies on the cooking ranges.

Then it was their turn to receive their portions of the ambrosia which was awaiting them. This was eaten slowly in appreciative silence, not wolfed down as might have been expected. Then followed copious draughts of hot tea, proper tea. This was tea as they remembered it, not the barely-warm, chlorinated, foul-tasting sheep dip of the trenches. No! This was tea as it should be!

After this banquet, they began to feel almost human again.

The catering officer then informed them that as the camp was not fully occupied at the moment, only the main cookhouse was in use. As there were two on the camp, the smaller one had been set up as a drying room until such time as it was needed for its proper role so that troops coming out of the trenches could dry their uniforms. This sounded too good to be true but came as very welcome news.

In the 'drying room', racks knocked together by the engineers covered the available floor space. There were more than enough allowing each man to spread out his kit to dry. Things were organised on a platoon basis to avoid confusion. In no time at all, the whole mob had stripped to the buff, and soon were revelling in the warmth whilst watching their clothing drying out. The heat in the room was stifling, and soon, steam filled the air.

Some shrinking took place as the uniforms dried, but this actually improved the fit in some cases. In the rush to equip everyone, a lot of uniforms were considered to fit if the buttons could be done up. The idea was that the camp tailors would make the necessary alterations and adjustments. The trouble was that there had been so many needing his services, some had been attended, some had not.

By the drying room door, there was a stack of wooden batons about eighteen inches in length. With these, the now dried mud was to be beaten out of the uniforms and puttees. This crude method worked surprisingly well. They now had reasonably clean clothing which was dry for the first time in three days.

They were then given the good news that tomorrow, there would be hot baths and an issue of clean underwear. This really was living! Was there no end to all the good things coming their way now that they were back in camp?

Then, back in their huts, they turned in for some genuine sleep and relaxation.

Tomorrow could take care of itself.

Chapter 9

Came the dawn, and with it *reveillé*. A good wash was followed by what seemed to be sheer luxury, a shave in hot water. Breakfast was then followed by muster parade where they were informed that the morning would be spent cleaning equipment and getting it back to parade-ground standards of perfection.

Brasses would be polished until they shone like gold. Uniforms would be cleaned to as high as standard as could be achieved, then pressed. Boots were to be treated with dubbin. After three days immersion in filthy water, there was no way in which the traditional high polish could be restored to the still wet leather. Hence the practical approach, the use of dubbin.

The midday meal at 1230hrs. for 'C' and 'D' Companies would be followed by them parading at the camp gates for transfer by lorry to Hazebrouck. Here, the brewery had ceased operations as such when overrun by the enemy earlier in the war, and was now, since the recapture of the town, being used as the Divisional bath house. Its massive boilers were more than capable of supplying the constant hot water needed to meet the demand. The mash tuns and other brewing vessels were now in use as giant bath tubs.

The bliss of wallowing neck-deep in hot water was indescribable. There was no other way of putting it. But alas, it had to end all too soon as there were others outside waiting for their turn.

Back in camp, it was 'make and mend' time, with no further obligations until next day. Fred, who had various ideas for trench weapons turning over in his mind, went down to the motor transport lines to see what facilities they had.

Emerging from behind one of the huts, he encountered Lt. Richardson heading in the same direction. Fred explained what he was hoping to do, and got tacit, if not open approval for his plans. On arrival at the M.T. lines, Fred vanished into the machine shops, found what he was looking for, and struck a bargain with the sergeant/mechanic in charge.

In the meantime, Lt.Richardson had tracked down the major who had overall responsibility for the set-up. He had already established that there was a lorry which had just been repaired, and which only needed road-testing. The lieutenant offered to do this with its usual driver at the wheel. Twenty miles, say, to Hazebrouck and back should constitute an adequate test? The major agreed. The lieutenant then made his bid. He would conduct the road test with a full platoon on board, out to the town mentioned, and back to camp. On completion of the test, Lt. Richardson would sign the certificate of roadworthiness. The major was quick to accept the offer. It neatly solved his problem of getting the test done when there was no-one else available to do it.

So, at 1900hrs., the 'test platoon' (who just happened to be Lt. Richardson's own lot) assembled at the M.T. lines, climbed on board, and set off to test the vehicle.

Their destination was, again by coincidence, an *estaminet* the lieutenant had checked out during the bath parade earlier in the day. Everyone de-bussed and vanished inside the hostelry. Despite a very convivial evening, no one got out of order. Then, when everyone had eaten and drunk their fill, the test was resumed. Back in camp, the 'testing officer' signed the requisite certificate with a flourish.

As an afterthought, on being given the certificate, the major asked what, if anything, Lt. Richardson knew about motor vehicles. The reply? "Not a thing, old chap. Absolutely nothing!"

So, if this was the case, why had he signed the certificate? The lieutenant replied that they had agreed that the lorry was to be returned after testing with the certificate duly signed. That had been the agreement, and, as he did not wish to default on his given word, he had signed it. He was after all, the officer present during the road test of the vehicle in question and so had signed the certificate. He had also qualified his status at the time of signing by showing himself as "Acting Testing Officer". So, it seemed to him that all aspects of the arrangement had been covered.

The major had to mentally concede defeat, realising that he had been too quick to accept the offer, and, as a result, had been duped. In consolation, he was promised a battlefield souvenir the next time the Lads came out of the trenches. This would be one of the much-coveted *pickelhauben*, the spiked leather helmets now being replaced by the steel 'coal scuttle' headwear.

In the end, it had all worked out satisfactorily. The Ledfords had been out for the evening, and the major's lorry had been road-tested. There was a war on when all was said and done. Compromises had to be made as and where necessary. Finally, the major was assured that his driver had been well looked after as regards food and drink, so there would be no complaints from that quarter.

This had been a very successful day in all respects, but no one could forget that it was also one day nearer to the inevitable return to the hell of the front line.

The next day, the routine first parades were followed by church assemblies for the three denominations. Yes ---three denominations. These were Anglican, Roman Catholic, and Jewish, each with their own clerics, and their own church parade.

The Army's view --- and it had a view on all things involving the rank and file --- was that three main religions would suffice. Minor persuasions were not allowed to exist, officially, and as for atheists and agnostics, there were no such beings. It was considered that no man would reject the chance of an easy hour or so at a church meeting if the alternative was doing fatigues.

Tom would be seen going into the church hut with his Jewish brethren, having already been Anglican and Catholic. On being challenged by the R.S.M., he said with a straight face that although nominally Anglican, he had been a back-slider all his life. Now that religion really mattered, he was undecided. He would therefore attend the services of all three faiths until he could make up his mind with certainty. It was not his fault if all three services took place on the same morning in the week, and that as a result, he would be unavailable for other duties for the whole of that time.

At the Anglican parade, the chaplain said his piece about how God was on the side of those fighting for a righteous cause, and that as the *Triple Entente* (Britain, France and Russia) had such a cause, they would prevail in the end. At this point, Fred asked permission to speak. He had seen a German belt which had "*Gott mit uns*" on the fastener. He had been told that this meant "God is with us". The chaplain agreed that was indeed the case.

Fred continued --- "If God is wi' t' Germans, then they must 'ave a righteous cause as well. If 'E is wi' them as well as wi' us, who'll get most support?"

At this, the chaplain went red in the face, and started to bluster. He burbled on about how that consideration was a matter of higher, divine logic, not to mention theology and philosophy, etc. etc. Fred interrupted once again, saying that all that sort of stuff was too deep for him. As a practical man, all he wanted was a straight answer, please.

By this time, the minister was looking decidedly uncomfortable and hot under his 'dog' collar, so Fred decided to let him off the hook. He stated quite bluntly that as he saw it, to have any chance of survival, it would have to be a matter of hedging his bets. So, he would attend church parades when ordered to do so, and pray for personal salvation. That should take care of the religious side of things. He would also make sure he had his 'lucky' penny with him at all times, plus, of course, his 'lucky' rabbit's foot, although, come to think of it, he was not too sure about this last item --- it hadn't done too well for its original owner!

As a last resort, he would try not to do anything stupid.

If, however, anything coming his way had his number on it, then that would be it. There would be nothing he could do about it. As the music hall song had it " Nappoo, toodle-oo, good byee!"

All the men present were, by now, arguing furiously about what Fred had said. Some agreed, some disagreed strongly.

The parade was dismissed.

The Roman Catholics now took over from the Anglicans to be followed in their turn by those of the Jewish faith. In the meantime, those not attending the service of their professed religion while away the remainder of the morning on general fatigues in and around the camp. Fred, on the other hand, had other ideas.

On the way back to camp earlier in the week, he had noticed that there was a battlefield salvage dump which had been set up the Royal Engineers for any re-useable equipment recovered from behind the front line. It happened to be located just beyond the huts in the far part of camp not in use at the moment. Fred had decided to check out this area to see what was available,

The boundary fence in that vicinity was in a poor state of repair. If challenged, he was there to check that the huts were still in good condition, and also to assess what needed to be done to repair the fence. If he was caught beyond the fence, and thus off camp limits without permission, he would have to think of another explanation, and quickly.

So, he strode off purposefully down the main camp road. He had soon realised that if he looked as if he was on official business, and moved briskly, he would not be challenged. It was all a matter of confidence, bluff, and sheer 'brass' neck.

When he was out of sight, he dodged away among the huts. All well and good, so far.

Reaching the furthermost line of huts, he stole forward towards the fence. It was as he had suspected. The hole was out of sight from the main camp road, which was probably why it had been made in the first place.

He dived through and doubled along the grass verge until he came to the dump. He soon found what he was looking for --- an entrenching tool still in its case, a bayonet and its scabbard, plus a steel helmet. All this was British issue. He also scrounged a brass shell case.

With his loot, he returned to camp the same way he had come out, but now, his footsteps took him to the M.T. workshops where he spoke to his sergeant contact. As the grinding wheels and cutters were not being used, Fred got to work. The bayonet, still in its scabbard, was cut down to half its length. The original eighteen-inch blade had been too long for what he envisaged. He then ground and sharpened the shortened blade so as to produce a pointed knife with a cutting edge on both sides.

A strip of brass, about three inches wide was cut from the shell case and worked into a "C" shape but with one end longer that the other. In this end, he machined a central slot parallel to the edges and wide enough to take the modified bayonet blade. At the other, shorter end, he drilled a hole to take the pommel of the bayonet hilt. The hand-guard he had just made was then offered up to the blade, and when correctly positioned, tack-welded into place. This was the "Fred Booth" trench knife. It could be carried in the cut-down scabbard in a standard-issue bayonet frog.

Now it was the turn of the entrenching tool. The first step was to cut away the digging blade leaving the socket still attached to the pick, the cut end being ground down to conform to the socket of the implement. (Fred was nothing if not a perfectionist.)

He now turned his attention to the pick end of the modified blade. It was the right length at about four inches, but with the wrong cross-section. This he reduced to a tapered finish of about 3/8in. wide at the striking end. At the same time, he gave it a circular section finishing in a point, not a needle point but somewhat blunter. It was still a point, however. This modified head was now assembled on its handle, knocked firmly home, and a small hole drilled in the side of the socket. A nail was driven in to secure things, cut off flush, and again tack-welding finished the job.

Now for a test. The helmet was placed on the workbench in the 'wearing' position. A good, solid blow against it, delivered with the spike, resulted in a satisfactory hole being pierced with the spike going through for about two inches. If it would do that to a steel helmet, then the unprotected, soft parts of the body of an enemy were in for a rough time.

This was the advent of "Fred's toothpick".

The R.E. sergeant was visibly impressed by the simplicity of these weapons and the speed with which they could be produced. Fred and he then came to an agreement. The sergeant would produce these items from material brought in by the customer, using Fred's ideas. He would charge what he could get for them for the time and trouble spent making them, and would slip Fred a 'bob' or two as beer money when the Lads were back in camp.

To add the finishing touch to the 'toothpick', a hole was drilled through the end of the handle to take a leather bootlace which could be passed round the user's wrist. The case was discarded.

On returning to his hut, Fred found that the rest of his lot had become as adept at 'dodging the column' as he had, and were now back there before him. When they saw the 'cutlery' he now produced, they were as interested as the R.E. sergeant had been. He told them how and where the basic materials could be obtained, and who to contact for the conversion job. They were to negotiate their own prices.

Off they went to set the production line in motion, and to arrange for the collection of the finished article the next day.

The remainder of the day (as well as the next) would be spent in camp on fatigues. As there were now so many men available to do them, the tasks would be of the soul-destroying kind so beloved by non-commissioned officers the world over when they run out of work for the men to do.

One favourite was moving the coal across the coal-yard, cleaning and washing the area just cleared, then whitewashing it. When the whitewash was dry, the coal was moved back and whitewashed in its turn!

Mad as it may seem, there was a certain twisted logic in what at first seems to be bordering on insanity. But no --- if any coal was acquired illegally by anyone wishing to supplement the meagre and inadequate allowance for his hut, the theft would immediately be obvious.

Duties over for the day, Fred and his merry men decided that as the next day would find them on their way back up to the front line, another visit to the *estaminet* was called for.

On arrival, Billy who had decided that speaking French was not all that difficult, was more adventurous in his choice (He had on the last occasion become quite taken with the idea of "--- spakin' to t' locals in their own lingo ---").

So, in addition to the ' *burf and pomm dterre*', he asked for '*bee-air, pang and burr*'. When the meal arrived, he was a trifle disappointed to find that the '*pang*' was not like the bread he had at home. It turned out to be (not surprisingly) the variety common to that part of France. It was a solid, heavy, brownish kind containing rye which gave it its characteristic taste.

Once they had tried it and become used to its texture and taste, it really was not all that bad. At least, a slice could be bitten into without fear of breaking your teeth, as was the case with the hardtack.

As for the '*bee-air',* although Hugo's booklet said that this meant 'beer', it was nothing like what they were used to. It was thin and sour, and much worse than the wine. This was strange as the beers of French and Belgian Flanders are normally very good. This poor quality was probably due to wartime restrictions on brewing materials with the brewer trying to get too much from limited supplies.

Then, all too soon, it was back to camp, and, as Samuel Pepys said in his famous diary, " --- and so to bed ---!"

Chapter 10

Dusk was falling, as once again, "C" and "D" Companies assembled at the camp gate where they would bear right in the general direction of Neuve Chapelle. They would stay together as a group, and follow the now familiar road as on their first visit to the trenches, almost as far as the fork where the communications trenches met. From that point onwards, they would spread out and continue by platoon, and ultimately by section. Apparently, German artillery activity had increased dramatically since their first stint in the line.

Their guide took them as far as the fork, then, having ensured that the guide tape had been found and that the leading man had it in his hand, sent them on their way, wishing them luck as he did so.

Fred found himself thinking about his discussion with the chaplain with a certain amount of embarrassment. He was, after all, a committed Christian --- well, not totally. He had been a choirboy, and then, a regular church-goer back home. As he pondered, he fingered his lucky charms.

At one stage, a random shell landed far enough in front so as not to cause any problems, but near enough to remind them where they were, not that they needed any reminding. They were now in a slight dip with the remains of earlier excavations available for cover.

Here, the platoon split into individual sections for the last leg to the trenches. Each then went forward in the artillery formation they had rehearsed in what now seemed like a former life. With luck, if they did come under fire, the spacing should reduce the number of casualties.

Fred's section arrived without any further excitement, and waited in the second line until the rest of "C" Company had reassembled. Then, a runner went forward to warn the outgoing troops to be ready to move.

The relief moved up into the storage sap immediately behind the front line and waited to move in. This was the moment when the line would be at its most vulnerable. Those being relieved would no longer be at their posts nor would the incoming troops have occupied the vacated positions.

"C" Company was taking over from its counterpart, "A" company. As the two units passed each other, the usual insults were exchanged as had become customary.

On a more serious note, Capt. Yorke was warned that there had been a change of regiments in the German lines. Whereas the previous lot had operated on a 'Live and let live' basis, the newcomers were more aggressive. Previously, it had been a token show during the morning 'hate', followed by a lazy day punctuated by the odd sniper's opportunist rifle shot from time to time as targets presented themselves. But now, all that had changed.

The new occupants were much more belligerent, being given to sweeping the British breastworks with bursts of machine-gun fire in the hope of finding gaps. This they had frequently managed to do until the sandbag wall had been raised and strengthened. But this had cost lives. The men working at the task had inevitably shown themselves. It only needed the slightest slip, and then, only for a split second. One shot, and the victim collapsed. As it was usually the head which was exposed, the wound was nearly always fatal. "A" and "B" Companies had taken nine casualties, seven having been killed instantly.

Such was "C" Company's welcome on returning to the front line.

There was not a lot that could be done about it apart from settling in as best they could. Capt.Yorke called a briefing for all his platoon commanders as well as those of the 'stiffening troops' who were to continue as the Bantams' battle instructors. He produced the sealed packet of orders he had been given prior to leaving camp. This was a new practice which had been introduced to avoid any leakage of plans to German Intelligence. Runners would also be used if necessary for any last minute change of intentions.

In 1914, Hazebrouck and the surrounding district had been surrendered to the invaders as much as to prevent the destruction of the town as due to the fact that there were no troops readily available for its defence. It was thought that suitable French-speaking Germans had been left in place to report back on French or British troop dispositions after the town had been recaptured. It was not too far-fetched to assume that there would be sympathisers in the local population doing the same.

No matter how it was happening, information was getting across to the other side. In the past, relief columns had come under enemy shellfire at exactly the right spot at exactly the right time. Coincidence could only be stretched so far. The pinpoint accuracy was just that --- too accurate. This had given rise to the 'sealed packet' routine.

H.Q. had decided in their wisdom that as many fighting patrols as were necessary would be mounted with the intention of taking a prisoner (or prisoners) in order to identify the present occupants of the line opposite. If prisoners could not be taken for any reason, then identifying material was to be collected. It was decided that the task would be assessed the next day once they had re-established themselves in their 'ditch'. Nothing else had changed --- 'home, sweet home' was still as foul as it had been the last time they had been there.

The following day, one "C" and two "D" Company men were killed by sniper fire. As a consequence of his success during his first session in the trenches, Tom was asked if he could do anything to discourage the enemy snipers operating in the vicinity.

The trench system had been dug as a continuous right-angled 'zigzag'. The idea was that enfilading fire could not be brought to bear on the occupants of the next bay in the event of intruders getting into the position.

Tom decided to investigate. To do this, he visited the locations of the killings to see if he could get a line on the sniper's hideout. He was very careful not to give the sniper (or snipers?) the chance to add to their score.

He found that the two "D" men, although killed at different times of the day had nevertheless been shot whilst in a section of their trench which ran parallel to that of the enemy, and looked in a southerly direction. The shots could not have come from directly in front. So, they must have come from somewhere off to the right.

In that direction, Tom spotted the ruins of what must have been a small pumping station used in happier times to drain the surrounding land. The stump of the chimney still remained.

He now went back to "C" Company positions and made similar checks. He found the set-up virtually the same. He concluded that probably only one sniper was at work, and that his 'hide' was almost certain to be the shattered chimney.

The big problem was that it was such good cover that there was no way the sniper could be seen even when in action. An even bigger problem was that there was no safe way anyone could risk crossing the open ground from the British lines to get at him. In short, it was a job for the Divisional Artillery.

But even that was not feasible. The ruins, whilst being in no-man's-land, were too close to British positions to risk such action. The quality of the fuses fitted to British shells at this stage of the war produced too many premature airbursts which precluded close infantry support such as this required. Short-falling shells would make it even more dangerous.

No! Artillery was out of the question.

Tom set out his findings and his conclusions to Capt. Yorke and all the other company commanders. As Tom's immediate officer, Lt. Richardson was also present.

Tom's proposal was this. The first time a fighting patrol went out, he would go with them. Whilst they headed for the enemy trenches, he would break off on his own and make his way to the ruins to have a look round. He would take with him a demolition pack which he would get from the sappers who had come up with them. He would demolish the chimney stump, and return independently. If, for any reason, the patrol had to withdraw prematurely, he would lie-up until the following night in a shell-hole he could see on this side of the ruins. He made two conditions. The first was that there must be no shooting anywhere in the vicinity of the ruins --- any movement might be him! The second was that another patrol should go out the next night if necessary so that all enemy action would be drawn to where they were in action, and so, away from him. He should then be able to get back to his own lines, he hoped! If he was not back the second night, he would not be coming back at all.

This was agreed, and a raid arranged for that night. Tom sought out the R.E. sergeant in charge of the sapper detail and explained what he was about to attempt. Tom learned that this type of chimney built on to the exterior wall of a boiler-house usually had a hinged door on its outside at its base. This was to allow for cleaning and maintenance as would the rungs up the inside of the chimney. It would be these that the sniper would be using to get into position if he was using the ruins for cover.

The sergeant then went on to tell Tom that he should place the charges inside, round the base of the chimney. Each charge would have its own fuse brought in to one central 'command' fuse which was the one to light when everything was in position. All the individual fuses leading from this would be the same length so as to burn for the same length of time thus igniting all the charges simultaneously.

When Tom had lit this command fuse, he should close the door from the outside, and, if the handle was still there and useable, pull it into the 'closed' position. If not, the door should be jammed shut with rubble. The design of the flues from the firebox should, to some extent, contain the force of the blast, and keep it where it mattered.

So, a suitable demolition pack was made up weighing some twenty pounds or so, with all the separate charges linked to one firing point on the central fuse.

The sapper's final question to Tom was as to what he intended to do as regards his own safety when the charges exploded and brought down the remains of the chimney. Tom mentioned the shell-hole about twenty yards away from it on the British side of the ruins. That was where he intended to take cover. At this, the sergeant commented that while it was better than being caught out in the open, it really was too close for comfort. "What goes up must come down, and that would be about where some of it would land! But, if that was all there was ------."

Dusk came, followed by darkness, and the usual stand-to. An hour later, the patrol set out with Tom bringing up the rear. Halfway across no-man's-land, Tom broke off, and took cover whilst the patrol carried on towards the enemy lines. Suddenly there were loud shouts in German followed by the sounds of fierce fighting. Intermixed with the general hubbub were the sounds of Tykes in full cry. This was his opportunity. He took to his heels, and dashed over to the ruins.

Sure enough, there was the access hatch on the outside of the chimney --- the sergeant had been right.

By the light of a flare, in the earth outside this entrance, he could make out the imprints of boots, German boots. The shape of the sole and the stud patterns were totally different to his. He had checked to make sure. Whoever was using the chimney was not British. Tom carefully pulled the door further open --- it had been partially open when he when he found it. Feeling around inside, he found the climbing rungs.

He rubbed his hand along one --- it was wet. At that moment, another flare lit up the sky. By its light, Tom saw that on his hand was fresh, wet mud. Somebody was up the chimney! As he listened, he was rewarded with the sound of someone carefully changing his position. The sniper was in residence. Tom would get a bonus when he destroyed the chimney!

He set the charges, lit the fuse, and slammed the door shut, hammering the locking handle down into place to seal the enemy soldier inside with the explosives. Then he fled from the scene and threw himself headfirst in to the shell-hole.

The charges exploded with a muffled roar. Soot, and what must have been the hapless sniper shot out of the chimney as if from a gun before the chimney collapsed back into itself. The bulk of the brickwork subsided into a heap for the most part, but sufficient was hurled into the air to worry Tom as he lay there with it falling all round him. He had all his breath knocked out of him when a chunk of masonry struck him violently in the back.

When all the commotion he had brought about had settled down, he addressed himself to the problem of getting back to his own lines and comparative safety. Flares and star shells showed the survivors of the patrol dropping back into their own trenches. There was now nothing to distract the enemy whose guns were even now searching no-man's-land for stragglers. Tom was trapped until the next night. There was nothing he could do apart from keeping his head down, and lying 'doggo' in the hope that he would not be spotted.

With this distinct possibility in mind before he set out, he had made sure his water bottle was full (with a drop of rum in it to kill the taste of the chlorine) and that he had some hardtack biscuits as well as a tin of bully beef. Not exactly a banquet, but he would not starve. It would do until tomorrow when he would be back with his mates, or not going back at all.

As the sun came up, he became aware of a nauseating, sickly-sweet smell which he immediately recognised. He was trapped in a shell-hole with a very badly decomposing German corpse, and there was nothing he could do about it.

Throughout the day, frenzied bursts of machinegun fire tracked the length of the British lines. This confirmed what they had been told about the aggressive nature of their new counterparts.

Darkness came at last, and not too soon as far as Tom was concerned. He had tried eating his iron rations but the smell emanating from his gruesome companion made him vomit every time he tried to swallow anything. All that would stay down was the water.

Then, as arranged, when the last traces of light had gone, out came another patrol heading for the enemy lines. Once they were in business, Tom legged it for home, and discovered that another enemy sniper must have worked out what had happened the previous night. This one must have realised that just possibly the demolition man might still be out there waiting for a chance to get back to his own lines, otherwise why was there another patrol going out again after the other bloody affair not twenty-four hours ago?

So, when tonight's patrol started out, he must have been keeping a watch on the area near the ruins because as Tom climbed out of the shell-hole, he had fired, striking the rim of the crater near Tom's hand. "That was too close for comfort" was Tom's immediate thought, and with that, he ran for his life.

Fear gave him wings as, ducking and weaving, he fled across the shell-torn ground, covering it with speed and agility he would not have thought possible. Arriving back at the British breastworks with unseemly haste, he threw himself over the wall of sandbags and vanished beneath the surface of the liquid filth with which the trenches were permanently half-filled.

It was significant that the toll previously being exacted by German snipers would now fall dramatically. In his report on the episode, Capt Yorke recommended Tom for a bravery award.

The second raid had proved more rewarding than the one the previous night. The enemy must not have been expecting another visit so soon. Not only had a good selection of badges and suchlike been amassed, but a prisoner had been dragged back, unconscious. As the opponents were now well-built Prussian Guards, the sight of the comatose body being hauled through the filth and debris of the battlefield by two diminutive Bantams must have presented quite a sight. Both captors would have been hard-pressed to reach five feet two inches in height but drag him in they did! This prisoner, together with the other bits and pieces, would now have to be sent back to Divisional H.Q.

It was agreed that because of the size difference as well as the atrocious state of the ground to be crossed, an escort of four could be justified. Two who were obviously eligible were the mighty midgets who had not only captured all six feet six inches of guardsman, but got him back to the British lines.

Tom would be another when all his exploits were taken into account. Apart from that, a corporal was needed to take charge of the detail.

The fourth would have to be a volunteer. Fred who had been unashamedly eavesdropping whilst all this was being arranged was there, on hand and readily available for the task. Quick as the proverbial Yorkshire miner's whippet, he was there in a flash, and offered his services. As ever, he was never one to miss a chance if it could be to his advantage.

They would go back as soon as it was dusk the next night as it was now too near daybreak to risk it. There would not be enough darkness remaining to cover their movements cross the more open stretches of their journey.

The prisoner was held under guard in the stores bay with his hands tied behind him until it was time to leave. Rations and water were shared with him. After all, why should the Ledfords be the only ones to suffer on their diet when you had one of the enemy to share it with?

With the arrival of dusk came the time for departure, so the little party set out. Whilst in the communications trenches, the prisoner went first with the escort following closely behind, bayonets fixed and with one round 'up the spout'. That way, there was no chance of a member of the squad being 'jumped' by the prisoner.

Once they were out on the lanes and roads leading back to camp, he was surrounded by his escort. Surprisingly, he seemed to have become resigned to his capture, strolling along and chatting to them in broken English. Apparently, he found the contrast between the Bantams and him to be rather amusing.

On their arrival back at the camp, he wished them well as he was given into the custody of the Intelligence Officer. Tom also handed in Capt. Yorke's report with details of the prisoner's capture, and, unbeknownst to Tom, details of the escapade in the chimney.

As it turned out, they were just in time to get places on a lorry on its way to the bath house in Hazebrouck. This suited Tom, who stank like a 'muck midden' (as he so prosaically put it).

Afterwards, back in camp, a good feed at the cookhouse was followed by an early night.

For the four members of the escort, tomorrow would turn out to be a very good day for them as officially, they did not exist in camp. They were of course, on the strength of their unit which was at present, out in the trenches. Records showed that 4 Platoon, "C" Company of the 17th. M.Y.R. was currently in the trenches some twelve miles away. As far as officialdom was concerned, they were not in camp. Ergo, as they could not be in two places at once, they could not be in the camp. So, it was 'hunky-dory' by them, they would not argue with official reasoning. No muster parades, no roll-call, in fact, no duties of any kind as nobody would be looking for them. Provided they kept out of the way, nobody was the slightest bit interested in them. So, having taken the first meal of the day, it was back to their billet to lie low until it was time for the next meal.

When midday came, they went for their meals at the cookhouse. The question as to whether they were there officially or unofficially did not spoil their appetites. Afterwards, they became genuinely 'unofficial' and went back to their hut to snooze for an hour or so until it was time to visit the local *estaminet*. This time, they would eat and drink in moderation as was dictated by their lack of funds until it was time to return to camp. This would be in time for the start at dusk, on the return to the front line. All in all, not a bad little interlude but one which had been earned.

They had decided on an early start so that it would be easier to pick out the remains of the trench leading back to their platoon's position in the line. It had been so badly shattered by the time they passed it on the way in that it would be well nigh impossible to pick it out when it was dark. They also argued that with a bit of luck, the Germans would think it not worthwhile wasting shells on such a small group of men.

Before they turned in for the night, four new, empty sandbags were filled with fresh bread from the cookhouse. The necks of the bags were lashed together in pairs to make them easier to carry. They also passed lengths of rope through carrying handles of four boxes of grenades. Earlier in the day, two lengths of fencing rail which just happened to be lying around were removed to the billet so as to tidy the camp. Each pole would be carried slung between two men, on their shoulders as they walked in file. On each, would be slung two boxes of grenades and two bags of bread.

As well as the reports on the day's action, Lt. Richardson had included a requisition for the grenades to supplement the few they had remaining. Cpl. Gardner had been authorised to sign for them at the ammunition dump.

Up at 0630hrs. having washed and shaved, they swallowed some bread and cheese as they were too early for breakfast. This meal had also been arranged at the time they had collected the bread.

So, with the poles loaded, the carriers hoisted them onto their shoulders and set out on their journey. As they went past the sentry at the gate, he commented sarcastically on the 'beasts of burden'. With a straight face Tom replied that he, as corporal in charge, had had to have these loads specially made up for his three men just to stop them breaking into a run. They had been so keen to get back into the trenches that he, the corporal, would have been left behind in the rush. He had to do something to stop them breaking into a gallop and slow them down so that he could keep up with them!

The look on the sentry's face showed that he was having great difficulty in believing what he had just been told in all seriousness.

When they arrived at the point where the communication trenches should have started, it was obvious that the area had suffered more heavy shelling since they had passed that way only two days ago. In fact, judging by the fresh reek of burnt explosives, it had been quite recent. The trenches had been totally obliterated, including the one they were looking for.

They stopped for a breather, and smoked cigarettes behind cupped hands. As they did so, they quartered the ground immediately to their front, and then in the general direction in which they should have been going. With luck, they might just spot something to put them on the correct bearing.

Just as they had almost given up hope of ever finding the trench they were seeking, and had decided just to push on straight forward and trust to luck, they found the faintest trace of what could have been what they had been looking for just about on the horizon. As it was roughly on the expected bearing, they set out for it, stumbling in and out of craters, dropping their loads, and cursing all and sundry for all they were worth. This, whilst not helping at all, did, to some extent relieve their feelings a little.

Providence must have been watching over them because not a single shell came their way as they crossed the open ground. As Tom explained later, this must have been because most of the time, they had been at the bottom of one of those bloody shell-holes!

The bombs were handed over to Bob and Charlie who were now the platoon's official bombers. With what they already had plus what had now just been brought up, they now had about eighty between them.

The bread was now shared out amongst 4 Platoon only as there was not enough for the whole of "C" Company. If further justification was needed for this restricted distribution, there was the fact that it had been 'won' by 4 Platoon personnel. Hacked into chunks using bayonets, it was shared out amongst the lucky few. Baked just before being collected, it was still fresh.

Charlie was heard to complain that it was full of 'hairy bits'. He was right of course, as the loaves had collected loose jute fibres from inside the sacks in which the bread had been carried. He had been in so much of a hurry that he had neglected to pick them off the bread as the others had done. He also moaned about the taste which the bread had picked up from the sacks along with the fibres ----- " It tastes as if it's been 'watterproofed' ".

This was too much for Bob. "It 'as, in case some silly sod like you drops it in t'watter. So shut thi'gob, an' stop thi moanin'! Ger it etten. If tha duzzent want it thissen, tha can gi' it tu me!"

Such was Bob's considered advice to his best pal.

Chapter 11

Darkness came and with it the customary stand-to. As nothing happened, everybody relaxed as much as possible in such appalling surroundings. The night dragged on as usual, or so it seemed at the beginning. There were the usual bursts of small-arms fire as well as flares. In short, a normal, quiet night in the trenches. But this was not to last. It soon became obvious that this early morning just before daybreak was going to be very different.

Fifteen minutes or so before what would have been the usual dawn stand-to, the morning literally exploded around them. Mortar bombs of all calibres as well as 'minnies' intermixed with more than the usual number of 'whizz-bangs' showered down on the British lines. Then, after about twenty minutes, the 'whizz-bangs' lifted to fall some way behind the trenches. This box barrage would effectively cut off any access to the beleaguered positions, and prevent any reinforcements getting through to the 'P.B.I.' who were beneath this assorted ironmongery falling on them from the heavens. (P.B.I. was how the infantry now cynically referred to themselves --- Poor Bloody Infantry!)

The 'minnies' and the 'Jack Johnsons' continued to fall on them with unabated fury. Trouble was on its way, and heading straight for them.

Word was passed along the line that the expected assault could not come whilst the bombardment was still in progress but could be expected the moment the shelling stopped. Riflemen were to aim at picked targets, and not blaze away willy-nilly.

They were to commence firing only when they heard their officer's whistle.

The two bombers set up their stall on ledges they had cut into the front wall of the trench. Here they placed their boxes of grenades plus all the spares they had collected from the riflemen. They had now amassed sixty or so grenades each, all fused in readiness.

As had been demonstrated in training sessions, Bob and Charlie had thrown '36' Mills grenades about forty to fifty yards This was about ten yards more on average than the normal distance. This extra distance meant that the grenade's four-second fuse had just about burnt its way to the detonator whilst the missile was in flight. With a shorter throw, if the intended target was quick or brave enough --- or even just lucky --- he could pick up the still-smoking missile and either throw it back where it had come from, or usually into the nearest crater. Bob and Charlie had devised their own method to stop this happening.

Ignoring what the training manual said (as usual), they would work as a pair, in tandem. Bob would throw the first bomb, then, just as this was about to land, Charlie would throw a second. This would be repeated for as long as was necessary. Anyone who chose to pick up the first bomb would suddenly find that he had a second one to deal with whilst he still had the first one in his hand! In his panic, he would forget about that in his hurry to get rid of the second. That was the general idea. Now was the chance to see if it would work.

The barrage stopped ----- THIS WAS IT!

A quick look through the loophole in the breastwork showed that the enemy had risked coming through his wire whilst his barrage was at its peak, and were even now threading their way through the British entanglement. At this point, it was about a hundred yards from the opposing lines, with the Ledfords' wire just thirty yards in front of them.

The enemy shelling had not done a very good job of cutting this wire, and had only managed to make one or two gaps leaving the bulk of the wire in place and undamaged. Bunching occurred at these gaps whilst other troops had to wait out in the open until further openings had been cut by hand.

When about half the attackers had managed to get through the gaps, the whistles sounded. The Guards at Mons, being regulars, had got off between fifteen and twenty aimed shots in a minute. The Bantams and the Fusiliers managed about twelve, but they all must have counted. As the enemy were not advancing in parade-ground files, but forcing their way forward *en masse,* the man in front overlapped the man behind him as he did the man behind him. As this was the case all the way through to the rearmost person, there were no gaps for bullets to pass through without hitting anyone so every round must have counted. By opening fire when the first men were through the wire, maximum confusion was created with resulting high losses for the attackers.

Bob and Charlie were in their element as their scheme worked like a dream. A continuous stream of bombs flew across the open ground to land in the melee in and around the British wire.

Despite massive losses, the attack was pressed home with determination. At one stage, a Prussian officer had reached a breach in the defence-works just in front of Bob. He, in the act of breaking out a fresh supply of grenades was unaware of the danger he was in. Some sixth sense must have alerted him. Seizing his rifle with its bayonet fixed, he turned round holding it pointing upwards at an angle of some forty-five degrees. The Prussian was on the point of emptying his pistol into Bob's head when a round from Tom, fired at point-blank range, took him full in the face which disintegrated in a spray of blood and bone splinters. As if that was not enough, Charlie waded in for good measure. Holding his rifle by the muzzle and swinging it like a club, he hammered it across the knees of the German who, pitching forward, impaled himself on Bob's bayonet, wrenching the rifle out of Bob's hands as he did so.

The frenzied attack continued unabated, so Bob had to resort to other means to defend himself. The 'toothpick' now came into its own. Thus equipped, Bob flailed about him at any of the enemy who were so unfortunate as to come within reach. Bones were broken when struck. If merely a soft target presented itself, the weapon gouged painful wounds, tearing out gobbets of flesh in the process. The recipient of such treatment suddenly lost any further interest in the proceedings.

At last the pressure eased and the enemy withdrew. Whilst the Bantams and the fusiliers had been fully occupied, the artillery Forward Observation Officer in the lines with them had called up a barrage on the German lines and the area behind it. This would be where there would be reserves moving forward to assist in the attack, and to consolidate any ground taken.

The survivors of the abortive assault were now moving back across open ground under offensive gunfire. They were trying to get back into battered trenches which were already crowded with the reserves waiting to move forward, and with more trying desperately to get in from the rear to escape from the shells falling all round them.

The F.O.O. was full of praise for the R.E. signals detachment who, after repairing the shell-damaged telephone cables, had had the good sense to bury them in the floor of the communications trench. This would give the cable a better chance of survival if the trench should be blown in. This had proved to be the case.

In the comparative calm which followed, each man checked his ammunition, drawing more from the reserve in the stores bay as necessary. Casualties were treated. Fred's lot had once again escaped with cuts and bruises. There was nothing disabling or life-threatening.

The rest of "C" Company had not been so lucky. Eight had been killed outright, and twenty-three wounded in varying degrees. On balance, when the ferocity of the action was taken into account, they had come out of it relatively unscathed.

As Bob recovered his rifle (and German officer!) from the depths of the flooded trench, Lt. Richardson grabbed the helmet, the much- prized *pickelhaube*. This would settle his debt with the M.T. major back in camp.

It was now that they were to learn that there were TWO kinds of noise on a battlefield. There was, of course, the din of the actual conflict itself. That was bad enough. Much worse, however, are the sounds which become apparent after the fighting has stopped.

There are the cries of pain of the wounded left on the field or hanging on the wire. There are the gut-wrenching sobs and shrieks of the fatally wounded, those left dying in mortal agony. There is the persistent whimpering of those with less severe injuries, which are not life-threatening, but painful nonetheless.

One German lad with his front ripped open had been left trapped on the wire. In between calls for his *mutti* (his mother), he would give vent to high-pitched screams as spasms of pain wracked his tortured body. It seemed that he had been in this plight for ever.

Suddenly a rifle gave voice. That single shot took the lad in the head and put him out of his misery.

The German barrage continued to fall behind the British lines, albeit sporadically. They were still cut off from relief and supplies, they were still isolated. And now, more trouble was in the offing.

The tot of rum was now distributed together with the tin of bully beef as it was now time for breakfast. It would also have to do for lunch, and possibly the evening meal, if they lived that long. There was no distribution of water as the all the tins holding the reserve supply of what passed for 'drinking water' had been riddled by splinters. All the water they had was that remaining in their bottles. Orders were given that in order to make this last as long as possible, only a small amount was to be taken at a time, and rinsed around inside the mouth before swallowing it. It was not to be gulped by the mouthful.

At that moment, the gas gong sounded. This was a shell-case suspended from a bayonet driven into the wall of the trench and struck with yet another bayonet in the event of a gas attack.

Hoods were donned with the skirts being tucked in to the necks of their tunics in the manner they had learned in what now seemed to be an earlier life.

Across the wastes of 'no-man's-land', a mist-like vapour slowly wreathed its way towards them. The claustrophobic struggle to suck air through the felt and canvas bag was now upon them, as was the gas. The eyepieces, as ever, started to cloud over. So, having taken a deep breath and holding it, the front of the mask was hauled out from the tunic, a handkerchief thrust inside and wiped furiously across the celluloid windows. Then, as much air as possible was now expelled from inside the device before replacing the skirt in the tunic. 'Normal' breathing was now resumed. There was a sudden smell of damp, musty hay. Phosgene was being used.

As some would inevitably seep inside whilst the eyepieces were being wiped, it was a risky business, particularly if the gas involved was phosgene. When inhaled in lethal doses, the victim would not suffer any great hardship at the time, apart from perhaps, a fit of coughing. But it did have an insidious delayed effect. Even small doses could become fatal some time later with the unfortunate individual collapsing without warning.

As the gas cloud drifted towards them, it did not reach all the way down to the ground, but for some odd reason floated about eighteen inches above it. As a result, the feet and lower legs of the advancing enemy could be clearly seen. Another interesting phenomenon was that as they walked forward, the movements of these men caused the gas clouds to swirl and eddy around them. So, the rifleman's target was in the eddy directly above those feet. The bombers also assessed the range by reference to the same feet. Despite what he might think, the cover given by the gas cloud to the advancing infantryman was not as complete as he would have wished. When fire was opened on the wraiths in the mist and bombs thrown in for good measure, the explosions further diminished the gas cloud.

The attack, when it came, was only a half-hearted affair, and not the pressed home with anything like the ferocity of the earlier assault. It wavered, then was no more.

On this occasion, there would be no post- battle noises as all the casualties from both attacks had been asphyxiated. Instead, there was an ominous, oppressive, sinister silence.

The hated gas hoods had, of necessity, to be worn for another hour or so until what little air movement there was carried the gas clear of the trenches to disperse in the shell-blasted wasteland behind them. After breathing through the chemically-impregnated fabric for so long, even despite the lingering traces of the phosgene, the comparatively fresh air would taste sweet.

Chapter 12

Eventually, it was considered safe enough to relax. Sentries were posted and weapons checked over. Repairs were made to the trenches and sandbagged fortifications which had taken a pounding. 'Jerry' must have been licking his wounds as well, and doing the same as the British. An uneasy lull had settled over the area.

The rest of the day passed in an atmosphere of uncertainty. German shells continued to fall from time to time, effectively stopping reinforcements being brought up as well as the much-needed supplies. Replacements for those killed could not come forward to where they were desperately needed, nor could the wounded be evacuated, no matter how severe their injuries.

Throughout the night which followed, bursts of enemy machine-gun fire would scythe across the Golgotha which lay between the lines. This would prevent wiring parties going out to repair the British wire.

When the German guns paused, British would take over. There was always the possibility that whilst the enemy guns were encouraging the Bantams and their comrades in adversity to keep their heads down, a new assault might be following lanes left between the arcs over which the enemy guns were firing. If that was so, then it had to be thwarted. Better to be safe, than sorry! The net result was that no one got any sleep, be they British or German.

Dawn stand-to came and went. They were already on the alert so it did not make any difference. The German artillery continued its incessant barrage, and the day was much the same as yesterday. The guns had been firing since --- nobody could remember when. The number of shells fired must have been considerable. The continuous explosions had numbed the mind.

The 'Dish of the Day' was cold McConochies straight from the tin as there was no means of heating it. Water was now getting dangerously low. Most men surrendered a good proportion of what little they still had left in their water bottles to give to the wounded, who by now, were beginning to suffer badly.

Day dragged into dusk with the inevitable routines being followed. The German guns continued their incessant firing. Would they never run out of shells?

Night was following its usual course when suddenly the sentry opened up with the Lewis gun. Somehow, unnoticed by all until now, German troops had managed to worm their way across to arrive unheralded almost at the breastworks.

When the initial panic was under control, it was simply a matter of 'kill, or be killed'. At one stage, the attackers actually got into the British positions. Anything which came to hand and which could be utilised as a weapon was used to deadly effect. One Prussian almost falling into a bay lost his rifle as he did so. Finding himself next to Charlie, he swung round and seized him by the throat. That was probably his intention, but with a guardsman attacking a Bantam, Charlie's throat was lower than expected. Instead of by the throat, Charlie was gripped round, the head with the German sinking his nails into his opponent's face to maintain his grip.

Fortunately, Charlie had a Fred Booth 'Special', a trench knife. With all the strength he could muster, he drove the blade through the enemy tunic and up into the ribcage. All nine inches of cold steel entered the German's chest cavity with dramatic results. The fingers relaxed their grip, and Charlie stepped clear of the corpse.

Then came a double blast on a whistle followed by shouted commands as the attackers withdrew.

With the arrival of daylight, the British took stock of the effects of the raid in force they had just repelled. There were more dead and wounded which was to be expected. Charlie had severe lacerations to his face which were more spectacular than dangerous. The medical orderly decided that as there was so much muck and filth about, not to mention what might have been under the German's nails, blood poisoning might set in. He applied what Charlie would refer to as his 'war paint' --- Gentian violet. This was liberally daubed over the affected areas.

Once again, the piteous cries of the wounded filled the air. Capt. Yorke was of the opinion that something had to be done and done quickly if any of the poor wretches were to have the slightest chance of survival. A large, white flag was constructed. As it was an ancient piece of tent canvas normally used to cover the stores, it was actually a light grey in colour, but it was 'white' enough for the purpose. When raised above the parapet, this off-white flag produced a similar response from across the way.

Slowly raising himself into view, Capt.Yorke climbed out into the open, calling on William to accompany him as interpreter (although he only spoke French).

They met an enemy officer about halfway between the lines. He too had a private soldier with him. It was soon established that he had very little English, and that the British had no German whatsoever. Luckily both interpreters were fluent in French so that would be the language used.

Capt.Yorke proposed that a truce be called until the Germans had recovered their wounded. He stipulated the conditions under which this would be allowed.

Any Germans who were on the British side of the wire would be carried by British soldiers to a point in no-man's-land near the German wire. There they would be collected by their comrades-in arms. (This would prevent the enemy taking note of any weak points in the British defences).

No repairs would be allowed to German positions which could not be done without climbing out into the open in full view from the British positions.

There was to be no sneaking forward of machine-guns into craters forward of the German lines under cover of the stretcher bearers. (This had happened elsewhere with advance defence posts being set up in this manner).

As a guarantee that these conditions would be adhered to, the German officer would stand in full view just behind the British wire to one side of the gap through which the wounded would be carried.

As there was no choice in the matter, the terms were accepted. In doing so, the German officer introduced himself as *Hauptmann* Heinrich von Etzeldorff. At this, Capt.Yorke announced his name whereupon they both shook hands. It was made clear that if there was the slightest departure from the agreed conditions, the *Hauptmann* would be shot without warning. That was why he would be standing out in the open in full view of the British lines. Tom, of course, had been given appropriate orders.

With the white flags stuck in the parapets, the evacuation of the wounded began. Twenty or thirty enemy injured were carried out beyond the wire as agreed. It was shocking to see just how youthful some of them were --- straight out of school by the look of some of them.

When at last, all had been recovered to the German lines, Cpt. Yorke and William walked over to the German officer and his interpreter who had remained with him, and told them to stay where they were until he, Capt. Yorke was back in the British lines. Then, and only then were they to return to theirs. Both officers saluted each other, and the two Britons set off.

Just as they reached the British parapet, Capt. Yorke tripped and fell to his knees. That stumble undoubtedly saved his life. At precisely that moment, a shot from as German rifle narrowly missed him.

Etzeldorff bellowed *"Nicht schiessen!"* Whether this was an order to his own troops, or a desperate plea to the British not to shoot him was anybody's guess. There was no shooting from either side.

Unbuckling his belt with its holstered pistol as he came, he strode over to Capt. Yorke offering his weapon. Following him like a frightened rabbit scuttled his interpreter. Apologising profusely for the *dummkopf* who had fired the shot, he offered his surrender. This was refused as apart from that one incident, all the other conditions had been met.

The two Germans went back to their lines, then, a moment later, the white flag was raised again in the enemy lines. After a short pause, a German soldier appeared followed by the *hauptmann* carrying a rifle. The hapless soldier set off at a shambling run away from his own lines managing to cover some thirty yards before collapsing, lifeless, as the rifle spat flame. This was then thrown after the guilty man who had been summarily executed with his own rifle.

After a moment standing with his head bowed as if in prayer, *Hauptmann* Etzeldorff saluted smartly, then dropped back into his own trenches,

It was now back to the war again. It was business as usual!

Then followed a period of comparative calm, although German artillery kept up its never-ending bombardment of the countryside behind the Bantams' lines. But even this was to ease off during the day. When a check was made to see how they stood should there be another attack, they found that ammunition was in desperately short supply. Water bottles were for the most part empty. As for food --- what was that?

As for the men themselves, they appeared to be dead on their feet. Tongues were swollen through lack of water. Their eyes were glassy and sunken in their heads. As well as carrying several days' growth of ragged stubble, their cheeks were hollow and haggard. This was not really surprising as they had had no sleep to speak of, and had been on short rations since returning to the line.

By now, the never-ending roar and the continual concussion of the explosions had so numbed their minds that the men existed in a state of stupefaction, as if in a trance. There was a perpetual ringing in their ears. When someone spoke to them, the words seemed to come from a great distance, and then, as if through cotton-wool. Reactions were slow and deliberate.

The question was asked as to how long they had been in the trenches on this stint. No one could remember, or even hazard a guess. They only knew that they had come in a long time ago in the distant past – or so it seemed. If they were spared, they might even be relieved sometime in the equally distant future. All concept of the twenty-four hour day had been totally lost. What they now endured was featureless time with variations in light and darkness.

The Forward Observation Officer sent an urgent message by means of the field telephone with a request for its priority transfer to Div. H.Q. In effect it said that if the position was not supplied with ammunition and replacements, IMMEDIATELY, then in the event of a further assault, the position would undoubtedly be lost.

Word came back that the relief was on its way with the supplies requested. The survivors would be withdrawn and replaced with new troops at the correct strength to restore the manning level to what it should be, " ---- and in answer to your query, the Mid-Yorkshires have been in the line nine days, the Fusiliers eleven! You went in at the same time as the Fusiliers!"

Chapter 13

Round about midnight, word came that the replacements had arrived at the stores bay, and that the outgoing troops could now start withdrawing from the line. The Fusiliers went first followed shortly by the Bantams.

The fresh men were horrified when they saw the condition of the creatures leaving the front trench. Filthy, unkempt, covered in mud as well as blood, they staggered and lurched from side to side as they went. The usual badinage fell flat as it provoked no response at all from the troops being relieved. These were men who had reached their limit and beyond, and who were asleep on their feet.

Onwards they staggered, back towards their goal. Arrival at the camp could not come too soon. Half the time they were out in the open as the trench system had been blasted out of existence. Not a single shell fell. It was if the Germans were in the same exhausted condition and hoped that if they did not shell the British, there would be no retaliation in kind. Whatever the reason, nobody gave it a thought, nobody really cared. They were past caring.

Because of the tortured nature of the ground, they proceeded in single file. The moment the line stopped, the leading man stuck the bayonet on his rifle into the ground, and resting his head on the butt, instantly fell asleep. All the rest leaned forward onto the man in front and did likewise. When it was time to move on again, N.C.O.s and officers had to go along the line and thump the men awake, or, more accurately, into a state of semi-consciousness. In this manner, they at long last tottered in through the camp gates and passed in front of the sentry who threw up a snappy butt-salute to the officers and the body of 'marching' men. He was totally ignored. Indeed, it was doubtful if they even noticed him.

The Accommodation Officer who had been expecting them showed them to their huts. Going inside, the men went to their allotted bed-spaces and fell asleep on the floor beside their beds. They stank to high heaven and were so filthy that if the beds had been used, they would have become so befouled as to be unusable under normal circumstances. A hot meal had been arranged for them, but starving as they were, no one stayed awake long enough to go and get it.

The next morning when *reveillé* sounded, the first task was to wash the filth from their hands and faces. Next to go was the luxuriant growth of whiskers that everyone sported. It was some task. When at last they emerged from behind the thickets, they all had sundry cuts and nicks to show as evidence of the struggle. Because of his face wounds, which, although healing nicely still carried suppurating scabs, Charlie was allowed to trim his growth into an elegant King George V-style beard.

They found that since they had last been in camp, the erstwhile drying room still operated in that role as well as its true one of mess-hall. Filthy troops could now take a meal in trench-fouled clothing the moment they arrived back in camp without having to clean up first.

Now, having eaten their first hot meal in over a week, they paraded at the Q.M. stores where new uniforms were issued to replace the rags they were wearing. These were not only ripped and foul, they were also rotting on the backs of the wearers.

Whilst drawing the fresh clothing, they discovered the reason for the severe itching and skin irritation from which they were all suffering. They had 'lodgers' ---- they were lousy! They had lice! The Ledfords had their own Yorkshire name for these little fellows, 'chats'. So, if members of a group were "chatting", they were not gossiping, they were bug hunting.

As the little blighters lived in the seams of the garments, shirts and trousers were turned inside out. A lighted candle would then be run along these seams, when, with any luck, satisfying crackling and popping noises would indicate that some of the unwanted visitors had been incinerated.

They had been ordered not to change into the new uniforms as there was to be a bath parade in about half an hour. They were to assemble outside their huts with the new clothing and washing materials in their kit-bags.

It was the same routine as before. Lorry to Hazebrouck where they would debus at the brewery, but this time, outside the building, they would check their pockets, strip off the old uniforms, and then dump them in a heap for burning. Some of the rags looked as if they could crawl away to the furnace unassisted.

Next came the shirts and underwear. These would be fumigated in the Foden 'bug cooker' (or delousing machine) which was standing nearby. According to the experts, this would destroy all the vermin before these garments were laundered.

Replacement items were now issued, which, in the best Army tradition fitted where they touched. If the 'fit' was too bad, or no fit all, they would be swapped around until the best fit possible could be managed. The quality of the Army laundering service was not too bad provided that things were not inspected too closely, and the recipient was not too squeamish. Or, to put it army-style, "That's all you're getting!"

Once inside, the men lay back, luxuriating in the hot water until they were told to get dressed and onto the transport back to camp.

The next stop was the medical room where they were subjected to a thorough going-over by the M.O. who seemed particularly interested in their feet. The next lot of Company Orders showed why. Privates Booth and Sugden were to be court-martialled in two days time! They immediately sought and were given an interview with Capt. Yorke. The M.O. had seen that both men had 'trench feet' or foot rot. This condition was brought about by prolonged immersion in filthy water, in other words, the conditions they had just left.

The skin on affected feet would literally rot, becoming white, soggy and with the texture of cream cheese. Skin in this state would come away at the slightest touch, exposing the raw flesh underneath. The smell was appalling. In bad cases, the toes would become distorted and twisted as the joints were attacked.

The charges were :-

1/. Failure to take good care of the person, said failure reducing the military efficiency of that person;

2/. Failure to obey an order in the face of the enemy. (Here, the prosecution would attempt to show that the whale oil had not been applied to the feet in question).

3/. Malingering.

4/. Conduct prejudicial to good order and discipline in the army of H.M. the King.

(These last two items were the universal 'catch-all' of the army, and were always included on any charge-sheet).

As the officer commanding "C" Company, Capt. Yorke had been instructed to prosecute. Lt. Richardson as platoon commander of both the accused was named as 'witness for the prosecution'.

A Lt. Edmondson from "A" Company had been nominated as 'Prisoners' Friend'. As the charges against each man were identical, the same defence would be required for both of them.

The following day, Fred and William were given permission to visit their 'friend' and take advice as to the manner of their defence. Along with dealing with the legal technicalities, they were told to ensure that they should create a good first impression on the Court by being smartly turned out. This meant their uniforms (being straight out of storage) would require a lot of hard work doing on them. As for their boots, after nine days immersion, they were still soaking wet, so the customary high polish was out of the question.

This problem was solved when Lt. Edmondson addressed a note to the camp R.S.M. and explained the situation. He was asked to find some boots with an acceptable, parade-ground gloss for the two to wear at their trial.

This proved to be no problem.

The President of the Court-martial was to be a Colonel Gilbertson from Div. H.Q. This was not as ominous as it first sounded. Although now a 'brass hat', he would know the score as he had been a frontline soldier until badly wounded. He was a Guardsman who had fought at Mons, then taken part in the fighting withdrawal to Le Cateau where he had lost an eye. He was above all else a soldier's soldier, and would have experienced all the hardships of active campaigning. He had the reputation of being thoroughly honest, no matter at what cost. They could have done much worse.

On the due date at the appointed time, the two miscreants were paraded by the R.S.M. and held in readiness for the summons into the hut being used as the court-room. On the command, they were double-marched inside to stand rigidly at attention until told to stand at ease.

The President introduced himself. He was an imposing figure with iron-grey hair, and a patch covering the empty eye socket. The other two officers on the Bench were the commanders of "B" and "D" companies of the Ledfords.

Having convened, the Court was now in session.

The accused were required to identify themselves. With that formality over, the charges were now read out and they were asked how they pleaded. On the instructions of their 'friend', the reply was "Not guilty".

The case hinged on whether or not the whale oil had been duly and diligently applied. When questioned on this point, Lt. Richardson stated categorically that it had been. He had issued it to them and had supervised its application. What was more, he had used his own portion on his feet at the same time. (As a prosecution witness, his evidence did nothing to advance the case).

Capt. Yorke, despite being the prosecuting officer now refuted the remaining charges. He reminded the Court that the 17th. Mid-Yorkshires had just spent nine days of sheer hell in the trenches, and that there was not the slightest shred of evidence to suggest that there was any substance at all in any of the charges. He would like to add to, and clarify what Lt. Richardson had said. They had all applied the whale oil whilst they still had any, before it had run out. They had also run out of food and water. They were also perilously near to running out of ammunition as well. Then there was the not-so-small fact that from about the fourth day onwards, the level of floodwater in the trenches had risen to about mid-thigh level. In the trench, it was impossible to raise your feet clear of the water to allow the oil to be applied, even if you had had any. To get your feet high enough, you would have to sit on the parapet. Then you would have been shot by the enemy.

So, to sum up, "Yes, the oil had been applied when they had some. However, in the later stages of the siege, they could not have done so even supposing they had had any!"

As both the prosecuting officer and the witness had virtually destroyed the list of charges before the Court, the President asked if the defending officer wished to add anything. Up till now, beyond acknowledging his identity, Lt. Edmondson had said nothing. Now he did.

He had found that the official preventive, whale oil, did not work in all cases. He had also ascertained that troops in flooded positions in the Ypres sector were issued with rubber thigh boots. Why were these not being issued in this sector?

He then craved the indulgence of the Court and invited Lt. Richardson to remove his leather gaiters, boots and socks. He then drew the attention of the Court to the fact whilst one foot showed signs of 'trench foot', the other did not. Both feet, however, had been treated with whale oil to the same extent. Why the difference?

Lt. Edmondson was aware of the Divisional order requiring the M.O. to inspect the feet of N.C.O.'s and other ranks, and to report those showing signs of the condition in question. Why was there no such order in respect of officers even though they could be affected as well, as he had just demonstrated?

Cpt. Yorke now stepped forward and removed his footwear. He too had 'trench feet'. When were Lt. Richardson and he to be court-martialled? If not, why not?

The President of the Court there and then pronounced both the accused "Not guilty" on all charges, and instructed the clerk to enter this verdict in the official record of the proceedings which were then formally closed.

He then spoke 'unofficially' to Capt. Yorke confiding that when he got back to Div. H.Q. he would ensure that no charges of this nature were brought against troops who did not have protective footwear whilst in the trenches. He would also pursue the question of supplying such equipment to troops in ALL flooded areas. His concluding remarks to the officers of the Court were "Where's the Mess? I'll have a double brandy!"

Afterwards, Lt. Richardson invited the defending officer to accompany him on the evening jaunt to the local *estaminet* as was customary when 4 Platoon was back in camp. This was when King's Regulations were ignored on a regular basis.

As was well known, it was an offence for officers to take drinks from the rank and file, but he had no doubt that Private Booth would make an exception in their case and pay for food and drinks out of his illegal earnings, about which he, his platoon commander, officially knew nothing at all,! Fred said that as William and he were innocent, at least, as far as the Court Martial was concerned, he would see what could be arranged. In any case, as neither of the two 'innocents' would lodge a complaint about either officer, there was nothing to worry about!

Over drinks in the officers' mess, the question was raised as to the ferocity and duration of the recent actions in which the M.Y.R. had been involved. Did H.Q. have any inkling as to what the enemy had intended as regards, perhaps, a bigger affair, or was it a purely localised, limited action?

Colonel Gilbertson said that in his opinion, and it was only that, the enemy had been trying to do what Intelligence had been expecting of them for some time. The British sector of the Front in the Festubert area projected in the form of a bulge into the enemy lines. It was this minor salient that they had been, apparently, trying to pinch out, thus straightening their front. That would have seemed to be their intention until they had come up against the Welsh and the Yorkshire troops.

Capt. Yorke commented forcefully, "It's a pity they didn't tell me, they could have had the bloody swamp for nothing! It's not worth one of those lives, British or German, hanging on to it. If anybody from Division had ever been up here, they would have realised that if WE had pulled back and made what is currently our second line the front line, then not only would we have been on slightly higher ground which would not flood so deeply, we would not be overlooked by the enemy. We would also have deeper, more easily defended trenches. Instead, we are ordered to hold on to a useless stretch at all costs. Very much a case of "Ours not to reason why!"

The colonel agreed, and, whilst sympathising with those views, commented that withdrawal, any withdrawal, would be unacceptable from a political standpoint. He would, though, drop hints here and there in the hope that with a bit of luck, some desk-bound general would come up with it as his own original thought.

Meanwhile, Fred and William had realised that as they were, on paper, still being court-martialled, they would not be expected to be available for duties of any kind. They decided to visit the workshops as a means of filling in time whilst keeping out of the way. Fred found that the sergeant-fitter was doing a roaring trade in what he was promoting as 'trench cutlery'. He handed Fred a pile of cash as the agreed fees for the use of Fred's ideas. The amount of cash was more than likely just a rough estimate only but more than enough to keep Fred happy.

It was more than adequate to pay for meals and drinks for the two officers as well as for William and Fred with enough left in hand to provide ' throat lotion' for the rest of the lads. (Charlie had bestowed this name on the thin, red wine available at the *estaminet*. He claimed that after a glass or two, there was no need to gargle, even if anyone had dared to).

As this was the only *estaminet* anywhere near the camp, there was no question of segregation, making one 'officers only' with others for lower ranks. The only way was to allow all ranks to mix at this inn when off duty.

It had been arranged that the first member of Fred's group to arrive at the hostelry would secure a table for four, and hold it against all-comers. When Fred and William turned up, the table would be relinquished to them the moment they came in. Thus, when the officers arrived a little while later, the only two free places would be at this table. They would have no choice but to sit with the lower ranks. In this way, army etiquette would be satisfied to some extent, if only on the face of things.

With William in attendance, there were no problems with the menu. A succulent meat casserole in wine gravy was followed by what Fred would later describe as an upside-down apple pie. They finished the meal with coffee. This was the first Fred had ever seen let alone tasted. He couldn't make his mind up whether he liked it or not. However, as he was paying for it, he would drink the stuff even if it killed him!

After a very enjoyable evening, during which the two 'offenders' were toasted by everyone present for beating the charges, the two officers who had defended them so ably were also the subject of alcoholic acclaim. Somehow, it was conveniently overlooked that one of them had been the prosecution witness!

Then, as always, it was time to return to camp.

Chapter 14

The morning after the night before, so to speak, Fred and William reported to the M.O. as ordered to be advised as to the best treatment for their feet. They were issued with what Fred recognised as lanoline, or purified wool grease. By the smell of it, coal tar extract had been added to it. In addition to this ointment, they were given what seemed like miles of gauze bandages.

The unguent was to be liberally rubbed into the afflicted parts of the feet before bandaging them. If they could get their socks on over the bandages, all well and good. If not, the bandages were to be carried up the legs to where the socks would normally finish.

As it was thought unlikely that their correctly-sized boots could still be worn over that lot, the M.O. wrote out what he referred to as 'medical requisitions'. These authorised the quarter-master to issue to each man, one pair of boots which were big enough to be worn over the bandages. The chits were duly stamped and signed, then handed one to each man.

Since their return after the recent fighting near Festubert, all those involved had been on light duties to allow them to recover from the experience. Kit still had to be cleaned and maintained, and brought back up to standard where necessary. P.E. was again part of the daily routine, as were short, sharp route marches undertaken with or without full equipment depending on the mood of the officer in charge.

As the next day would involve a full kit lay-out and inspection prior to going back into the line in the not too distant future, everyone in Fred's hut was slaving away cleaning and polishing, when the platoon sergeant came in. Charlie, who had just cleaned the rust from his bayonet and was now polishing it vigorously asked why this was necessary as the moment they were back in the trenches it would be filthy again in no time.

The sergeant looked at him, pityingly, and said, "Nay, lad. When tha sticks it in Jerry's guts, if it wur mucky, 'e'd dee o' blood poisoning, like as not. Tha wouldn't want that on thi' conscience, would yer?"

Inevitably, all good things must come to an end. They were now considered to be so battle-hardened as to be capable of front-line service without the support of the stiffening troops. From now on, they would be responsible for their own section of the line.

The map references showed this to be near Laventie, a little to the north of Neuve Chapelle, and looking towards Aubers Ridge. The map contours suggested that the new location was slightly higher than the swamps they had just left. With luck, they might even have dry trenches, or even just drier ones. They could only hope that this would prove to be the case.

Their orders stated that the section was to be held against any assault, and maintained in good, defensive condition. Offensive action was not required and should not be initiated unless specifically called for, in which case, orders would be sent up by runner. It was to be a case of settling in, and not disturbing the neighbours.

Their route would take them part way along the roads which had become so sickeningly familiar. But this time, when the ruins of Merville had been reached, they would follow the River Lys until they reached Estaires (or what was left of it) instead of continuing to the south as on previous occasions.

Capt. Yorke had been advised that the ground in the vicinity of their new home was shelled only occasionally, and then, only lightly. He had sent a runner forward advising the current residents of the relief's estimated time of arrival. These residents were, as it happened, Grenadier Guards. The changeover would be quite a sight!

The 17th Mid-Yorkshires would move off at 1400hrs. and had slightly more than ten miles to cover. Forewarned by their recent experiences, they carried as many extra supplies as was humanly possible. In addition to the rounds in his pouches, each man had a further 250 rounds in bandoliers festooned about him. Extra grenades were carried in boxes slung on carrying poles between two men. As for food and water, so much was carried they could hardly stagger, let alone walk.

They reached Merville, and then struck out into countryside or rather, 'devastation' which was new to them. Alongside the river they went until they came to a different lot of ruins. As Merville was now behind them, (or so they thought), and as the expanse of rubble was bigger than the last lot, then this must be Estaires.

The river crossing at this point was by means of a very shaky footbridge. The R.E. notice warned all users that it was only 'temporary', but gave no indication as to how long the bridge was expected to last! As they stepped onto the shaky structure, the order was given to break step' (not that they could be 'in step' with the loads they were carrying, and the condition of the ground). Breaking step would prevent the build-up of any regular vibration which, if it happened to be the correct frequency would cause the bridge to collapse.

A mile south of the river were more shattered buildings. These were surrounded by unburied dead from both opposing armies. As they approached, a 'corpse' stood up, stretched and yawned. He scratched himself vigorously and with obvious satisfaction.

It was a guide, but not theirs. Theirs had been killed back up the road by one of the very occasional shells! None of the craters or holes had been deep enough at that point, so, as a guardsman, there had been nowhere for him to take cover. He would not have had that problem if he'd been a Bantam -----

This guide was waiting for another relief column who were going in between the 17th. Mid-Yorkshires. and Festubert. As his lot were not due for about an hour, he would see them on their way. He led them to the entrance of a trench which was not only dry underfoot, but in not too bad a condition. They were to follow this until it forked, with both forks heading in more or less the same direction.

On arrival at this point, according to the guide, they would have no problem picking out the correct branch. "A dead 'un is pointin' t' way." With that cryptic remark, he bade them farewell, and left them to their own devices. He then retraced his own steps back to the rendezvous where he had his own replacements to meet. The 17th Mid-Yorkshires were not his responsibility.

They reached the fork, and sure enough, there was nothing to choose from between two trenches leading more or less in the same general direction. The dead 'un turned out to be a British casualty mutilated more than a little by shellfire sometime in the past. What remained of him had fallen with his right arm flung out, his hand still clutching his rifle and bayonet. The bayonet was pointing directly into one of the trenches. As that was obviously the one (they hoped), in they went.

They were now passing over ground which had been well fought over earlier in the war. Then, it had been in the French sector. Unburied dead were still exposed to the elements, some almost reduced to skeletons by the effects of the weather and the depredations of the rats which swarmed all over the wasteland.

They noticed that the duckboards under their feet had an unusual springiness. They tried not to think too deeply about the probable reason as to why this was so, at the same time trying to ignore the fearsome smell.

Then, at a bend, they came upon a skeletal hand and wrist poking out from the wall of the trench. The scraps of uniform still remaining were the 'horizon blue' of the French infantry. At first, the men were shocked at the sight, then, as often is the case, the macabre sense of humour of the British 'Tommy' took over. As they passed, each and every one solemnly shook hands with it.

Finally, the changeover point was reached.

For some reason, when the man nearest to the reliefs saw that they were Bantams, he went berserk. He shouted that it was an insult to the Guards to be replaced in the line by dwarfs, by bloody pygmies etc. etc.

William just happened to be opposite the guardsman when this tirade, this flood of invective was in full spate.

The situation was now on the point of becoming ridiculous. Five feet of irate Bantam now squared up to about six feet nine inches of fuming guardsman, who, if he had been wearing his bearskin would have been getting on for eight feet from the top of his head-dress to the ground.

As William put it "You overgrown bean-poles are all the same. You can be more bloody-minded than anybody else because there is more of you in one lump. You think you are better than anyone else --- well you're not. You think you can walk all over little blokes like us and get away with it. You're wrong. Put a sock in it. Shut your mouth. There's one very important point you have overlooked. Blokes our size don't need as deep a hole for cover. The reason we came in without a guide was because your mate, as a guardsman, was too big to find a deep enough crater when Jerry started shelling back there. Check it out as you go by. He's lying by the side of the track, dead. On another point, you'd better watch yourself. You haven't seen me really angry, so you don't know what I'm like when I am. So far, I'm not even annoyed!"

This last sally was so outrageous that everyone within hearing cracked out laughing and the tension in the air immediately vanished (which had been William's intention when he made it). The usual exchanging of the time-honoured, over-used traditional insults and quips were bandied about. Jokes took the place of animosity.

William's potential adversary looked down at him, and, patting him paternally on the top of his helmet said " Calm down, Tiger! Save that for Fritz".

William would frequently be addressed as 'Tiger' in future.

At last the handing over was completed and they were able to assess their 'home' for the next seven days. As they had hoped, their line of trenches was on a gentle rise. This had the effect of producing some slightly better drainage. The flooding was nothing like that at Festubert. There was now only six inches or so of liquid mud covering the duckboards ---- and their boots!

There was a fairly large dugout complete with stinking, muddy floor. Crude wooden benches and a rough table furnished this hovel. This must have been Company H.Q. and would continue in that role.

Deep 'funk-holes" had been dug into the walls at right angles to the run of the trenches. These, which had to be entered feet first with the head to the outside, had been where the previous tenants had got what little sleep they could. As they had been cut for guardsmen the holes were more than adequate for the Bantams even with all their kit.

But this disparity in height now produced difficulties. The Ledfords, on average, were about fifteen to eighteen inches shorter than most of the guardsmen. This meant that the heads of the Bantams were that distance below the parapet, even when they were standing on the fire-step. The remedy was to lift the duckboards and fill in the floor of the trench with earth and sandbags from the *parados* and behind it. A new firing-step had to be cut.

One amenity was found which lightened everyone's hearts – they now had a latrine dugout!

A short spur had been dug in the rear wall, with a small dugout to one side. In this had been placed the ubiquitous Army, chemical latrine bucket. In place of a seat, a German rifle had been jammed between the two opposite side walls to be used as a support by anyone in residence. Here was luxury indeed! At last the Company 'honey boy' would have something to do with his time when he wasn't busy fighting the enemy.

Shortly afterwards, the evening stand-to was attended to, after which, apart from the sentries, all souls crawled into their burrows. Although a deep sleep was not possible in the circumstances, they were at least able to doze off. But the big thing was that they were off their feet.

The following morning, they were amused to see hoisted over the German lines a large banner in English. It said: "We take breakfast at 0730hrs. We then rest for two hours. After that, you may shoot if you must. Please respect the rules of the house. Thank you"

As the orders they had been given stated quite distinctly that they were to hold the line against assault, but not to provoke enemy aggression, the attitude shown by this request suited the Ledfords down to ground.

Breakfast was taken from what had been carried by each man in the now familiar ration bags. This was eaten at 0730hrs. without any disturbance by the Germans as this when they would also be eating.

Lt. Richardson then sought permission to take a small, working party back to some ruined buildings they had passed on their way in, about a mile behind the line. He wished to see if it was suitable for a purpose he had in mind.

Fred's half section, who had 'volunteered' when ordered to do so, set out laden with picks and shovels. When they arrived at the ruins, they were found to be those of a farm and its outbuildings. It had been built in the style common to this part of France. Attached to the two sides of the farmhouse at right angles had been two barns. Across the ends of these and completing the 'square' was another lot of outbuildings. Entrance to the enclosed yard had been through a double gate set in one of the barns. The two side barns had been partly destroyed but the buildings at the end of the yard and at the opposite end to the farmhouse had been reduced to a mound of rubble.

What was left of the house was just about useable, the more so as nothing else was available. Most of the roof had gone as had about half its walls. The chimney wall and chimney were still standing. It was amazing how often this would prove to be the case in shelled buildings. Short stubs of walls were still attached. A cellar (still in reasonable condition) was found.

What Lt. Richardson had envisaged was a cookhouse for "C" Company.

When some of the rubble had been cleared away, a bundle of steel, reinforcing rods was found. These were of the type the Boche was using in the concrete of the pillboxes he was now constructing all over the place. With the fireplace cleared and the hearth extended forward, a grid constructed from these rods would support the cooking dixies, if only they had some. Smoke from the fire would find its way up the chimney, if only they had some fuel for a fire.

But these were early days. A British soldier when short of something he desperately needs is the world's best scrounger, although he would describe what he is doing as 'organising'. Nothing is safe, even if it is nailed down.

The kitchen area dealt with, the remainder of the floor space was tackled. As the broken brickwork was removed, it was stacked up along the three remaining wall locations to form windbreaks but with gaps to allow access. Now there was wood for the fire. Door frames and doors, windows and rafters, all had been buried under the fallen masonry. There was also an abundance of the wooden strips which in better times had supported the roof tiles. Things we beginning to look better every minute.

Then while clearing away more rubble, a two-section hinged flap was found which gave entry into a second cellar in addition to the one found earlier. This turned out to be a dry, brick-lined room with a row of storage bins across the back wall. Two of these were almost full, one holding still useable potatoes, the other turnips. Whether these were for humans or cattle was anyone's guess.

Back upstairs, rubble was replaced on the hatch to conceal its existence and the treasure beneath it. Using an oil lamp, also found below, the message "C Company, 17th.MYR property. KEEP OUT" was smoked on the chimney wall as well as outside so that it was immediately obvious.

Having done this much, the squad returned to their unit. Four men were now detailed to return to camp with a requisition which Capt. Yorke now wrote out. He required four dixies, ladles, kitchen spoons and four 'hay-boxes'. These latter items were double-walled, insulated chests with lids. Each box would take a dixie of hot food or tea straight from the kitchen, and if carried out to troops in the field, the contents would still be piping-hot on arrival.

As they set off, Capt. Yorke took Fred (now known as an inveterate and skilful scrounger) on one side. Fred was reminded that whilst the dixies could be carried back inside the 'hay-boxes', it would be a great shame if the space inside the dixies was wasted. "I'll see what I can do" was Fred's response to this very broad hint.

The small group arrived back at camp just in time for the evening meal, after which, a bed for the night was arranged.

The following morning, the dixies and other items were drawn from the stores and signed for. Fred and his cronies then made their way to the cookhouse to arrange for the dixies to be suitably utilised in transit, if possible. With Fred, most things usually were.

A deal was struck with the cookhouse sergeant. He would trade, unofficially and illegally, a selection of supplies he just happened to be holding 'in case of an emergency', and which, by sheer good luck also happened to be 'surplus to inventory'.

In order to prevent a potentially embarrassing situation developing for the sergeant (such as would be the case if the stores were checked), he would, for a suitable consideration allow these 'surplus' stores to be to be put to good use. A deal was struck. When Fred was back in camp again, a goodly selection of battlefield souvenirs would be delivered to the sergeant who, once again by coincidence, just happened to have an outlet for such things. This would be on a continuing basis ---- while Fred or his nominee brought souvenirs to the cookhouse, he would not return empty-handed to the trenches.

Off they went, two hay-boxes to a carrying pole slung between two porters. By the weight of them, the containers which had earlier been left empty with 'cookie' were no longer in that condition.

Another acquisition had been a stout hasp, staple and padlock for the cover to the cellar where the food-supplies would be stored. As Fred mused "What'd be the point us workin' our socks off if some thievin' bastard could come along and help 'imself?" He had a point. If anyone was to profit from their nefarious activities, it would be "C" Company. After all, Capt.Yorke had more or less hinted at this!

Back at what was now thought of as their cookhouse, they unpacked their ill-gotten gains. Two dixies held tins. One was full of bully beef, the other McConochies meat and vegetable stew. The third held hard tack biscuits. These were looked a bit 'sideways' until the last dixie was unpacked. This had a sack of raisins crammed into it. On top was a note. It was recipe of sorts. If the biscuits were pounded into meal, mixed with water and some of the raisins, two hours slow cooking would produce an acceptable 'duff'.

When all the supplies and the cooking gear had been locked away in the cellar, the group reported back to their lieutenant listing the supplies they had acquired. Fred and William were detailed off as duty cooks. This would keep them out of the trenches most of the time, and give their feet a chance to heal. As the two officers would have to remain, the two 'cooks' handed over half their supplies of foot ointment to help out them to eke out the personal supplies of each officer.

The cooks would be required to produce hot tea in the line at least twice a day, together with a hot meal in the evening. If more could be achieved, then all to the good, but the minimum specified had to be produced.

Back to their new abode the pair went, taking with them three cans of water as well as their own kit. As of now, they would bed down in the comfort and safety of the first of the two cellars.

Next morning, they were up and about just before first light. They required neither alarm clock nor bugle, their 'body clocks' by now having become fully attuned to the hours kept in the trenches. When it was full daylight, they brewed tea and filled the dixies. They found that boiling the water from the ex-petrol tins got rid of the lingering taste of fuel and the tang of chlorine. It was a great improvement.

As they made their way up to the trenches, they felt somewhat naked and exposed to any enemy observer who might just happen to be looking in their general direction. They were to get through unobserved, or, more probably, ignored. Two minute figures were obviously not considered to be worth the wasting of ammunition.

On its arrival, the tea was greeted as if it was nectar from the gods. Such sallies as 'one no milk' etc. etc. were dealt with politely and efficiently. They were ignored! The 'squaddies' took what they were given. In any case, there was only one recipe ----- tea, sugar (if there was any), milk (similarly), and hot water. At the moment there was plenty of sweetened, condensed milk for some reason. The connoisseurs had two choices --- take it or leave it!

The empty containers were now filled with some of the tinned food from the stores sap to be taken back for safe-keeping in the cellar under lock and key to be drawn on as the hot meals demanded. About half the tins would remain in the stores bay in case of an emergency. They could be used cold if the need arose.

Back in the kitchen, it was now time for prepare for the next tea run.

Fred, who was naturally inquisitive investigating anything and everything, went for a look round outside to see if there was anything further available, and if there was, could it be put to good use. In the collapsed side barns, he found plenty of wood in the shape of timber which had been used in their construction. It was wet but would dry out if brought under cover. He set to and stacked a good supply near the chimney wall where heat from the fire would hasten the drying. He then resumed his explorations. He found more wood for the fire in the shape of the gate which had obviously taken a direct hit. This wood did not have to be cut to be useable, it was just a matter of collecting the shattered fragments.

Behind what had been the house, he found a spring of clear water bubbling from the ground. A brick-lined basin had been constructed round it with an outlet to let surplus water flow away as a small stream. It had a device like a small crane dangling over the water. The spring must have supplied the farmer and his family with their drinking water. Despite the wreckage, human and material, lying around it, it still ran crystal clear.

Fred tentatively tried it --- it was completely tasteless. Its source must be so far underground as to have escaped pollution. After some discussion, it was decided to heat some to a good, round boil for about fifteen minutes, then let it cool after which, they would try some. If they suffered no ill effects, they would get Capt.Yorke's views on its use in the drinks and the cooking. If it was considered safe to use, then there would be no need for water to be carried forward by fatigues men. Food and ammunition could be carried instead. An added benefit would be that it would also be sweeter than the stuff in the tins.

On balance, they thought that it could be used with a reasonable degree of safety. Out where they were, in the front area, it was a toss-up how your end would come when it did. This could be just another way to go.

It was now time for the next trip.

When all the tea had been dished out, the question of the spring-water was raised with their platoon commander. He thought that if it was well boiled so as to kill any germs, then it should be safe to use, but the company commander would have to have the final word on the subject. That worthy agreed that it should be safe enough subject to adequate boiling. If not, then the M.O. would be busy, if they lived. Better let him give his opinion to be on the safe side.

More stores were taken back to the cellar, and then it was time to get cracking on the evening meal. The 'recipe' per dixie went as follows: one tin of meat and vegetables with the same amount of bully beef for every two men. Add a pint or two of water and set to heat. Potatoes (already peeled) were put on to cook in the second dixie. The turnips, although slightly woody would be edible if the customers were hungry enough. The cooks decided that they would be --- once again, there was no choice in the matter --- their 'customers" could always spit out any hard bits they came across. So, turnips were on the menu as well.

The fourth dixie was left empty temporarily as space would be needed to mix the lot together when all had been cooked.

With the stew fully mixed and all four dixies now in use, there was still space in all of them, but the meat content seemed a bit low. The recipe would have to be adjusted. A further four tins each of bully beef and McConochies was added for good measure, and the mixture topped up with water. Now it was a bit thin. This was remedied by the addition of a handful of hard tack biscuits to each container. Now, the meal, whilst not *haute cuisine* was without doubt hot and filling. The cooks themselves were quite pleased with it --- they had to be, they had created it! Now to try it out on their unsuspecting, captive customers.

Out into the twilight they trudged, struggling with the four loaded dixies in their 'hay-boxes'. They would have to ask for two men to be sent down each evening to help carry the cooked food up to the trenches. It would be easy enough bringing the empties back.

Four dixies did not allow for large helpings, but at least, the denizens of the trenches were now getting something they had never enjoyed on previous stints in the line. The effect on morale was well worth the effort. Reasonably dry underfoot, the men could now look forward to a hot meal in the evening as well as good tea twice a day. Things were improving.

Whilst the meal was being dished out, a runner appeared out of the gloom with a message from Div H.Q. They required a fighting patrol to go out to capture a prisoner for interrogation. The usual 'flap' was on as there had been a rumour as to the change of the enemy regiment opposite. Intelligence had heard from an undisclosed source that fresh troops who were reputedly more aggressive had taken over from the previous easy-going lot.

Fred and William regretted that they would be unable to join the party as they had left their rifles locked in the cellar. They had had to choose between bringing them with them, or leaving a dixie of stew behind. Then, apart from their lack of rifles, they still had the washing up to do, unfortunately ------- .

The raid turned out to be a complete success. The enemy, the Saxons, were taken by surprise. As a race, they were totally relaxed in their approach to war which they regarded as not only unfriendly, but dangerous in the extreme. They had not been replaced, but would be in the near future.

Tom, finding a machinegun unattended, smashed the firing-pin and operating mechanism with the butt of his rifle. The Maxim would have to be withdrawn for major repairs. Remembering the friendly welcome the Saxons had given the Ledfords when they had arrived in the line for the first time, he left a note on the gun --- "Sorry for the damage, but orders are orders".

The Yorkshire troops were intrigued to find that the cap badge of the one prisoner taken on the raid bore the legend "Waterloo". In recognition of their spirited action in that engagement of 1815, the Mid-Yorkshire Regiment had been awarded the place-name as one of their battle honours. The forebears of the regiment they were now opposing had been their allies in that earlier campaign, and had fought alongside them against the Napoleonic French.

When it was daylight, another notice appeared above the trenches opposite. "Please save that kind of activity until next week when the Prussians take over again". Not only did they have a prisoner, they now knew who would be taking over, and when.

Tea arrived and it was swallowed gratefully by everyone, including the prisoner. He seemed quite happy with life now that he had been captured. The realisation that his life expectancy was now much better than it had been could have been the reason for his cheerfulness.

Tom volunteered to escort him back to camp, and, in company with the two 'tea boys' and the prisoner, set off with his rifle slung over his shoulder. After what turned out to be a pleasant stroll on a crisp, frosty morning, they parted company at Fred's Place. (This was the name the establishment seemed to have been given now by all and sundry). Before he left the cookhouse, Tom filled his water bottle with some of the spring water so that the M.O. could test it.

In the kitchen, all four dixies were filled with water and put on to boil, this being the easiest way to wash them out.

All the chores having been attended to, there would now be about an hour or two slack time for doing nothing. So, out with the Woodbines ('gaspers', 'coffin nails', however they thought of them), a mess-can of tea, then stretch out on a greatcoat in front of the fire. These were the hardships which the two frontline soldiers they now were had to endure on active service!

Tom, meanwhile had gone on his way with 'Heinie' as he had dubbed the prisoner, both of them enjoying the weak winter sunshine. Heinie was chatting away, twenty to the dozen and obviously very happy to be out of the war. Tom offered the occasional choice comment in his broad Yorkshire accent from time to time. That neither understood the other did not seem to matter at all. In this companionable manner, they arrived at the camp gates where the prisoner was handed over to the Regimental Police against a signature. On returning to the platoon, Tom said his biggest problem at this stage was finding an R.P. who could write!

Chapter 15

The following morning on his way back to the trenches, Tom made a detour to the R.E. dump where he looked for, and found what he needed, a spare haversack and sling. He picked it up and checked it over as he went on his way. A mile down the road, he decided that as he had 'forgotten' to put it back on the pile, he might just as well keep it as it could come in handy.

On the way in, he had seen that despite the devastation, there were quite a lot of rabbits, not to mention pheasants running about all over the place. There were also numerous chickens on the loose. Tom, the peacetime poacher, had his rifle and now had the 'game-bag' he had just 'found'. In a short space of time, he had three rabbits, a brace of pheasants and four chickens. That would have to do for the day as the haversack was now full.

He stopped off at Fred's Place to leave these additional items for the menu. There he found Lt. Richardson sitting in front of the fire enjoying a cigarette and a mug of tea. When Tom tipped his 'kill' onto the floor, everyone was intrigued to see that each bird or rabbit had been taken with a head shot which had decapitated the victim. When this was commented upon, Tom pointed out that a ·303 round through the body of a rabbit or a bird would shatter any bones it struck producing fine splinters which could be fatal if anyone eating the meat swallowed one. Even if all the bones were missed, but the round passed through the guts of the beast, the resulting leakage would not only spoil the meat, but could even poison it. The best thing to do was to knock the head off so that the edible parts remained untouched. You didn't eat the head, so it wasn't wasted. It was obvious really, if you thought about it. It only needed a crack shot (who also happened to be a skilful poacher) to do it.

The reason for the lieutenant's visit was that in two or three day's time, they were to be relieved. He had come down to see what could be arranged in respect of "C" Company's kitchen. He found that Fred was mentally there ahead of him, and had thought of a plan to deal with that inevitability. He had decided that the handover would be 'official' and done in the approved Army manner.

. So, on the morning of the changeover, Lt. Richardson would go back to liaise with the C.O. of the Manchesters (another Bantam regiment), with whom they would alternate on a week by week basis until further notice, and tell him what had been set up.

In the unlikely event that he should bump into anyone back in camp who knew that the lieutenant should still be back in the front line, even this aspect of the changeover had been covered.

As this would be the first time that the Ledfords would be unsupervised when handing over their positions in the Front Line to raw, new troops, Lt. Richardson had come back to camp to explain to his successor just what the process would entail. This 'explanation' sounded plausible, and would be if delivered with a straight face.

On arrival in the trenches, the new C.O. would give a receipt for all the stores on hand against an inventory which Fred would prepare at the last moment. The C.O. would also sign for the key to the cellar at the same time. As these ideas could not be bettered, the lieutenant agreed to go along with them.

And one other thing Fred mentioned ---- they were getting low on wood for the fire. If some duckboards were to be brought up with them, they could be stored under cover until they were 'needed in the trenches'! A dozen or so could be stacked away under cover ---"so as to stay dry".

Lt. Richardson would return with the reliefs and supervise the handing-over of the kitchen and stores, ably assisted by Fred. The incoming stores would be locked way in the cellar and the handover would be complete.

When they were relieved again by the Ledfords in due course, the Manchesters would leave an equivalent amount of stores they would have to 'acquire' to replace those they had used.

As Fred saw it, it was nothing to do with the Manchesters how he got his supplies. The fact that he got them illegally was none of their business. The Manchesters would have their own arrangements as did most of the units now in France. On their way in, perhaps they could bring in a sack or two of potatoes as well.

Whilst the discussion had been going on, the officer had been watching with interest as the evening meal was being prepared. This time, it would be meatier than usual. Tom and he would help carry it up to the hungry troops waiting for it.

The rabbits and the fowl had been prepared by Tom who showed as he did so that he had lost none of his peacetime skills, illegal though they may be. After the fur or feathers of the game had been removed, it had then been gutted. This was followed by simmering until all the meat had fallen off the bones which had then been removed and discarded. This rich broth had then been divided evenly between the four dixies which already held the usual mixture of bully beef and McConochies. The potatoes and turnips were then added. All in all, a feast fit for a king!

On the due date, the changeover took place with the chit-chat bandied about having a 'Wars of the Roses' theme as regiments from both Yorkshire and Lancashire were involved.

Now they could get on with the war!

All the business of the day having being dealt with, the Mid-Yorkshires made their back to camp happy in the knowledge that not only was there a substantial hot meal with gallons of hot tea waiting for them, this time they would be in a fit state to enjoy it when they got there.

Tom had taken upon himself the role of souvenir collector, and had a sandbag full of various items of German origin, some complete with genuine blood stains. There were more than enough to settle the account with the cook-sergeant for the first lot of supplies and still have some left to ensure that there would be more 'surplus' foodstuffs available to be taken back when the Manchesters were relieved.

Then it was heads down and total oblivion until some idiot with a bugle woke them up at daybreak.

The usual camp routine followed ---- meals, then bath parade, followed by an issue of clean shirts and underwear from the Divisonal laundry. As always it had been processed to its usual standard ---- better not to be too fussy.

Then, all too soon, they were on their way back to the line.

Fred and his bunch called round to say "Cheerio" to the cookhouse staff, and, in passing, help the sergeant balance his stock accounts by removing any surplus goods.

Official stores were now distributed amongst the rest of "C" Company together with six or seven duckboards. These were, of course, to replace any which had been broken by enemy action since the Ledfords had last been in the front line.

The unit's officers stood and watched in amazement the quiet and speedily efficient manner in which the stores, official and otherwise, were distributed amongst the men without dissent or argument. As no good would come from disrupting such a well-organised display, the men were left to get on with it.

Apart from the fact that all involved would benefit from the illicit activity, the officers watching no longer had any idea which were the official, the legal supplies! Although it was only Army personnel involved, the spirit of Nelson was called upon, and the proverbial 'blind eye' was well and truly turned.

On arriving back in the trenches, the relief and the exchange of intelligence took place. That done, the important business of the hour was next --- the handing over of Fred's Place. Given that the Manchesters came from the wrong side of the Pennines, Fred had to concede that they had done a good job as regards his cookhouse. Stores more or less agreed. He did not ask how they had achieved this ---- they obviously had their sources, just as Fred had his.

There were now more potatoes in the bin than when Fred had left it. The place was in profit from a material point of view. The Manchesters could come again!

The Mancunians had left another pleasant surprise behind them when they left --- firewood, and plenty of it! Out of boredom seemingly, their two duty cooks had been investigating the heap of rubble at the opposite end of the 'square' in the hope that some of the timber used in the building could be recovered. What they had found was that that particular building had been used to store the cut logs which were used as fuel for the farmhouse in its better days. Not only were there more than enough to last them for some considerable time, they had been cut ready for use, and were accessible through one of the walls which had not totally collapsed ---- it still had a door which opened!

Chapter 16

During the handing-over, the Manchesters' C.O. confirmed that now the Saxons had gone, their place had being taken by another lot of Prussians as had been expected. The situation now was that trouble could, and should be expected at any time of the day or night.

Because of an increase in sniping activity, the trench to and from Fred's Place had been deepened. It had also been modified by the addition of two 'doglegs' where, before, it had been almost straight. Before they had done this, two men carrying a brewing of tea had been shot. Fortunately, they had escaped with flesh wounds but the tea had been a total loss. On checking the lie of the land, it had been found that the stretch of trench in question could be taken under enfilading fire. Either the Saxons had not spotted this, or they could not be bothered to do anything about it. With this new lot, it was a totally different matter. Whilst it was a case of back to the old routine now they were back in the line, this time, they had to be much more careful.

Before he left, the Mancunian passed on a message the Saxons had left for the 'York Sirs'. They bade everyone farewell, and wished them good luck with their new neighbours.

The Ledfords approved the new 'title'. They were quick to stress that it was NOT a mistake. It was also rammed home that even if it had been, there could never be any possibility of a similarly accurate 'mistake' being made with either 'Manchester' or 'Lancashire'.

Bearing in mind the change in things insofar as the opposition's intention of carrying the war to the Ledfords, --- or indeed, any other regiment for that matter, it was still easy to slip back into the old established routine with minimum effort.

Whilst the Manchesters had been holding the line, and taking advantage of the lack of aggression shown by the Saxons, the artillery Forward Observation Officer had decided to survey the area to his front over which he could range his guns. He particularly wanted to tighten his ranging on no-man's-land.

On this sector, the distance between the two opposing front lines was, on average, one hundred and twenty yards or so, but varying from one hundred and ten to one hundred and sixty. In the event of heavy assaults on the British positions, he would risk bringing down fire at about sixty to seventy yards to his front (say, two hundred feet), provided he knew the exact distances involved at various points along the line. Even with the somewhat suspect quality of the fuses currently in use in the shells, it would be a case of balancing the risks involved. Trading a few casualties from British 'shorts' could prevent a greater number being inflicted by a successful enemy assault as well as the loss of the position.

He had been out with his orderly on several nights to measure the distance from the British wire back to the parapet; he had also estimated the width of no-man's-land as well as the distance from the enemy wire to their trenches

A plan of the sector had been drawn up, and, down the middle of no-man's-land, a line had been drawn. This he referred to as his 'S.O.S. fire line'. It sounded most impressive when he used this phrase, particularly as he at least sounded as if he knew what he was talking about. A table had been incorporated in this plan showing the distances from this line back to the British trenches.

One red rocket would bring down fire on this line; two 'reds' together would cover the ground from this line to the German trenches whilst a group of three would blanket all the ground from that line to the rear of the German positions and include the area where enemy reinforcements could be expected to be waiting.

During their first night back, the Ledfords were attacked in the early hours of their morning. As the first wave was already through the British wire when spotted, two red rockets brought a curtain of shells down along the S.O.S line and the open ground back to the German trenches. Troops of the second assault wave were caught out in the open and battered into oblivion. Three 'reds' switched the bombardment to cover the German trenches and hit the reserve troops waiting to move forward to consolidate any captured ground.

The survivors of the first wave were now trapped. They could not go back nor could they continue forward because of the hail of small-arms fire lashing them from their front. They were caught on the wrong side of the British wire.

There was no choice for them but to surrender. But how to manage this in the heat of the battle was the problem. By this time, the surviving Germans had taken what little cover was available in shell holes if they were lucky enough to be near one, or in any dip in the ground if they weren't. Shouted commands in German stopped them firing. Then a grubby handkerchief spiked on the bayonet of a rifle was tentatively waved from one of the craters.

At this Capt. Yorke bellowed "Stand fast, the Ledfords. Cease fire!" This bought a temporary halt to the killing. But what could the Ledfords do with such a large number of prisoners? As one Prussian officer spoke reasonable English, Capt. Yorke gave him thirty minutes in which to collect his wounded and get back to his own trenches. When that time was up, anybody still out in the open would be fired on without warning no matter what they were doing.

All those now caught out in the open were to dump all their weapons in the water in the nearest shell hole and leave them there. Any attempt to recover them would immediately terminate the truce and the offender shot.

And so were the Ledfords welcomed back to their primitive existence holding their line. Things had changed for the worse with a vengeance.

It was now late March. The weather had turned bitter with sleet and snow in abundance. Hard frosts during the night were a regular occurrence. Snow introduced a yet another hazard to the trench dwellers. After a fresh fall, the footprints told enemy snipers where someone had gone. So, if there were no return tracks, all the sniper had to do was wait patiently in case the potential victim returned the same way.

All through this hard winter, the Ledfords were having a hard time. For some reason, the trenches which had been reasonably dry up to now had started to fill with water. As well as manning the line, they were kept busy on trench maintenance, laboriously pumping out the water now flooding them. The walls also had to be shored up with wooden revetments.

Entries in the battalion War Diary did not waste words describing the conditions.

One entry read: "Trenches flooded; snowing a blizzard; heavily shelled; not good!"

The following day: "Trenches still flooded; still snowing; still being shelled; no better!"

On the third day, the writer was even more laconic: "No change!"

During his wanderings behind the trench, Tom had come across a section of the old French defence-works. Most of it had been destroyed by shellfire, but one length had only partially collapsed. Projecting from under the earth was a length of woodwork. On investigating, he found what appeared to be a stack of duckboards and other sawn timber. In Tom's eyes, it looked just like firewood for the kitchen.

Setting to with a spade, he poked around in the debris. Not only did he find an abundance of 'firewood', he also came across a pile of tins. The labels had long since gone, but their size and shape suggested some sort of canned food. As a corporal, when circumstances demanded, he had to use his initiative. This he now did. He quickly organised a carrying party, packed the tins into empty sandbags and transferred the lot to Fred's Place. This would also be the destination of the woodwork found at the same time.

There were some fifty tins in all, one of which when opened disclosed chunks of pork with white haricot beans in a rich gravy still in good condition. A strong smell of garlic filled the air. Here was something else to add to add to the stew. If the men didn't like garlic, they soon would.

The days dragged by, and it was changeover time again. This time, the relief troops would be the Hallamshires, otherwise known as the York and Lancaster Regiment. It would have been interesting to know what the enemy intelligence made of this. This section of the line had a Yorkshire Regiment alternating with a Lancashire Regiment, and then for good measure, one whose title carried the names of both the cities of York and Lancaster. Perhaps something might be lost (or gained!) in the translation!

The established routine as regards Fred's Place had been explained to the newcomers so the handover went smoothly.

Towards the end of April, they met Australians for the first time. They had just arrived in the locality for their introduction to trench life and all it had to offer, which was not much. The Bantams were now regarded as sufficiently experienced as to be available as stiffening troops in their turn, and as such, competent instructors for raw troops coming into the line for the first time for 'battle inoculation'. (This was the latest jargon, and had replaced the earlier term 'blooding', with all that that implied!). That the Bantams were competent went without question -- the majority of them were still alive. What they had learned the hard way, they would now pass on to the 'diggers'.

The Aussies it seemed made no distinction with regard to the size of the man. If he was fit enough, he was in. They were a mix of characters from all walks of life. They came from the towns and the cities, as well as the farms and cattle stations of the outback.

However, when they saw the size of their instructors, they were quite taken aback. But that was until they realised how tough and aggressive the Bantams could be. The Aussies were also impressed by just how attuned the Ledfords had become to living in the appalling conditions to which they would now have to adjust.

They also found that they had a lot in common. When they spoke, they both destroyed the English language, but in different ways. Neither lot minced matters when it came to describing things ---- they were equally frank and blunt, not to say inventive in their choice of adjectives.

The Bantams soon learned to accept being referred to as 'bleddy Pommie bairsteds', and 'cobber'. Things were a bit fraught at first in the early days when the Bantams found they were addressed as 'mite'. But that was until they realised that that was 'Strine' for 'mate, so that was 'fair dinkum'. Both lots had the same opinion for officialdom of the Div. H.Q. variety and higher. They were also in total agreement with the concept of the unofficial cookhouse and its rather questionable means of keeping it well stocked with supplies. They approved of the fact that it existed apparently, with local official blessing and connivance.

Then, as they put it "In the spirit of our pioneering forefathers", they produced two dixies and four or five sacks of supplies which they insisted had somehow become mixed up with their baggage when they were passing through some place or other "--- as it does!"

These 'extras' had also been 'surplus to inventory' but were no longer so. There was of course no inventory entry for them now that they had been, shall we say, stolen.

As Aussies, they believed in the old adage "The Lord helps him who helps himself, but Lord help him caught helping himself!" As the Bantams also believed in that outlook on life, it was a meeting of kindred souls!

So far, they had not been caught. But then, neither had Fred and his contacts. When the time came for the Hallamshires to take over, they too entered into the spirit of the enterprise becoming as it were, full partners. They too would get their supplies from the sergeant who supplied Fred, and on the same terms. The Australians had their own source of supply which they did not divulge. This was not a bad thing, really. If one source dried up (i.e. got caught) there would still be an alternative.

The Manchesters too were still involved in the scheme of things. As they handed over to the Mid-Yorkshires on completing their spell in the line as part of the three-way rotation of stiffening regiments, they said that they had had two killed and three wounded, all at the entrance to the latrine bay. A sniper, or snipers, must be keeping an eye open for visitors to the latrine. Something had to be done, and done quickly.

Once the length of old French line had been cleared of useable material, Tom checked it out. If he roofed over a section of it with some of the rubbish lying about, he would have a hide from which he could see most of the enemy positions without being seen himself. A further consideration would be that he would be in an unusual position, and not where a sniper could be expected to be. The hide would be behind the British lines, and not in them, or in front of them in a shell hole, for example.

He set to, and built his 'hide', then reported back to Lt. Richardson who in turn had a word with his Aussie counterpart who nominated his best shot. The two marksmen returned to the hide, and prepared for as long a wait as was necessary.

Having made themselves as comfortable as possible, they mentally divided the enemy trench opposite into two killing grounds, each man taking a section on either side of an agreed dividing point. In this way, they would not both be firing at the same target. Once this had been decided, they settled down to wait. Two hunters watching would have a better chance of spotting the enemy sniper than if only one was trying for him. They might even get both of them if there were two out there. A lot of patience would be needed

Then, after what seemed like an eternity, Tom caught a quick, minute flash of light from what could only have been the telescopic sight of a sniper's hunting rifle. So, taking aim, he took a deep breath and exhaled slowly. He took first pressure on the trigger. Even as he watched the enemy rifle came slowly in to view together with the head of the sniper taking aim.

It only took one shot.

While Tom had been holding himself in readiness for his shot, the Aussie had been checking as well as he could on the German's intended target. The soldier who had just gone to the latrine would have been so much dead meat when he left it had Tom not been there.

Eventually, it became obvious that the hostile sniping had stopped for the day, probably as a result of Tom's shot. On reporting the 'kill', Tom suggested that a hessian screen be set up to hide the entrance to the latrine bay. It would not be bullet-proof, but it would deprive the enemy of any visible, guaranteed targets.

A screen was set up immediately.

Then it was changeover time once more. The first lot of Australians were replaced by a second lot, whilst the Ledfords handed over to the Hallamshires the next night. This would be the pattern for the next week or two until the Aussies had acquired enough trench 'savvy' to be able to survive if left to their own devices.

As there were now urgent rumours that the 17th. Mid-Yorkshires would be moving to another sector of the front at a moment's notice, the problem was what to do about Fred's Place. The solution was surprisingly simple and totally in keeping with the manner in which it had been conceived and run. The commanding officers of the units taking over this sector would be offered the chance to 'buy' it from "C" Company as a going concern.

When the day arrived, the offer was accepted and a bid made for the place. The price agreed upon, two demijohns of rum, was accepted with alacrity. These, when produced, bore an uncanny resemblance to those of the official issue. The same style and size of containers, these were made of the same glazed, brown pottery as the official issue, and were even stencilled 'SRD', (Service Rum Diluted). They even had a broad arrow on the front. It was thought best not to risk causing offence by enquiring as to how they had been obtained, but to accept the payment in the 'spirit' in which it was offered!

Business (official and unofficial) having been concluded, it was back to camp in the Forêt de Nieppe for the usual cleaning sessions and never-ending fatigues. Whilst they were there, Fred brought his business arrangements up to date. First and foremost, 'cookie' was advised of the change of proprietors of what would still be known as Fred's Place, and which would continue to trade in the well-established manner.

Next call was to the mechanic-sergeant. He was now so busy with the venture that he had taken on an assistant, a corporal. His logic was that an n.c.o. working in the machine-shop, no matter at what hour, would be less likely to be challenged than would be a private soldier. Such was the way the official mind worked, and so far, they had not been bothered.

With the cash handed over to Fred, the next stop would be at the *estaminet* where he would be able to settle the bill for the whole of his section as well as those of the platoon sergeant and their lieutenant.

During the evening, Billy who had been toying with the menu which William had translated for him. He was obviously not impressed. "Ah cud murder yan o' mi Mum's meat an' tatie pies wi' onion gravy" he sighed. "This lot's all forrin'!" At this, William said gently "That's because we are in a foreign country. Mind you, to the French, it is us who are the foreigners".

This was too much. Billy exploded. He could not take that. "Ah'm not a forriner, Ah'm from Yorkshire!"

Whilst true sons of the Broad Acres the world over would agree with that sentiment, that claim was not one which could be argued successfully in a court of law.

At their now favourite watering-hole, the proprietress as usual omitted to make out a separate bill for the lieutenant if he just happened to be there at the same time as his men. In that case, for some reason the bill usually went to Fred.

This time, the officer had already left the building by the time the account had been prepared, so, as usual, Fed settled it. This was to save embarrassing the officer by calling him back. Fred would pay for the lot even though he was well aware that by doing so, it would be an offence under the King's Regulations.

But then, so were a lot of things Fred was involved in. To keep things in balance, he would settle the account from his illegally amassed funds.

Lt. Richardson was equally aware of the situation. That was why he had left before the bill was produced. After all, he had no wish to be present when a member of his platoon committed an offence by paying for an officer's meal and drinks!

Chapter 17

During April, the whole Division moved to a different stretch of the line near Richebourg l'Avoué to the south of Neuve Chapelle. Would they never get away from this detestable part of France? They seemed fated to spend their tours of duty in flooded ditches which the papers from home would insist on referring to as 'the trenches'.

They were no longer based in a hutted encampment but would have to do with ancient bell tents which had seen better days, probably during the Boer War. All the administration units, such as stores, cookhouses and the like were housed in good, solid huts. As usual, the permanent staff were well looked after. It was only their 'customers', the frontline troops who actually did the fighting who had to put up with the rough end of the stick.

When the Ledfords moved into their new stretch of trenches, the Germans once again demonstrated the efficiency of their Intelligence branch. As the British troops arrived, they were greeted with loud shouts of "Cock-a-doodle-doo" together with loud clucking and cackling noises. It was obvious that the Hun knew who had come into the line opposite.

When they tired of this, they subjected their new neighbours to heavy shelling. At the same time, smoke was released which drifted slowly across to the Bantams' lines. Gas hoods had to be donned immediately, not so much for the smoke as for any poison gas which might have been mixed in with it. This was the latest ploy to be adopted by the Germans --- sometimes gas would be present, sometimes not. As there was no means of knowing, the discomfort of the hoods had to be endured until it was all clear again. The enemy was all too aware of this which is why he did it.

The new F.O.O. knew his job very well indeed just like the one they had just left behind. He too was fully conversant with the various distances along the stretch held by the Ledfords. By means of signal rockets, he too could bring down a heavy barrage on the hostile lines to discourage any thoughts of an assault while the replacements were getting organised in their new surroundings.

Five days in the line with a similar period 'resting' was to be the pattern for the next two months. There would be no change from the squalid life-style to which they had become accustomed apart from the fact that they no longer had their own cookhouse. They now had to rely on what could be brought forward by carrying parties. Hostile raids would be received and dealt with, and return visits made. This was what passed for 'normal' in a 'quiet' sector nowadays.

One occasion was to be different. That was when a raid was mounted to destroy a German forward observation and listening post which had been established in a deep shell hole just in front of their wire. How long it had been there was anyone's guess. It was well camouflaged, and was only spotted when a wisp of tobacco smoke was seen rising in the early morning air.

The first indication that something was not quite right was when Tom caught a whiff of the acrid smell of the smoke peculiar to the cigars to which the Germans seemed to be rather partial. His first thought was that there was an enemy patrol out and about. No matter how much he looked, he could not spot anybody. Then he spotted a very fine strand of smoke. Even as he watched, it disappeared only to reappear then vanish again. The smoke was vanishing and reappearing as the smoker inhaled then took the cigar from his lips. Capt. Yorke's attention was drawn to the danger.

As the post had not been set up for the benefit of the British, the sooner something was done about it the better. There were also two machine-gun nests reasonably close to this forward German post, so they could be dealt with at the same time by a large enough party.

"C" Company personnel would mount the raid. One section would knock out the listening post, two sections would deal with one machine-gun each, while the remaining section would create chaos in the length of trench in between. Charlie and Bob, as bombers, would each accompany one of the sections involved in destroying the guns, All four sections would come from 4 Platoon.

The plan of attack had the first section silencing the forward enemy post. This was to be done quietly if at all possible. A full section had been allotted to this task as the strength of the opposition in the post was not known. Depending on what the raiders found, any surplus men were to attach themselves to the section attacking the trenches. All assaulting troops were to assist in this when their primary roles had been accomplished.

When it was fully dark, the first wave slipped over the parapet and wormed its way towards the enemy-held crater. This had been roughly roofed over leaving a viewing slit at the front, and an exit at the rear. Fred and Billy slipped quietly round to the back intending to either enter and deal with the men inside, or take them as they emerged from their post. Either way, it would have to be done with the minimum of fuss.

Just as the pair arrived at the exit, there was a heart-stopping moment when a face appeared at the slit at the front. Tom, as corporal, was in charge of this part of the raid. In a flash, he threw himself forward lunging with his rifle and bayonet as he did so. The only noise his victim made was a choking gurgle as the bayonet passed through and severed his windpipe.

Seeing this, the *feldwebel* in charge of the post dashed to the rear intending to raise the alarm. There he met Fred who swung his 'toothpick' at him. The German collapsed as the terrible implement ripped away most of his lower jaw. The third occupant of the post stood rooted to the spot as he stared at the remains of his sergeant lying on the ground drowning in his own blood. He was bayoneted by Billy. There had only been these three on duty in the post. Now there were none.

So far, so good. The first part of the plan had gone without a hitch. There was now no danger of the raiding parties being spotted and the alarm raised. Tom now flashed a signal using a masked lamp he had brought for the purpose. Now that the German post had been snuffed out, Tom's lot would join the section attacking the trench and its occupants.

The two sections veered off towards their machine-gun targets whilst the main body headed towards the central section of trench, spreading out as they went. With only nine or ten feet left to cover, someone became snagged on a stray length of barbed wire. As he struggled to free himself, the ensuing noise alerted the enemy who immediately manned their parapet. In the free-for-all which followed, it was a case of every man for himself. While this frenzied struggle was going on, the sound of exploding grenades indicated that the guns had been attended to.

Then it was all over and the two flank parties – or what was left of them --- appeared and joined the main group whereupon Lt. Richardson blew three sharp blasts on his whistle, the signal to withdraw.

As the Ledfords retired from the fray, the screams and shouts from the Germans confirmed that the raid had indeed caused chaos, and that the defenders had been thrown into total disarray by the ferocity of the sudden attack. They were still defending themselves, but now, it was against each other, their assailants having already left.

Halfway back across no-man's-land, the raiders sent up two green Verey flares. This was the agreed 'success' signal. At this, the British guns opened up on the area of the enemy trenches. The German guns which had been in action against the British positions ceased fire the moment the two 'greens' lit up the sky. The Intelligence officer had been correct when he said that this was the signal used by the enemy forward infantry to tell their guns to stop. Whatever it meant to them, it worked whoever used it.

Back under cover, an assessment was made as to the results of the raid. A large number of casualties had been inflicted on the enemy, but about an equal number had been suffered. On the positive side, two machine-guns had been destroyed as well as an observation post being taken out.

Once again Fred's lot had come through virtually unscathed, apart from the usual collection of minor cuts and bruises. So far, they had been lucky, but they knew that inevitably, by the law of averages, their luck just had to run out. Their good fortune could not last forever. Each tour of duty in the trenches shortened the odds against them. The risks were stacking up. The five days in the line mounting or repelling raids always involved killing or being killed. Fate had to have something in store for them.

Whether or not they were achieving anything worthwhile with all this activity, they would never know. What was certain was the increasing number of casualties. As the 'Top Brass' had ordained that it should be so, they had no choice but to obey orders. That would continue to be the position until they were no longer able to do so.

April became May, and then, before they realised it, the weather was balmy with the promise of summer.

Five days in the line were followed by five days out, 'resting'. 'Resting'? That was a laugh and no mistake! The only rest they got was that of being out of the danger zone for some of the time, otherwise they were back up, but not as combatants. On these occasions, they were doing very passable impersonations of pack mules, or so it seemed.

No. Out of the line, 'resting', meant providing carrying parties for whatever needed to be carried to wherever it had to be taken. Failing that, 'resting' troops were a very handy source of labour for all other needs.

The one hot meal a day was taken up to the trenches by those who were 'resting'. All the ammunition, replacement barbed wire, all the R.E. stores, all this and much more was carried by troops who were 'resting'. They were frequently under shellfire whilst so employed. Yes! It was good to be out of the line, 'resting'!

But all good things must come to an end, so they say.

Chapter 18

During the first week in June, they were on the move once more. This time, they ended up in a reasonably civilised encampment situated in the open countryside near a small town to the west of Béthune. As a headquarters town it had been subjected to intermittent shelling since the previous year. A lot of the ancient Flemish buildings had been destroyed or badly damaged as a result.

Once again, they were in bell tents, but this time, these were almost new. These had been fitted with duckboards which had been tailored to fit the floor space. The occupants would now be out of the mud when sleeping. Duckboard paths had also been constructed to all admin. units, ablutions and the cookhouse.

On checking company standing orders, the Ledfords found that they would no longer be required for trench-holding duties in the foreseeable future. Nor was there any indication as to how long this would be the case, nor why it should be so.

By now, the Ledfords had been in the Army long enough to realise that when there was any change for the better in their conditions, there had to be a catch in the improvements somewhere. As sure as eggs are eggs, there just had to be a snag.

For the next four weeks, they would be subjected to intensive physical exercises mixed with route marches with full equipment over progressively increasing distances. If they paused to consider the reason why they were being toughened up, there could only be one answer. The immediate future was also going to be tough.

Then, for a change, they would be on 'general' duties, or, once again, employed as carrying-parties, their favourite pastime!

The nearby town of Chocques was an important railhead, and as such was the destination of huge amounts of stores and ammunition coming in for distribution to units deployed across this part of France. When not slogging along the local roads route marching, doing P.E., or enjoying themselves carrying, they would be required to unload and stack these incoming stores to await onward delivery as needed. Supplies would also be unloaded from rail trucks onto lorries and wagons for delivery direct to the unit if an official requisition was already to hand and had the mandatory stamp impression in the proper section. Otherwise, the crates and boxes would be stacked in the railway warehouse to await demand in the future.

There seemed to be yet another unwritten rule in force amongst the P.B.I., this one governing the handling of these stores. Anything going direct from the train or shed to where it was needed was handled correctly and without any interference with the goods. If, on the other hand, the *matériel* was going into storage, albeit for a short period, then if it was food, particularly the new, self-heating tins of soup, it was vulnerable --- very!

The reasoning behind this 'rule' was simple, and very practical. Direct delivery goods were going to where they were needed immediately. Lives could depend on the correct quantity being delivered. That was the moral consideration. The practical approach was that it was impossible to hide the deficit if you could not control both delivery and receipt. With storage goods, you could.

On the station platform, a tallyman recorded the number of packages leaving the truck. At the warehouse door, another tallyman recorded the number of packages crossing the threshold into the building. In an attempt to reduce pilfering, only one commodity was dealt with at a time. In practice, this had the opposite effect

The tallying system employed was the 'five bar gate'. With this, four vertical strokes indicate that four items have been counted. When the fifth has been seen, a diagonal line is made across the block of four thus completing the 'gate'. When making the final total at the end of the session, the number of blocks of five can be seen at a glance. This is not only quicker than counting the individual strokes but is more accurate.

So, at the truck door, (say), as the forty-ninth case passes, the appropriate vertical stroke is made on the tally sheet. It is swiftly followed by the diagonal line, but without another case having gone by. When this case reaches the storage shed door, the tallyman similarly tallies it in as two cases. This will, of course, have been agreed between all parties involved in the petty pilfering.

As there are hundreds of cases etc. in the shed already, stacked and being stacked, there was no way of challenging the accuracy of the tally, without doing a total, physical check of everything in the building, particularly as both tally sheets would agree. So, the 'accuracy' of the tally has to be accepted as everyone knows that in the shambles resulting from a full stock check, there would be even more losses.

So, the 'spare' case has to be removed from the scene of the crime and disposed of.

Again, this is quite simple. A wooden case dropped a foot or so, so as to fall flat on the floor makes a good, solid 'slapping' noise which sounds much worse that it is. No damage is done to the case or its contents. But it does attract attention which is the object of the exercise.

On the other hand, if the spare case is gently thrown down so as that the point of one corner strikes the ground, the case is so knocked out of shape that it literally falls apart, doing so fairly quietly. So, two cases would be dropped simultaneously, one to draw attention from the other.

Along the front of the sheds opening onto the road ran a raised wooden platform, set at the height of the load bed of a lorry or wagon. The underside was supported by wooden beams and posts. More importantly, the underside was accessible and cluttered with the rubbish and dunnage of ages. It afforded ideal concealment for the loot and dismantled cases. Waste not, want not --- the broken cases made valuable firewood.

For some reason, no watch was kept on this area, nor was it ever checked, apparently, for hidden loot. It is possible that to the official mind, the practical approach of allowing a little 'slack' would mean that there would be petty pilfering only, and not theft on a larger scale.

All this treasure would be collected after duties, and shared out. In most cases, the tinned soup was not for immediate consumption but would be kept as an extra emergency ration against the next time they were in the trenches. So, it could be argued that the food was going to be used more or less legally, but not in the manner the Army intended.

In a strange way, the men involved found that they were actually enjoying the hard physical labour involved. The weather was fine and sunny, and they were working in a pleasant locality well away from trenches. They were recovering the muscles and fitness that had been lost while trench-holding. They had regular, hot meals, and there was a canteen in camp; they had a hot bath once a week. Life was not too bad after all.

Once again, the bath house was a brewery which had been commandeered for the purpose. But even this had not been without its problems initially.

It was like this.

There were two breweries in Béthune, one considerably larger than the other. The Army had requisitioned the smaller of the two to be used as a bath house. This had led to a deputation headed by the town mayor complete with his tricolour sash descending on Army H.Q. Having demanded and been granted an immediate meeting with the Town-Major in charge, the mayor insisted that the brewery be returned at once to its peacetime use. He was politely reminded that it was no longer peacetime which was the only reason the Army was there in the first place. The Town-Major then added that if the mayor insisted, the Army would relinquish the brewery.

The mayor and deputation were then given a choice.

The town could offer "of its own free will", the use of one of the breweries, either would do. To that end, the mayor should return the following day with a legally drawn-up document authorising the Army to use said premises for as long as there was a need for them. That would be the end of the matter with no hard feelings. Failing that, the Army would take over BOTH breweries.

As was pointed out to the townsfolk, troops coming out of the lines were filthy and needed such facilities. The only reason that they, the British were in France and in such a state was that they were defending them, the French, against their enemies, the Germans. They, the British were risking their lives in doing so.

The next day, the mayor returned alone, and without his sash. The smaller of the two breweries would continue as the Army bathhouse as before. The only difference now was that it would be used for that purpose as an act of friendship on the part of good citizens of the town, and would continue to do so for as long as was necessary.

Chapter 19

During the last week of June, orders were posted putting the 35th (Bantam) Division at full readiness for an imminent move to the Somme. The component battalions would move out on an individual daily basis in accordance with the displayed schedule. The 17th Mid-Yorkshire Regiment (The Ledford Bantams) would move on July 2nd entraining at Chocques where they had spent so much time of late.

Kit was checked and replaced if at all suspect. Boots were soled and heeled where necessary, but all studs, heel and toe plates were replaced as a matter of course. Some Divisional stores were loaded in readiness on the lorries which would be driven down to Albert to await the arrival of the troops. Other necessary items would be drawn from stores in that sector when the Division reassembled.

The day of departure came and they set off for the railhead. Here, on the 'bush telegraph', they heard that the Somme offensive had started the previous day, July 1st. Rumours were rife as to the terrible casualties the British forces had taken when they had come to grips with the Germans

The air of levity, the fooling-around, all vanished to be replaced by a mood of apprehension tinged with fatalism. Conversations now included such comments as "– while we still can", or "-- while I still have time".

But as ever, such moods did not last long and the customary joking and horseplay was resumed. The attitude now was that of accepting one's lot, such as it was, while hoping that if you were going to 'cop one', it would be a clean, instantaneous death. Ideally it would be a 'blighty' wound. This would be one which while not being serious enough to cripple the recipient for life or mutilate him beyond acceptance, was still bad enough to get him off the battlefield and back to England (or 'Blighty') for hospital treatment and eventual recovery. Two or three months in hospital, waited on hand and foot by pretty nurses, followed by a spot of convalescent leave was now the height of ambition for the P.B.I. in the trenches.

The train backed into the siding where the Ledfords were patiently waiting. It was the usual collection of box vans ---*10 chevaux, 40 hommes* --- for the rank and file. These had the normal sliding doors on either side of the vans. In they climbed. The vans were clean on this occasion as they had been used by earlier drafts going south. As it was now mid-morning with the sun roasting anyone out in it, both doors were left wide open so that the forward motion of the vans would provide a cooling breeze.

The officers as befitted their exalted status were given passenger carriages. If the faded numerals painted on the doors were to be believed, then at some time in the past, they had been 'First Class'. By now, they had seen better days. Battered, dirty and with broken windows as they were, the seats were worse. Springs poked through the upholstery which, when new, had boasted a floral pattern. It was still vaguely discernible beneath the filth which covered it.

During their last evening in camp before the move, Fred and his cronies had discussed the forthcoming move with their lieutenant, and, with the help of his maps, had tried to work out just how far the train would take them. They had heard the name Frevent bandied about, along with several others. Working on the assumption that as the majority of the guesses favoured Frevent, then that could be where they would finish up. They estimated that a journey of some twenty-five to thirty miles lay ahead of them.

With a snort and a back-breaking jolt, the train shuddered and wheezed out of the marshalling yard. This forward movement was achieved in what could only be described as 'instalments'. One convulsive jerk followed another as the train staggered forward enveloped in clouds of steam and choking black smoke only to expire after no more than a quarter of a mile or so. Then, about an hour later, it would try again and resume its progress, (if that is what it could be called).

So, clanking and groaning, wheezing and shuddering, the asthmatic train staggered onwards out into open countryside as yet unmarked by the war. Its progress was so slow that men climbed out of the trucks and walked alongside the train to stretch their legs and break the monotony. When it was time for the mid-day meal, ---- the inevitable bully beef and 'whatever was available' stew---- two men from each truck visited the cookhouse wagon and collected their group's rations. The dixies would be returned after they had been emptied.

Shortly afterwards while several of these van orderlies were returning to their vans, the train suddenly and without warning put on speed. Despite prolonged shouting, the driver and his fireman chose to ignore the stragglers, one of whom was Tom. As he ran alongside the van he should have been in, he called for his rifle which was tossed out to him. He fired a shot towards the cab, deliberately aiming wide, but making sure he hit the metalwork. The shot whined off into space. Although the driver looked back with a big smirk on his face, he showed no signs of slowing down.

Tom's next shot broke the small circular window just in front of the driver's face, showering him with broken glass.

The train stopped!

Tom strode up to the engine, but being a Bantam (and so too short) couldn't reach the driver who retreated to the far side of his cab .With William's help, he told the Frenchman that although he (Tom) could not reach him, a bullet could. So saying, one was fed very ostentatiously into the chamber of Tom's rifle.

William then told the train driver that he had three choices available to him. The first was that he should get down from his cab without further ado. The second was that if he did not do so he would be choosing to be shot through a leg. The third choice was as to which leg it was to be!

The speed with which he left the cab was truly remarkable considering the size of the man.

With the driver standing in front of him and within reach, Tom held the muzzle of his rifle about two feet in front of the Frenchman's face and fixed his bayonet with a loud click. The point was now close to the driver's nose, and almost in one rather endangered nostril.

Tom now asked William to translate: "This blade 'as killed at least two men. One 'ad his throat cut, t'other got it through 'is guts!" Having set the scene, William was now to tell the now terrified driver just where and exactly how Tom would thrust the bayonet if the driver did not stop playing "silly bugger".

When the driver and his fireman were asked if they understood, they both almost nodded their heads off in demonstrating how well they had done so. William than added one more comment from Tom: "When everyone is back on board, would the driver get a bloody move on". To mark the end of the conversation Tom helped the driver back into his cab by the application of a size nine boot to the seat of his overalls.

It was noticeable that the train now set off in a more determined manner than before, and moved forward at a much more acceptable speed. It was obvious that the driver had only needed some encouragement. Its effect was obvious.

It was gone 1600hrs. when the train pulled into the station at Frevent. As it turned out, they had guessed correctly. It had taken the best part of six hours at an average speed of little better than walking pace. The track had followed a route which was more or less parallel to the Front, and about twenty miles to the west of it. The countryside was as yet very little damaged by all the military activity taking place in the vicinity.

Having left the train without any regrets whatsoever, they set out at a steady, easy pace along the Doullens road until they came to a small, side-lane heading in an easterly direction to the little hamlet of Le Souich. To its south, woods provided shelter for the overnight bivouac.

As they turned off amongst the trees, they saw to their delight that their camp-cookers had been set up and were in full operation. They had last been seen as they were being loaded onto lorries back near Béthune. Things were not so bad after all. Not yet, anyway.

The encampment was very pleasantly situated being as it was in a wooded valley with the accommodation consisting of a mix of good quality tents, and wooden huts. When their billeting area was pointed out to them, the quickest off the mark (and fleetest of foot) found themselves in huts. Not surprisingly, Fred's bunch was among them.

Once again it was case of making the best of their surroundings and getting organised. In the five months the Ledfords had been in France, they had become very skilled in the finer points of scrounging and fixing things to their advantage. It was not long before they were as comfortable as circumstances would allow. It was late afternoon before this had been managed.

Next morning, up at first light, and breakfasted, they were on their way by 0600hrs. Fifteen miles had to be covered to their next overnight stop. This would be at the *Bois de Warnimont* which was halfway between Doullens and the British trenches at Gommecourt.

Up till then, they had not realised that their steps would take them ever nearer to the front line which was now less than ten miles away, near enough to hear the sullen muttering of the guns. Here, they would be held as an emergency reserve until a very uncertain situation had resolved itself one way or another. They were now in limbo until someone decided where, when or if they would be needed.

Chapter 20

They were to spend the next seven days in the *Bois de Warnimont*, as good a place as any in which to pass the time waiting for orders. There was a bathhouse which although somewhat primitive was still effective. There was a good cookhouse, so plentiful, hot meals were guaranteed.

As there was not much doing in the way of fatigues, a spot of route marching was undertaken from time to time, but only enough to stop their muscles stiffening up. Nothing too strenuous was undertaken.

For entertainment, there was a resident concert party made up of members of the camp's permanent staff. They rejoiced in the name "The Cough Drops!" With hindsight, a better choice might have been "The Masochists!" After one of their shows, one had to feel some sympathy for them. They were, after all, amateurs doing their best. On the other hand, there is no audience more cruel than one of soldiers when they have decided that they do not like the show, no matter who the performers might be. Still, in the absence of anything better, it helped to pass the time. The Lads went four or five times on the trot, not because they liked the show but to see if the same mistakes would be made in every performance.

One day, a notice went up alongside daily orders. A gala entertainment was to be staged by The Cough Drops and a guest artiste. This would be a Madesmoiselle Térése, *danseuse exotique.*

William translated. "A young lady named Teresa will be performing exotic dances." He went on to say that she was very probably a striptease dancer.

The evening of the big show arrived. Queuing for the best seats, or indeed, any seats, started early in the afternoon. The best efforts of The Cough Drops were endured till at long last, the high spot of the evening arrived.

The house lights were extinguished leaving total darkness. Then, with a roll on the drums, approximately, three spotlights lit up a figure completely hidden by two huge ostrich-feather fans. The drums stopped, giving way to music of a vaguely oriental nature. The top fan moved and a face smiled seductively at the audience in what was presumably meant to be a 'come hither' manner. (The French equivalent *'Venez ici'* does not hold the same suggestiveness ---- something gets lost in the translation!) The result was not what she must have hoped for. Despite the derisory whistles and catcalls, she pressed on with her performance.

The lighting changed to a mixture of alternating colours. More or less in time to the beat of the music, the fans were wafted about while ensuring that the strategic parts of the 'young' lady were kept more or less covered. It was possible that if the spectator used his imagination, he would think he was seeing what was suggested.

Suddenly there was a change of mood. With another flourish on the drums, the lighting changed back to the spotlights, and Térése bared all! Striking what she must have imagined to be a provocative pose, she flung back her right arm (and fan) up into the air. At the same time, her left arm (and fan) were extended horizontally to the left, away from her body. She stood there waiting to take the rapturous applause which she obviously thought her performance merited. Instead, all she got was stunned silence broken only by one voice. It was Bob's.

"Bluddy 'ell! All that meat an' no taties!"

The burst of laughter that comment produced was too much for *mademoiselle* who dropped her fans and fled from the stage in mortification, losing one of her shoes as she did so.

At this, the entertainments officer stormed onto the stage and tried to tell the licentious soldiery that the rest of the show would be cancelled forthwith. As he could not make himself heard above the laughter and the catcalls, the R.S.M. also climbed onto the stage to help. When the audience realised that neither of the two currently holding the stage was having the slightest effect with their shouted orders, the two became the targets of witticisms and downright obscenities.

Eventually order was restored, but only when the 'heavies', the camp Provost Staff, arrived on the scene. Discretion being the better part of valour, (particularly if nothing further was to be gained), the audience quietly filed out of the auditorium when ordered to do so, and made their way back to their billets.

That show would long be remembered as the best put on by The Cough Drops, particularly with regard to the guests who would, of course, include the officer and the R.S.M. who came on at the end in the guise of comedians!

One afternoon, Tom asked Lt. Richardson for permission to "scout our flanks". Seeing that Tom had his rifle and 'gamebag', the officer, although suspecting that Tom was up to something decided that it would be wiser not to ask what. If anything went wrong, it would be better to state truthfully that he had no idea what Tom was going to do. It was not too difficult to guess, however. In the past when Tom had gone off like this everyone (including the lieutenant) had benefitted as a result.

So, without enquiring what this manoeuvre would entail, and with his fingers crossed behind his back, the officer gave permission. He then went and found a nice, inconspicuous spot in which to be 'unavailable' until Tom got back.

When Tom returned, the bag was more than half-full of mushrooms. With one hand, he carried his helmet by the strap. It was brim-full of hens' eggs. In the other hand, by its legs, he carried a headless chicken. In the back of that hand was a deep, triangular wound which was bleeding freely.

As he crossed the boundary fence, Tom came face to face with Captain Yorke. There was no way that Tom could salute without his head-dress and with both hands full. So, he snapped smartly to a halt, and then to attention.

Standing him at ease, the captain enquired as to the nature of the goods that Tom was carrying in his helmet. In answer, he was told that they were "wild chicken's eggs". The rooster was also of that variety.

When asked how he had known that the chickens had been "wild", Tom replied "Ah just knew they were. When they saw me tekkin' their eggs, they all went for me! See what this 'un did to mi 'and! It soon stopped though when its 'ead fell off! " Tom went on to add that "Ah 'ad to defend missen with mi bayonet. Onny road up, there were no point in wastin' 't rest of t' fowl when it cud be etten. T' foxes would 'ave 'ad it if Ah'd left it."

For the sake of appearances, Capt. York warned Tom that 'finding' hens' eggs could lead to the 'finder' being charged with looting. He also reminded Tom of the warning he had been given back in England.

Tom agreed, saying he had not forgotten the warning. But the warning had been given England, and this was France. He agreed that an offender, if caught, could be charged with looting, but added "It'll tek more nor a Frenchie tu cop me! Ah'll tek mi chances!"

Once again, and not for the first time (nor would it be the last!) Capt. Yorke had to mentally concede defeat. He would have to be up early in the day to outsmart someone with Tom's approach to life. In the meantime, he presumed, inwardly, that as usual he would be invited to sample whatever Tom 'found'. It was always worthwhile, and livened up the monotonous army fare.

When it comes to living off the land, a country boy definitely has a head start, particularly if he just happens to be a skilled poacher. That evening, Tom's section as well as the two officers dined on scrambled eggs and mushrooms with roast chicken, prepared and cooked by the resourceful Tom. When all had been consumed, the two dixie lids used in the cooking were returned to the cookhouse before they were missed.

The next day or so also passed very enjoyably but far too quickly. They were all too aware of what lay ahead of them ---- they could hardly ignore the thunder of the guns in the not too far-away distance.

July 10th saw them on their travels once more. This time, their destination would be Varennes, a mere five miles behind the lines. They were moving inexorably nearer to the Hell's kitchen that the Somme battlefield had become.

The distance covered on this march was much shorter than of late, some six miles in all. This was covered by lunchtime after which settling-in was the order of the day. Billets were empty civilian houses taken over when their owners had fled the district. A cookhouse had been established in a large farmhouse on the western outskirts of the town.

On the way in from Léalvillers, the Ledfords had noticed with not a little apprehension that there was a large military cemetery at the side of the road. As they passed, they eyed the long line of ambulances parked by the verge waiting to discharge their loads. Judging by the insignia painted on them, all the Divisions in the area were well represented.

The cemetery was a new one created to accommodate all those who had died in the hospitals in the locality, or who had been found to be dead on arrival when brought in from casualty clearance stations at the rear of the lines.

The next place they passed were the R.E. carpenters' workshops. Stacked outside were what must have been several hundreds of wooden crosses, painted matt white so as to take the pencilled details of the poor blighter who finished up beneath one of them.

So far, not the cheeriest welcome to this part of France.

Fred and his immediate circle could consider themselves very fortunate to have lasted as long as they had done without any of them being killed or seriously injured. In spite of what they had endured, all they had collected along the way had been a bit of trench foot (now healed) and the usual assortment of cuts and bruises. When would their luck run out, they wondered?

As if to emphasise the thoughts which were going through their heads, the noise of the artillery fire was much louder here, and would continue for much longer at a time, with one lot or another joining in or dropping out.

The night of arrival as well as the next was spent in Varennes, and then they were on the move again. Once again, only a short distance had to be covered. Five miles later on, they arrived at a place by the name of Bresle, a short distance to the west of Albert.

The next day was a rest day. This time, they were actually allowed to take things easy for once. While they were there, they heard disquieting reports on the first day's efforts in the Somme offensive. It seemed that the British had taken some 60,000 casualties killed or wounded on July 1st alone. Figures like that were hard to take in let alone comprehend. To say that the Ledfords were shocked would be an understatement. It was into that maelstrom that they were now heading.

Whatever the truth of the matter, they were in that theatre of war and they would just have get on with it.

Quarters were basic in the extreme consisting of waterproof wagon sheets stretched over holes in the ground. To make matters worse, their cookers had got lost or delayed on the way so there would be no hot water or cooked meal that night. It was back to hard tack and bully beef. That would be breakfast as well the next day. This was when a tin of the self-heating soup 'acquired' at Chocques would come in handy.

The following day, they headed towards a spot to the south of Montauban. Their destination was a narrow strip of woodland thrusting forward at right-angles to the line of the front, but at the rear of the trenches.

This was *Talus-Boisé*. They arrived on July 14th. It had been the scene of desperate and fierce fighting when Montauban had been captured. The trees had been reduced to shattered stumps with the ground in between a mess of overlapping shell craters. It was littered with the debris of battle, and stank of burnt explosives and putrefying corpses.

Accommodation again consisted of tarpaulins stretched over holes in the ground, but this time, they were slung between stumps above the shell holes.

But now there were rats. They were fat and fearless. Above all else, they were loathsome creatures feeding as they did on the unburied dead which still lay around.

If the smallest scrap of food was saved for later, it could not be left in a haversack or even a tunic pocket. The detestable animals would gnaw their way into the haversack, or, if in a pocket would climb up the wearer of the uniform and chew through the material to get at it. If an attempt was made to brush them off, they would inflict severe bites on the soldier. Considering where the rats had been, it was hardly surprising that the bites very quickly turned septic.

The only way to safeguard personal food supplies was to hang the comestibles well above ground level if possible, preferably on a long length of wire. The men soon learned to eat standing up in the open. If they didn't, it was not unusual to find a rat joining in the meal and actually in the mess tin!

Meals would be taken with a bayonet stuck handily in an available stump so that it could be quickly reached. It was amazing how adept one became at decapitating the rodents with a quick swipe of the blade.

This was to be 'home' until further notice. To make matters worse, as if that was possible, they were now within range of the German guns, with shells landing among the shattered stumps at irregular intervals.

It really was "Home, sweet home" with a vengeance!

Chapter 21

Over the next few days, the Ledford Bantams provided carrying parties --- what else? They brought forward reserve supplies of tinned food, ammunition and any material needed by the Engineers. Intermediate forward dumps were established near Carnoy. These forward dumps would reduce the distance to be covered on the last leg of a 'carry' to the troops in the front line.

Attempts were also made on two successive days to bury cables which the R.E. signallers were laying up to the forward positions through the fringes of Bernafay Wood. On each and every occasion that an attempt was made to do anything, the working parties would come under immediate and accurate shellfire. It was uncanny.

While sheltering from the inferno, Lt. Richardson noticed that all the other parties in the vicinity of the wood seemed to attract the same accurate gunfire. This was strange as all these 'targets of opportunity' for the enemy gunners would be passing through what should have been 'dead ground'. They were in a hollow just below the ridge, and on the blind side, away from the enemy. From the enemy positions, there was no way that the guns could be directed to fire so accurately on targets which they could not see. There must be an enemy observer on the British side of the hill.

The lieutenant set about meticulously quartering the ground to his front. There was nothing which could conceal a spotter. There was nothing on either flank, nor were there any enemy aircraft or balloons in the sky.

His eyes were always drawn back to a French farmer industriously ploughing his land, even though it was almost in the front line. What was even more surprising was that no shell, not even strays fell anywhere near that field.

Even to a townsman, there was something odd about the manner in which the field was being worked. Not only that, but when ploughing towards the wood, he would don a large, French beret, yet when he was going the other way, he would take it off and put it in the pocket of his *bleu de travaille,* the traditional light blue smock worn by the farmers in the north of France. It could be that the beret was worn when heading towards a target, but removed when going away from it.

A bit imaginative, perhaps, but the more he watched, the more the officer was convinced that the ploughing routine was some form of signalling to the enemy guns, particularly as the field was high on the side of the slope facing towards enemy positions. It was almost certain to be visible to a suitably sited observation post in the German lines.

He decided to test his theory, so he sent for Billy. As a ploughman before he volunteered, he would know if there was anything odd about the technique of the suspect farmer on the hill. When all was said and done, there should not be much variation, if any, between French and British ploughing methods.

Billy watched for a few moments, then said "No plahman in 'is reight mind would muck abaht like that. Ah'm buggered if 'ah know why 'e orlus stops in t"middle! 'E nivver gets to eether 'edland". (To the uninitiated, the " headland" is the strip of ground at each end of the furrow where the plough is turned to go back the other way).

That was a sufficiently damning verdict for the lieutenant. He called Tom over, and a plot was hatched. Tom and Billy would make their way unobtrusively to the hedge bordering the field where they would hide. They were to avoid being seen by the man at all costs.

A target would then be offered to the German guns -------- 4 Platoon would start to move forward! If the theory was correct, at this point the farmer should start ploughing in their direction, wearing his beret, then turn back from the 'target' area having removed his beret. Seconds later, the German artillery should open fire on 4 Platoon!

The lieutenant would therefore allow the platoon to take five steps then blow his whistle whereupon everyone would dive for cover to avoid the incoming shells which could be expected.

Tom was given orders that in the event that things turned out as predicted, he was to kill the 'farmer'. It would have to be with one shot only to prevent him giving warning that he had been unmasked.

Billy was to dash over, calm the horses, and put on the dead man's smock and beret. He was then to turn the outfit and plough in the general direction of the bottom right-hand corner of the field. He was then to pause, remove the beret, and then plough back to the centre of the field as the dead man would have done.

If Lt. Richardson's reasoning was correct, and the German spotter had not seen what had happened to their 'farmer', their fire should now lift from the Ledfords and switch to the direction in which the plough was heading when Billy was wearing the beret. The range was probably indicated by the distance 'ploughed'. As the area had previously been held by the enemy, they would have realised that there was a large expanse of dead ground which could only be controlled by means of ranged, directed artillery fire in the event that they lost the area. With this in mind, it was possible that a distance-related scale had been worked out together with a means of signalling it.

It sounded far-fetched, but if such a scheme *had* been devised, then something would have to be done about it. As it was, the Ledfords were effectively pinned down. They could neither go forward nor pull back. If nothing was done, the moment they tried to move, they would be shelled. As they would have to move sooner or later, they had no choice. They might as well try the plan.

With Tom and Billy in position, 4 Platoon stood up as arranged, somewhat hesitantly it must be admitted. As they did so, the lieutenant kept a close watch on his 'farmer' friend. Sure enough, he turned his plough and headed towards them, donning the beret as he did so.

After the five paces had been taken, the officer blew his whistle and everybody hit the ground and prayed like they had never prayed before. Seconds later, a salvo landed nearby showering them all with earth and stones. A single shot rang out and the ploughman collapsed across his plough.

As they watched Billy dashed across the field, tore the smock from the Frenchman's (or German's) body and put it on. Cramming the beret on his head, he went to the horses and quickly brought them under control. Then he stepped back, undid his flies and urinated. Obviously, here was a man with no worries in the world and where he had every right to be. Or so it appeared. The plough and team were then skilfully and calmly turned round, and off they went towards the corner of the field suggested to him.

Reference to the trench map of the locality had shown that the British positions between Montauban and Bernafay Wood formed a slight salient which protruded a little way into the enemy lines. On the Ledfords' right flank, the enemy line swung round so as to be slightly behind the British. It stayed that way until it reached the French sector at Maricourt.

So, if the German fire plan had been correctly deduced, then it might be possible to get him to fire on his own lines

Earlier in the day, the French had ground to a halt during an unsuccessful attack. If they had managed to regain momentum and were now moving forward again, then troops under attack would require defensive fire from their guns. In this situation, such a switch in direction would be logical. That he had no idea what the French were doing, if anything, did not worry the lieutenant one little bit. He had his own problem to solve.

Having reached the corner of the field as instructed, Billy took off the beret, spat on his hands and turned the plough. He brought it back to the centre of the field and stopped. After removing the smock, he then sauntered back to the edge of the field and sat down next to the hole in the hedge through which he had got into the field. He then slid backwards through the gap, picked himself up and ran for the shelter of the woods and the companionship of his pals.

As if by magic, the next salvo of shells was aimed well away from the woods and in the direction indicated by the ploughing. Whilst congratulating the pair on their coup, Lt. Richardson asked Billy what had inspired his touch of genius, his master stroke.

Billy replied "Nay, it were nowt like that. Ah were that scared stud art in t'oppen like that, if Ah 'addent done it proper, 'appen Ah'd 'a' peed missen!"

A case of asking a silly question?

Taking stock of the cable-burying task, it was obvious that as all the drums of cable had been reduced to so much rubbish and firewood by the hostile shellfire, there was effectively none left to be buried. Most of the trenches which had been laboriously and dangerously dug for the cables had been destroyed by the same shellfire. As for the signallers who had come up to lay and connect the stuff, they had all been killed.

As there was now effectively no task to be completed, there was no point hanging around. They would call it a day, and what a day! But before they left the scene, there was one more thing that Billy had to do. He released the horses and brought them back with him and handed them over to the Army Service Corps horse handlers.

Next stop was "Sleepy Hollow", the derisory name given to their hovels back in *Talus Boisé* by the Ledfords. With time in hand, they would improve them.

The original shell holes were dug deeper and roofed over. These would not only give better protection from the elements, but would afford some protection from the sporadic shelling to which the location was subjected.

The roofing was supported by the branches cut from the trees by the shelling and consisted of the tarpaulins with a deep covering of earth. The entrance was formed in the side away from the enemy, and opened into a short length of trench.

This would be 'home' for the foreseeable future.

There was nothing that could be done to get rid of the rats. William summed it up very neatly when he said there would be no point in trying to get hold of the Pied Piper of Hamelin as he would probably be in German uniform by now getting rid of their rats.

The next day, the cable-laying having been tasked to some other lucky souls, the Ledfords worked their way forward into a position known as "Southern Trench". This was to be found, not surprisingly to the south of Montauban. To their right lay the shambles of the brickworks, with just forward of them, the boundaries of Bernafay Wood. Between the west side of the wood and the eastern outskirts of Montauban was open ground. This was where they were to be employed.

Their task was to search the bodies of British dead, and recover personal papers and possessions to be returned to the next-of-kin back home. More importantly in the Army view, pay books and identity discs had to be collected so that official records could be kept up to date. That aspect of the job was most important. If the records were out of date, how would anyone know who was winning the war?

Personal effects and pay book went into a white, cloth ration bag, bundles of which had been brought up for the purpose. On each corpse, there were two identity discs, one red, and one green. One was to be left with the body, the other taken and tied round the neck of the ration bag. It no longer seemed to matter which colour went where so long as one was taken and one left with the remains.

The task was to prove beyond description. Some bodies had been fearfully mangled, most having been there since the start of the offensive on July 1st. All had been attacked by rats. The stench was foul in the extreme. The whole day would be punctuated by the gut-wrenching sounds of grown men retching and vomiting as the body they were searching literally came apart in their hands.

The day passed in this ghastly manner, then it was time to return to camp such as it was. Despite the nauseating filth with which they were covered, there would be no means of getting rid of it as there was no water supply apart from that in the tins, and that was for drinking only. Even that was getting low.

4 Platoon assembled at the crossroads near the corner of the wood, and set off towards Montauban where the road would fork. The left fork would take them directly to *Talus Boisé*

That had been the intention, but it was not to be.

They were halfway between Bernafay Wood and Montauban when they heard the shriek of incoming shells. They had been caught out in the open and were totally exposed. There was not a scrap of cover anywhere. They now realised why there were so many dead in the area.

In came one salvo followed by another. These were followed by a third and a fourth in quick succession. It was what one would imagine Dante's inferno to be like. There were blinding flashes all round them together with a continuous succession of deafening explosions.

They were choking on flying earth and dust, together with the acrid fumes of burnt explosives. The air was punched violently out of their lungs. The ground rocked and boiled all round them as they were buffeted from side to side by the series of blasts.

Lt. Richardson was hit full in the face by a large clod of earth and stones. Just at that moment, the platoon sergeant was lifted clean off his feet by the sheer force of a shell which exploded next to him and flung straight at his officer. Both finished up in a tangled heap at the side of the road. Protruding from the sergeant's back was a large shell splinter.

As Fred was looking in horror at the carnage all round him, he was punched violently in the midriff, all the air being driven from him. A fireball expanded on the road about fifteen feet in front of him, incandescent white in the centre going through yellow and orange to red and black at the edges. He felt two savage blows, one to each arm at the very moment he saw the flash. The feeling that he was flying through the air was followed by a body-shaking impact as he landed in a heap at the other side of the road. After that, he knew no more.

Sometime later ---- he had no idea how much later --- he thought he could hear voices. They were a long way away, and seemed to be coming through cotton-wool. Then, through a haze, he became aware that people were bending over him, calling his name. He found that he had sustained severe lacerations to his chest and abdomen, as well as deep wounds to both biceps. The front of his tunic had been torn to shreds. He was bleeding heavily.

Standing near him was the lieutenant. The majority of his front teeth were missing, his mouth bruised and battered. His left eye was closed. Even as one watched, the left side of his face was swelling visibly, and taking on a strange assortment of hues.

Then there was Tom. He had taken splinters in his right shoulder and was bleeding profusely.

Charlie, with a bemused look on his face was still on his feet, staggering around in circles. His face was streaming with blood. He was holding his helmet in his hand and burbling on about the fact that he had been wearing it correctly. He was, of course, harking back to the training session where he had been told to wear the strap round the back of his head. The splinter which had ripped the helmet from his head had been able to do so without breaking his neck. It was pity that in doing so, that same splinter had penetrated the 'tin hat' and gouged his scalp resulting in the copious flow of blood.

Of the men of 4 Platoon, only these four were able to stand, if only precariously. The lieutenant, Fred, Tom and Charlie were all that were left. Billy would never see his eighteenth birthday. As for William and Bob, they had vanished without trace. Of the original six who enlisted more or less at the same time in December, 1914, only three remained. It was possible that other men of the platoon might be removed from the field as stretcher cases, but it did not look too promising.

The luck of the Ledfords had run out!

Chapter 22

The four wounded lurched off in the direction of a regimental aid post which had been set up in a large shell crater just inside the wood. Between them they half carried, half dragged the sergeant. Although at first he had seemed to be done for, he had started to bleed from the mouth and from the entry wound in his back. There was a bloody froth on his lips and from the wound itself. That was a certain indication of damage to his lungs, and not a good sign at all.

The M.O. took one look, and shook his head. The sergeant was in need of urgent specialist treatment he said, but did not hold out much hope for him. What was needed was way beyond anything that could be done in the aid post. The splinter was left where it was as removing it other than surgically would aggravate the wound and result in more vigorous bleeding. He did, however, pad the protruding sliver of metal, and applied several field-dressings to the site. That was the best he could do in the primitive pit in which the first aid was being administered. An orderly wrote out a label and tied it to the patient's buttonhole.

Fred was next. Dressings were swiftly lashed in place on the wounds in his arms. As his tunic and equipment had been shredded, there was no point in trying to undo buttons and fastenings, even if they could have been found. Using Fred's bayonet, no time was wasted in cutting the tatters away from the frontal wounds.

Exploring the lacerated area with his finger tips, the M.O. concluded that whilst there had been severe wounding to the site, there had been no penetration of either the chest cavity or the abdomen. If Fred managed to avoid blood poisoning, he had got himself a very nice 'blighty' wound which would give him several months back in England.

Bandaging the wounds on Fred's torso posed a problem as there was no dressing to hand which was large enough to cover such a large expanse of lacerated flesh. Then the M.O. had a flash of inspiration. From his personal valise he took two towels one of which he folded to a quarter of its size. This produced a pad big enough to cover the wounds. The other towel was passed round Fred so that the ends came together behind his back. He then produced a ball of string and laced the two ends together like an old-fashioned corset. That was the best that could be done until Fred was at the casualty clearing station.

Medically speaking, Tom's wound was of similar severity to the selection that Fred had collected. He also would be a 'blighty' candidate. A fragment of shell had struck his right shoulder narrowly missing his neck. It had torn a deep, ragged gash close to the point where the neck rises from the shoulder. In doing so, it had exposed and broken the collar bone.

As for Charlie, the verdict was that while the wound looked spectacular, all it needed was tidying up and a few stitches. He also had concussion to some degree. A field-dressing was tied in place and he was dismissed with the comment "You'll live!"

The M.O. now turned to the lieutenant. As the dirt was washed from his patient's face, the verdict was delivered. "Apart from a black eye, split lips and having your teeth knocked out, you haven't done too badly. One thing is certain, you'll never have problems with your front teeth ever again!" And with those cheery words, he turned to deal with the long line of wounded who still awaited his ministrations.

As all that could be done for them in the forward are had been done, they were consigned to the Casualty Clearance Station, but advised to call in at an Advanced Dressing Station they would pass on their way to check for any deterioration in their condition.

Lt. Richardsdon said that as there could be no question of the sergeant having to wait for stretcher bearers, he would carry him. It was obvious that the man was in urgent need of a higher degree of medical skill that was possible at the moment. That attention was needed with the least delay possible.

The badly wounded sergeant was draped across his officer's back, 'piggy-back' fashion, but with his wrists tied together under the lieutenant's chin. Of the other three, Charlie was the fittest. If the truth be told, he was not so much the 'fittest' as the least wounded. He would help Fred and Tom.

From Charlie's left side, Fred draped his right arm round his pal's neck. Tom, from the other side used his left arm. Charlie then reached round both of them and seized hold of whatever clothing or equipment was still available. In Fred's case, Charlie grabbed his trousers waistband and belt.

Off the human wreckage staggered. Now officially classified as 'walking wounded', they would have to make their own way back for the hospital treatment they all needed.

Fred could not feel anything from the wound in his arm, even where it pressed against Charlie. By this time, the morphine which had been injected into him was beginning to take effect leaving him vague, and unaware of what was going on.

Away they tottered, eventually arriving at the A.D.S. where they were checked over. There was nothing more which could be done in addition to the treatment they had already received, so they set off once again.

By now, they were near Carnoy. Onwards they lurched to be greeted by the sight of an immaculately groomed and polished 'brass hat', complete with swagger stick. On his arm he wore the blue and red brassard of a staff officer.

The road at this point was thronged with soldiers from all sorts of units, from carrying-parties going forward, to unladen troops on the return trip. Intermingled with them were the walking wounded. Probably because of their diminutive stature, this officer saw fit to pick them out from the rest of the scruffy troops. He did not seem to be very pleased with what he saw. Purple with rage, he screamed at Charlie, "You there! That fellow with the 'bird' on your arm!"

Without slackening his already slow pace, Charlie retorted over his shoulder, "Yon's not a 'bird', it's a bluddy Bantam!" From then on, he totally ignored the apparition.

The next to come within range, and so become another target because he too had a 'bird' on his arm, was Lt. Richardson and his burden. He was, of course, wearing the uniform of a private soldier. In this guise he appeared to be just another ranker.

Through his battered lips he mumbled "Who, sir? Me, sir? I am Lt. Richardson. My unit? I no longer have one! We *were* 4 Platoon, "C" Company, 17th. Mid-Yorkshire Regiment. The three in front and me are all who can stand. With the sergeant on my back, we are all who are left from my platoon. The rest are stretcher cases if they were lucky, or dead if they were not. Our orders were to bury British dead near Bernafay, which we did. The snag is that we replaced them with our own, unfortunately."

"Yes, sir. I'm sure Charlie would have saluted you if he hadn't had his hands full with his wounded mates. But then, he's only half-carried them for over two miles. He's also got a head wound and concussion, but that's no excuse for ignoring army etiquette. He could see what you were the moment he clapped eyes on you. I'll have a word with him in due course, if I remember. You will have noticed that I didn't salute you either. You may also have noticed that I too am rather busy at the moment with this dying man on my back. Sorry, can't hang about all day gossiping. Must toddle. Got things to do, old chap. Ta-ta!"

With that, he resumed his lurching progress towards the C.C.S. leaving the staff officer fizzing with barely concealed rage.

The C.C.S. was reached after a veritable lifetime, or so it seemed. With this establishment being in effect a mobile hospital, it could set up 'shop' as far forward as possible but out of range of the enemy guns. This meant that quite sophisticated treatment was available at the earliest opportunity for all who could get there. Treatment would be there for all who needed it, irrespective of nationality.

On arrival, the little group collapsed in a heap, totally exhausted. A very young-looking doctor dashed out from behind a desk in the reception area and, with a nurse, classified them in order of priority.

The sergeant no longer needed treatment, urgent or otherwise. The lieutenant had been carrying a dead man the last mile or so.

Tom and Fred were immediately whisked away in the direction of the main surgical unit. Charlie and his officer received more first aid. Charlie had his scalp shaved and stitched. He would be on light duties until he was fit enough to resume full active service.

Then what?

Given an adequate supply of bombs, and provided the war lasted long enough, Charlie would happily bomb his way to Berlin, if he lived. But knowing Charlie, he would very likely be killed in the thick of action before long. But on his way out, he would almost certainly win a medal for bravery ----- or insanity!

Lt. Richardson's face was washed and thoroughly examined. Apart from a cut at the side of his mouth which had to be stitched, the only real damage was his now non-existent teeth. As for his eye, this was deftly washed out and checked for damage. Provided he reported regularly to his regimental M.O., it should sort itself out given time.

On emerging from the treatment room, they both waited until Fred and Tom had been installed in a ward to await their turn in the operating theatre.

Considering the time they had spent together, and what they had endured, the farewells could have been rather emotional. But as Fred said, the occasion was not overly mawkish, but more a last chance of getting in as many insults as possible, one to the other, before they went their separate ways.

On his return from the C.C.S., the lieutenant reported to Capt. Yorke to be told that as the commanding officer of "D" Company had been killed in the same strafing which had destroyed 4 Platoon, he, Lt. Richardson was to take charge. He had accordingly been made a 'brevet' captain. When he asked what that was , he was told that such a being had all the responsibilities and worries together with taking all the risks of a substantive captain, but not the pay! Once again, the Army got the best of the bargain.

So what of our two in hospital?

A visit to the operating theatre resulted in the odd splinter or two being dug out of Fred together with, more importantly, shreds of uniform which had been driven into the wounds. All these had now been properly dressed.

Tom, whilst not carrying any scrap metal also had material from his tunic removed from his wound. The collarbone was set, the wound dressed and the arm immobilised.

Bed rest was now the order of the day for them, with both being kept under observation in case of any delayed shock or other reactions.

By the following afternoon, both Fred and Tom were feverish, and running dangerously high temperatures. The doctor was of the opinion that when scraps of their uniforms had been driven into their wounds by the shell splinters, battlefield filth picked up on the burying detail must have been taken in as well. It must be this which was now poisoning their wounds. Drainage tubes would have to be set up to remove the noxious fluids.

With these in place, the two were transferred to the 10th. Field Hospital, Rouen.

It took fourteen or fifteen days before the suppuration showed any signs of diminishing, but eventually it stopped altogether. Two more days elapsed without any deterioration in their condition, so arrangements were put in hand for their shipment back to England.

They had made it!

They were going home!

Despite the boost that this knowledge brought to them, they knew all too well that the respite back home would only be of a temporary nature. When they recovered, --- and they knew they would --- they would be shipped back to another hell similar to the one from which they had just escaped. Next time, it would be different. The tight little group of which they had been a part no longer existed.

There and then, the two of them vowed that if it was at all possible, they would go back to their next unit together, and stick it out until it was all over and done with, no matter what the outcome.

Then the great day arrived when they were put on the train which was to take them to Le Havre in transit to England.

Netley Hospital near Southampton was to be their next resting place. Ultimately, if they could wangle it, a transfer to

Fulford Military Hospital in York would do very nicely, thank you.

For the moment, that was so much wishful thinking. So long as they were somewhere in England, that would be good enough to start with.

When they got there, Le Havre seemed to be from far back in a different lifetime. How many centuries had passed since they had first set foot on the quay? Had they really bleated like sheep at the antics of the harassed and confused Port Control Officer? Had Charlie really tipped that thieving Frenchman into the river? Had they really ----------------?

And so it went on. If all that, and more, had happened, it must have been during the last century at the very latest, they seemed to have been here for so long.

But it had only been six months ago, in February to be precise, when they had first landed on French soil. It was now only August. There was no denying that they had been to the gates of Hell and back since February. That short period of time seemed to have been the longest in their lives, and no mistake!

But enough of such thoughts. They would have to try to put it all behind them, and ignore the future. They would have to concentrate on making the most of their convalescent leave when they got it.

For the moment, all that mattered was that

THEY WERE GOING HOME!

Chapter 23

It was now October, two months since the two Bantams had been shipped back to England after that disastrous day near Montauban. Their wounds had been dealt with efficiently, as had the septicaemia which had followed. They were now at Netley in the huts built as an extension to the palatial Victorian hospital which overlooked Southampton water. This establishment was now working at full stretch in an attempt to cope with the flood of casualties resulting from the Somme offensive.

When patients had recovered sufficiently to allow them to be transferred elsewhere, they were moved as quickly as possible. This would free beds near to the Channel ports so that there was hospital space available for the large number of wounded being brought back from France virtually every day.

Casualty Clearance Stations and hospitals over there had almost been overwhelmed by the sheer numbers involved. So, the moment a man could be moved with a reasonable degree of safety, he was sent back to England. Whilst this freed beds nearer to the fighting it tended to overload hospitals in the south of England. This knock-on effect meant that wounded already in England had to be moved further inland as soon as possible. Where to did not matter so long as it was away from the Channel ports. So, after a few not so subtle hints, the two friends found themselves in residence at Fulford.

One immediate benefit was that they could no longer hear the guns giving voice along the Western Front. At Netley, on a quiet night and with the wind from the south east, they could often be heard quite distinctly. Thankfully, this was no longer the case at York.

Despite the fact that their wounds no longer produced the copious discharge of earlier days, they did leak from time to time, and just would not heal. Tom's collar bone had knitted together very well indeed. If it was not for the discomfort and inconvenience of the unhealed injury, he would have regained full use of his right arm.

Fred was in a similar state. Although his lot had only been flesh wounds, they would not heal either. They would skin over, but it was an unhealthy, unnatural-looking membrane. At the slightest suggestion of strain on it, it would split wide open.

One doctor in desperation suggested that rather than droop around the ward making the place look untidy, they should be out in the fresh air, taking advantage of the bright, late autumn sunshine. They should spend as much time out in the hospital grounds as they could, and take things easy. If they could find a spot out of the wind but open to the sunshine, they should try its beneficial effects on their wounds.

They followed his advice, found a sheltered arbour facing the south west, and, following the best army traditions, scrounged a couple of easy chairs and occupied the position.

On sunny days, this was where they were be found, stripped to the waist. It became an established routine that if they were needed for any reason, the arbour would be the first place to be checked. Their meals were automatically taken out to that spot if the weather was fine. As a result, some colour returned to their faces, which was not a bad thing. On arrival, their cheeks had been sunken, and their skin a yellowy-white. This waxy pallor was not the best advertisement for the quality of army Medical Corps nursing.

One day during the course of a daily examination, the M.O. noticed a difference in the texture of the new skin covering Tom's wound. It looked more like normal skin, and not the shiny, transparent stuff which had been giving all the trouble.

Greatly daring, he applied gentle pressure with his thumb. The new tissue held firm and did not tear. What was more, when the pressure was released, the skin returned to its original contour.

That was Tom, how about Fred? It was exactly the same with him. Whatever the reason, be it the sunshine, or the poison having worked its way out of their systems, they were on the mend at last.

Progress was continued until the day came when, if they wished, they could to spend their days in York. They could visit the Minster, stroll along the river banks or walk the walls of the city.

They were issued with 'hospital blue' uniforms to wear. Bright blue jacket and trousers would be worn with a white shirt and red tie. Their normal head-dress and regimental cap badge completed the outfit.

They would find that when they went into a café or restaurant for a meal, or just a cup of tea and a cake, the uniform would produce immediate service without having to wait for a table. When they came to leave, they would often find that their bill had already been settled by one of the other customers.

Our two wounded heroes always made a point of thanking the generous donor if at all possible, and would never take such acts of kindness for granted, or as a right.

In this manner, time passed until they were ruled fit for further active service after they had spent some time toughening up at the regimental depot a short distance down the road from the hospital.

They were given fourteen days leave on discharge from the hospital after which they were to report to Fulford Barracks.

Furlough passed all too quickly, then it was back to York, but this time, to the regimental depot at the barracks. Bedding was drawn, and bed-spaces allocated. The Q.M then issued each man with a complete set of equipment as well as khaki uniforms to replace the blue ones they had worn while on leave, and nominally still on the patients' roll at the hospital.

All their previous issue had been stripped off them and left behind at the C.C.S. in France. At least, Tom's had. Fred's had been shredded by his collection of shell splinters. Their tunics, or what was left of them had been cut from them by the medical orderlies over there. As for trousers and boots, they had taken away and burned, covered as they were with evidence of their last task before being wounded. That had been (as if they would ever forget) the burying of British dead in varying stages of decomposition!

Now, newly kitted out, the immediate task was the rebuilding of their wasted bodies. Slowly this was achieved. Good, solid food, and plenty of it, together with exercise and route marches over varying distances gradually restored their lost fitness

Christmas was now imminent with the promise of five days' leave. This would effectively be embarkation leave as well in anticipation of being sent back to France early in the New Year.

Back in barracks, Fred disclosed that he and his girl had come to an 'agreement'. Although not officially 'engaged', they had decided that if Fred survived, they would get married as soon as he was released at the end of the war

The year rolled on until it was the last week in February, 1917. Fred and Tom were now almost as fit as they had been in 1914. According to the M.O., they were 'A2'. With this medical grading, they were as fit as the majority of the men currently with the Colours. They were now back on the "Available for Draft" list. It was now simply a matter of time before they were on their travels once more.

Then, one evening, company orders instructed them to report to the Orderly Room the next day. On doing so, they found they were to be posted to the 9th Battalion of their regiment. They would not be returning to the 17th. They were no longer officially "Bantams", despite their lack of inches. When they queried this posting the Adjutant told them that it was in accordance with the latest War Office directive. This meant that ex-wounded were to be sent to units other than their original outfits in order, eventually, to spread casualties (apparently) across the whole of the United Kingdom. This would prevent the recurrence of such lists as had been published when purely local regiments had been slaughtered *en masse*.

Those returning to the Front, other than from leave, would be allocated to whichever regiment needed topping up with replacements. Traditional recruiting areas would be ignored, the men being rebadged as necessary. Tom and Fred were lucky to be going back to their original regiment, albeit to another battalion. With that, they would have to be satisfied.

Although proving to be huge success in persuading men to enlist, the Kitchener recruiting ploy of "Pals" battalions and similar groups had drastically misfired with appalling consequences. With units such as 'Pals' battalions of the West Yorkshire Regiment from Leeds and Bradford, when they had been massacred at Serre on July 1st., whole streets in those cities had lost all their young men. Some streets had lost someone from every house. Some had even lost both brothers from one dwelling. The impact on civilian morale had been shattering.

So, officialdom had come up with a solution. All ex-wounded being sent back to France would be posted not to their original regiments, but to others. Although this would in no way reduce the rate of attrition, the casualties would now seem to be distributed across the whole of the United Kingdom as was the intention. It would also make it extremely difficult, if not impossible for the editors of local newspapers to extract details of the casualties pertinent to the locality covered by their journals. They would have problems in collating and publishing such lists as had been published for the Somme battles. Whilst the figures were not being falsified to reduce their impact, in the form now published, it was impossible to relate them to any specific area.

But back to Fred and Tom who were setting out for France for a second time. Before they left the depot, they had drawn rifles and bayonets from the armoury to replace those lost or destroyed at the time of their wounding.

York station saw them on the train to London and thence to Dover for the short sea voyage to Calais.

Part Three
"Survivors, but for how long?"

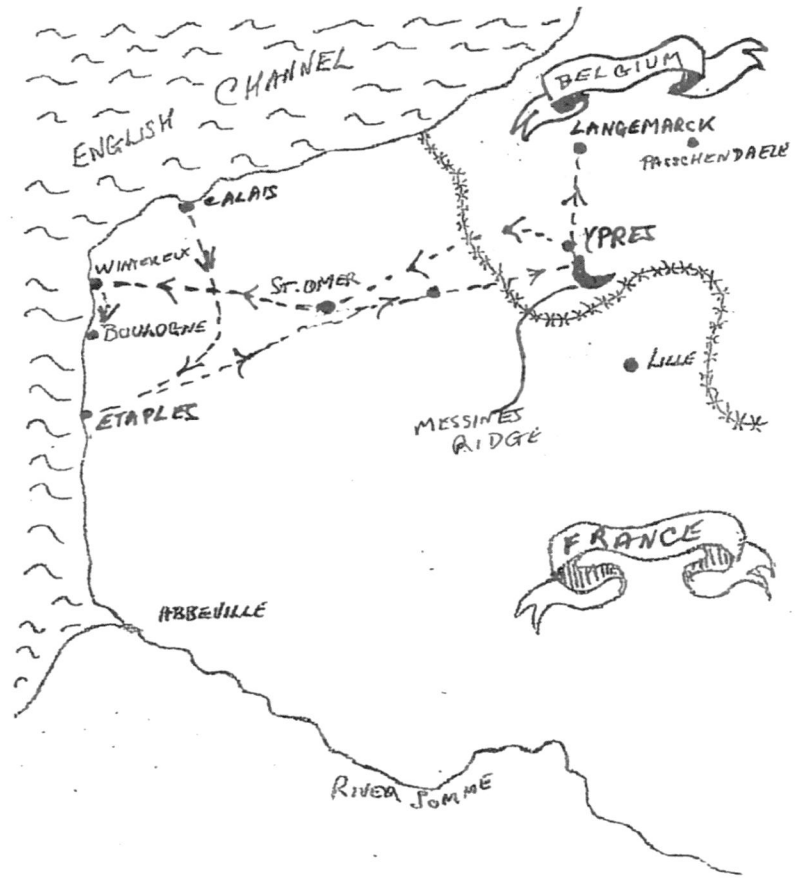

*Fred's Travels in France & Belgium
February, 1917 – September, 1917*

Chapter 24

After an uneventful crossing, they found on disembarking that all troops had to report in at the transit camp just outside Étaples ('Eat apples' in the *lingua franca* of the day). With scant regard for the units involved, everybody was herded onto the lorries waiting on the station concourse in Calais which left when they were full. On his lorry, Fred found about twenty bored Aussies and their sergeant who had been waiting for the last three hours. They had been held until the next cross-channel ferry had docked and discharged more passengers for Étaples.

As all the lorries were now fully loaded, the vehicles set off in convoy. As might have been expected, the Aussies' comments on the lack of organisation in the "bairsted Pommie Army" were quite educational. As before, they had a turn of phrase the like of which was not normally heard in Yorkshire.

On arrival at the encampment, (the 'Bull Ring', as it was known), they found that it had been set up to 'instruct men in the art of survival in the trenches, and to harden them for battle'.

Everybody jumped down from the lorries and formed up with their kit. They were all too aware of the baleful glare of a sergeant who was waiting for them. He was immaculately dressed with razor-sharp creases in his tunic and trousers. His boot toecaps could have been used as shaving mirrors.

He wore a bright yellow brassard on his arm. While the little group were sorting themselves into some sort of order, he stood there, like a ramrod, shrieking obscenities at them through a froth of spittle on his lips. This was their first encounter with an Étaples 'canary'!

These creatures had been given this soubriquet because of the colour of their armbands. An alternative, more popular version was that it was the colour of the streak up their backs. Whatever the origin of the nickname, they were universally detested by all the troops passing through the camp.

They were sadists to a man, everyone a bully. They operated on the principle that if they were seen to be chasing their victims into the ground, they would be thought to be so good at their job as to be invaluable. As such, it would therefore be unlikely that they would ever have to go out and do some of the fighting about which they professed to know so much.

One peculiarity common to all the 'canaries' was that very few had been anywhere near the forward areas let alone the front-line trenches.

These, then, were the staff who were to 'instruct' those who had.

No exception was made for those men who had been out there already, been wounded, and were now returning for more service in the trenches. Similarly, those who had been lucky in the leave 'lottery' and were also returning to the front lines, they too had to be battle-hardened and taught how to survive by those who had never required these skills.

All the newcomers were double-marched to their billets no matter how far they had come nor the state of their health. The amount of kit being carried was not the concern of the instructor unless, of course, anything was dropped. Then all hell would descend on the man who dropped it. They would have to endure this kind of treatment for the next five days.

They found that they had been put in one of the hundreds of weathered bell-tents which covered every inch of what once had been open ground. They spread over the landscape like some sort of scabrous growth. Each one had a rough floor of planks which fitted where they touched. The gaps between the ill-fitting boards did however prevent the build-up of the sand which was blowing everywhere.

Having made up their beds in no time at all, they were doubled down to the cookhouse where the meals were swallowed without wasting any time. Then they were doubled back to their tents, and told that although nominally they were now off duty, they were to hold themselves in readiness in case they were needed for anything.

They discovered later that evening that this was, apparently, a 'canary'-type joke, aimed at ruining the spare time of any newcomers. When they realised that there would be no call on their services, the Aussies, Fred and Tom adjourned to the canteen.

Over the beers, the Aussies revealed that they had been inducted into trench warfare near Laventie by some 'little blokes' just like Fred and Tom. Apparently these little blokes were 'fair dinkum' characters who even had their own cookhouse just behind the lines. They ran it because they had established what they called 'trading rights' with a cookhouse sergeant who always had 'spare' stores for disposal. When this sergeant had been caught selling stores to civilians as well, and sent to the army prison for his sins, the Aussies allowed all users of Fred's Place (as it was called) to use their source of supplies which was equally illegal, but as yet, undetected.

It was at this point, Tom said " Meet Fred!"

From then on, they were treated like mascots by the Aussies. When it was discovered that they were all on their way to Messines, the two ex-Bantams were adopted as honorary 'diggers' but because of their size were nicknamed 'Joeys', that being the name for baby kangaroos.

Two days passed with them taking and ignoring all the abuse and ill-treatment to which they were being subjected. Because of their size, the two ex-Bantams were regular victims. All the so-called training was conducted on the beaches and sand dunes just outside the town. The loose footing made foot drill and marching with any sort of precision well-nigh impossible. The 'canaries' knew this to be so, but made it an excuse for more and more bullying.

Having completed several tours of a circuit marked out in the loose sand, Tom stumbled in a particularly loose patch. Although Tom had been the only one at fault, both Fred and he were made to do 'press-ups'. To do these, they had to lay down their rifles on the sand. When these were subsequently recovered, there was, of course, sand sticking to the oiled woodwork. This unleashed a further screech of hatred with more 'press-ups' being inflicted. Both Fred and Tom having just recovered from wounding to arms and shoulders began to find it hard going.

The 'canary' immediately planted his boot in Tom's ribs. He then turned to do the same to Fred only to find his way blocked by a line of grim-looking diggers, all with their bayonets fixed. In a quiet drawl, the Australian sergeant told the bully "Right! That's it! Cut it out! I shouldn't do that, if I were you!"

At this, the instructor looked as if he had suffered an attack of apoplexy. No one had ever challenged him before at Étaples.

The Aussie hadn't finished. He continued. "You and I are both about the same size. We are both sergeants. I've been wounded, you never will be. Why not have a go at someone your own size and rank for once, like me? You can even have first poke!"

The 'canary' stood there, spluttering, but said nothing.

"Right" said the Aussie. "Bugger off! Go walkabout!" Having effectively dismissed their instructor, he called the group to attention, and marched them back to their tent.

Talking things over later in the day, someone mentioned the electric tension in the camp, the strong feeling of resentment at the treatment that was being dished out. The camp was like a keg of gunpowder with its fuse already smouldering. Before long, the place would explode, with rioting between the troops in transit and the permanent staff. They all hoped to be long gone before that happened as they had no wish to be caught in the savage official purges which would be bound to follow.

Then, daily orders were posted showing them moving out at 0200hrs. the next day but one. Fred and Tom, now in the 9th Mid-Yorkshires would be going to the 11th (Northern) Division currently under canvas near Dikkebus. The Australians were also in the same neighbourhood. They would all travel by train to Bailleul, and from there, they might get a lorry, if they were lucky. If not, as they were infantrymen, it would have to be 'Shanks's Pony'--- they would have to walk.

Especially for the occasion, the Australians has prepared what they referred to as their contingency plan. What they intended to do was to kidnap the two 'canaries' who had made life hell for their group, and take them up into the front line. As the Aussie sergeant said, "It will complete their education!"

So just after midnight, two Aussies took off with their kit, and hid themselves in the vicinity of the station in the town. That left a gap in the squad which would be filled by the two chosen 'canaries' who would be forced to wear slouch hats. Around the same time, the Aussie sergeant and his corporal had been keeping watch on the appropriate instructors' rooms. When their lights had gone out, the two walked up to the doors of those rooms, and tapped gently. As the victims opened their doors to see who was there, they were felled with lead-weighted coshes and dragged back into their rooms. On recovering consciousness, they were made to get dressed.

A group of Australians who had quietly assembled for that express purpose then escorted them to the Australian tent to await the time when they would assemble for the march to the station.

With slouch hats crammed on their heads, the unfortunate pair was herded into the middle of the squad. As the number of men passing the guardroom would be correct, there would be no identifying each individual. This was why two Australians had already sneaked out of camp early so as to leave the 'correct' number in the squad.

The two 'canaries' were warned that all the men surrounding them had flick knives and would not hesitate to use them if there was any trouble when passing the guardroom. The Aussies' view was that as they were almost certain to get it when they were back in the trenches, what did it matter if they were shot at Étaples if they took a couple of these bastards with them? What the hell, they had nothing to lose. It was a good risk with good odds. On the other hand, the 'canaries' had everything to lose, including their lives. If they did not make a fuss when passing the gate, at least they would still be alive at the other side. Then after that, it would be a matter of luck.

Out the mixed bunch marched, and into the town where they were joined by the two who had gone on ahead. Once the troops were on board the train, it clanked out of the station and headed towards the sound of the guns in the east.

When it was well out into the countryside, the Australians set about their reluctant guests. All regimental and divisional insignia as well as badges of rank were removed from their uniforms. Paybooks, any other official documents and all private papers were consigned to the night air via the open doors. The 'canaries' were now devoid of any scrap of identification --- there was not even a cap badge between them.

As was pointed out to them, if they were caught behind the lines in the forward areas in this condition, the Battle Police would shoot them out of hand as deserters. Their best chance of survival would be to attach themselves to some Pommie outfit. Apart from the fact that that neither sounded remotely like a digger, the Aussies wanted nothing more to do with them. They would be able to pick up rifles and equipment from the R.E. salvage dumps, and there would be plenty of cap badges to be had on the dead lying around the place. They would be able to have the regiment of their choice.

Paybooks could be had from the same source if they had not been collected from the bodies. However, if caught with one, as they would have been assuming a false identity, they would be shot, that is, after a 'fair' trial.

So, with no paybook, they had no official identity, or indeed, any identity of any kind. With no identity, they would not be attached to any unit. So, no unit would have any responsibility for feeding or housing them. Nor would they get any pay! If apprehended, they would be automatically classed as deserters.

They were now in the ideal position to demonstrate how good they were at surviving in the real world, and not the artificial set-up of the Bull Ring.

When the full implications of all this struck home, one of the pair started to plead with their captors in an attempt to get them to vouch for them, and to explain how they came to be in their predicament. This was a ridiculous request and showed just how far from the real world the pair were. They were appealing to the better natures of men they had only yesterday been abusing and humiliating. Apart from that aspect of the situation, there was no way the Aussies could make such a move without confessing that they had kidnapped these two lost souls.

Not unexpectedly, the answer was blunt "Get lost! And keep quiet about the fact that you are 'canaries'. Just hope that nobody recognises you otherwise half the army will want to have a go at you!"

Arriving at Bailleul, the Aussies found that there was a lorry drawn up outside the station, waiting for them. So, with suitable expressions of good will and farewell, the erstwhile partners in crime went their separate ways.

The two Ledfords looked around to get their bearings and spotted a lorry being loaded with stores. It was emblazoned with the emblem of their new division, the 11th (Northern) Division) picked out in red, black and white. This was the "ankh", an ancient Egyptian symbol of good luck and long life!

They made their way across to where the driver was taking a breather, introduced themselves, and asked if there was any chance of a lift.

"If they helped with the loading of the stores, there would be".

The two badge-less characters now approached and tried their luck. The driver looked at them, then at Tom and asked who they were. "Dunno" said Tom. "Nivver seen 'em afore in mi life!". Fred then added his two-penn'orth. "Ask 'em 'oo they are, an' wot lot they're with. Where've they bin?"

At this, the driver realised that something was amiss and said that he didn't want to know, nor was he interested. But he did warn them that there was a squad of Battle Police combing the area looking for a bunch of deserters. They were shooting first, and asking questions afterwards.

Disconsolately, the two 'unknowns' wandered off towards the station's marshalling yard. If that was the best they could do, they were in for a rough time as well as taking a very great risk. It was well known that Provost Staff regularly and routinely searched railway wagons when checking for absconders.

It looked as if the survival techniques as taught by this pair were not a lot of use in reality, particularly in such a quandary as the one in which they were now caught up.

What the ultimate fate of these men would be, Fred and Tom would never know, not that they cared all that much.

Chapter 25

The 11th Division was in camp just to the north of the two hills, Mont des Cats and Mont Noir. Together with Mont Kemmel, they ran approximately from west to east, forming a low ridge which eventually became the sickle-shaped Messines Ridge.

Having completed the usual formalities of reporting in and drawing bedding, it was a matter of settling down in yet another bed space in yet another billet. Looking round their new home, the two ex-Bantams found it to be clean and tidy, but without too much emphasis on 'spit and polish'. That was how they liked things. All being well, they should fit in with their new lot.

As it was now the end of the working day when out of the lines, the hut started to fill up with their new comrades-in-arms. Introductions over, 'war stories' were swapped in earnest.

The 9th had just come direct from the Somme so they all had that much in common. Before that, they had been involved in the Gallipoli fiasco. They did not have much, if anything, to say in favour of the High Command who had run that show.

For their part, not only had Fred and Tom their experiences at Laventie and Festubert to offer, they also had their jaunt to the Somme where they had both been blown up and wounded.

The 9th turned out to be a mix of men not unlike the old 17th with the same outlook on life. They held the same views on authority and King's Regulations as did the Ledfords. All in all, there was not much to choose from between the two units (apart from height!)

The next two weeks were spent on more toughening-up exercises and drill. Stress was placed on skill-at-arms. Newly devised infantry procedures and tactics were explained and practised. The platoon was now to be in effect a self-supporting unit, at least, as far as small arms were concerned.

The platoon structure continued as before with four sections. Although each section still had seven to ten men, it was now to have a distinct, separate role

Thus, the bombing section would have two bombers. There would also be bayonet-men who would be first into the target zone after the bombs had exploded. Their job was to deal with any survivors. They would also be the barricade-men who would block off each end of the captured length of enemy trench.

This section would also have spare riflemen, according to how many there were in the section after allowing for any casualties. These would act as 'protection' men.

There would also be a rifle-grenade section, again of about eight men. Four of them were the specialists, the others riflemen to protect them.

There would be a Lewis gun section made up of about eight men. Between them, apart from the gun itself, they would carry the spares and tools for the weapon, about two thousand spare rounds as well as forty loaded magazines (or drums). As these drums each held forty-seven rounds, this section could deliver getting on for four thousand rounds from the Lewis gun, together with whatever rounds the riflemen fired.

Last, but not least, there was the rifle section. This would be the realm of the sniper and the marksmen. It was also the home of the section scout.

At company level, there would be a Stokes mortar section providing a form of light artillery support.

To round things off, a Vickers heavy machinegun would form part of the new line-up.

The infantry would no longer advance in line abreast, shoulder to shoulder as they had done in the past. These tactics were the substance of history. Now, forward progress would be achieved by small groups or pairs dashing forward from cover to cover in their turn. Each rush would be covered by fire provided by other sections.

The harsh lessons learned on the Somme had provided the reason for these radical changes in tactics. In reality, the slaughter on the Somme had forced the adoption of tactics which were not only in use by the light infantry but had been so since the Peninsular Wars.

The thinking relative to the use of artillery had also changed. The prolonged bombardment up to and ceasing the moment before the assault began would no longer be the norm. Instead, just before the 'off', the gunners would lay down a barrage just in front of the enemy positions. Then, when the advance had commenced, the barrage would lift and move forward ahead of the troops to land on the enemy front lines. This was the advent of the 'creeping barrage'.

This would continue until it was falling on the enemy second line and the areas behind it when it would become 'stationary'. This would effectively prevent any reinforcements or supplies getting through to the beleaguered position.

So much for the theory, but would it work in practice? They were soon to find out.

At the beginning of June, the 9th. Mid-Yorkshires along with the rest of their brigade assembled at a place called Scherpenberg. It was here that the engineers had constructed a scale model of Messines Ridge, complete with all the enemy trenches and defence-works currently known to Divisional Intelligence. It was as accurate as could be, down to the smallest detail. All round the model was a raised, wooden walkway from which an almost aerial view could be obtained. Each unit had its role in the forthcoming operation explained to it in depth, then they were 'practised' on the model as far as possible. This, of necessity, took the form of a 'question and answer' session with a problem being put to the men who then had to come up with a solution to it.

The 9th Mid-Yorkshires would be held in reserve with the rest of IX Corps. The role of their particular division was that of an assault unit in Phase Two of the attack.

The Ridge was to be destroyed by the exploding in Phase One of vast, underground mines. These had been put in place during the past twelve months by 'clay kickers', the majority of whom were experienced miners, or tunnellers from civilian life, specially recruited for the task. If all went well in this first phase, then the German second line, the Oostaverne Line, was scheduled as Phase Two. If on the other hand, things did not go as planned, the Phase Two troops would be used as necessary to hold the present British lines.

The actual time and date of the first phase assault was a closely-guarded secret, being referred to as 'H-hour and D-day'. Any questions were met with such replies as "Don't worry, I'll make sure you don't miss it! We won't start without you!", or "You know as much as I do, and that's bugger all!"

With that, they had to bide their time, and be patient.

For the past week or so, British guns had continued in action twenty-four hours a day, despite the so-called new thinking in artillery application. There had never been such a concentration of guns. They were lined up wheel to wheel, the gun lines stretching as far as the eye could see in both directions. The number of artillery pieces in action was later said to be in excess of two thousand along the assault line.

Then, on June 3rd, the barrage intensified, suggesting that the attack was imminent. That was odd as no one was standing by in readiness for such an event. Life all round was carrying on as usual as far as the P.B.I. were concerned. Then the barrage eased off, almost stopping, only to resume again at the high intensity of a few moments ago. Shortly afterwards, it reverted to its normal daily level.

The reduction in intensity must have been to fool the enemy into thinking an attack was on its way and cause them to man the parapets. The resumption of the barrage would catch them out in the open.

Then the day was announced --- June 7th.

At dawn, nineteen deep mines were to be exploded simultaneously (or as near as could be managed) under the length of Messines Ridge. The most northerly one was at Hill 60 with the southernmost at "Birdcage" and "Trench 122" in Ploegsteert Wood. (This was 'Plugstreet Wood' to the troops.) In all, more than 400 tons of ammonal would be fired to take the top of the Ridge together with anything that happened to be up there.

With the assault due very shortly, church parades were arranged, again for the three main faiths. Fred and Tom attended the Anglican service where the main theme was that of self-sacrifice.

"Greater love hath no man than this, that he lay down his life for his friend" intoned the chaplain. He then continued by asking individuals to put forward their views on the subject, for discussion. To say that he was leading with his chin (to borrow from boxing parlance) was, to say the least, putting it mildly. He was, after all, asking the best part of a thousand Yorkshiremen what they thought of putting their lives at risk. They told him!

He got an assortment of answers for his temerity, all plainly put. That the sons of the Broad Acres are renowned for their plain speaking was demonstrated there and then. They didn't mince matters. There was no beating about the bush.

Put politely, the general feeling was that although one might actually do what the sermon suggested in the heat of battle, it would not be done in cold blood after taking time to think about what was involved. If the chaplain wanted to do that, then that was his choice

Fred's thoughts were that he would still pray for his own personal survival while he was in France. In fact, since the Somme, he would pray with the greatest of enthusiasm. All the rest were more than capable of doing their own praying. His system had worked reasonably well as far as he was concerned. He was still alive, although a bit knocked about, but he had got a 'blighty' out of it.

He would still hedge his bets though. He would check his gas mask. His rifle would have a magazine of ten rounds firmly in place. In addition, there would be an eleventh round in the breech. His ammunition pouches would also be full. His bayonet would be fixed and securely locked in place. Then, as his 'banker', he would have a couple of grenades in his pocket with the pins nicely splayed. After that, with Fred having done all that he could to avert personal disaster, it would be up to Providence,

By 0300hrs.all the first phase troops were in their positions in the trenches of the 'start line'. On the dot, all the British guns stopped firing. The silence was uncanny. The enemy must have thought so too. Flares and rockets were sent up to illuminate no-man's-land. A few hesitant artillery rounds were sent over.

What was happening? Was anything happening? Was this just another ruse like the ones earlier in the week?

Not this time!

Even as Jerry was still trying to work out what was happening, the whole length of Messines Ridge appeared to rise ponderously and majestically into the air. Columns of earth, concrete bunkers, guns and men hurtled skywards. What they could see mixed in with all the debris and earth were human beings, men like themselves. Yes they were the enemy, but they were still human beings when all was said and done. Fred in particular could feel for them. He too had been blown up, but not on such a grand scale.

While the British struggled with their feelings, they were at the same time, over-awed by the sheer magnificence of the spectacle unfolding in front them.

Great tongues of multi-coloured flame leapt after the debris. The ground shook and vibrated wildly. A sullen rumble issued from the bowels of the earth, and increased in magnitude as it escaped from the craters. It was as if the ground was crying out in anguish. The quivering and shaking made it almost impossible for the watchers to keep their balance. It was akin to trying to stand on jelly in a howling gale.

The tremendous attack on the senses was almost sensual. The reaction was to laugh or to cry, or even to try to do both at once.

Then all at once, the British guns opened fire again. A creeping barrage progressed towards what was left of the enemy positions, staying just ahead of the first wave of infantry. This was what they had been told would happen.

As Fred watched, he could see officers blowing their whistles, then looking at them, shaking them then trying again. As no sound seemed to be coming from them, the officers just waved their men forward. As normal hearing returned, they realised that although the whistles had been working, they had been unable to hear them. Ears had been numbed by the intensity of the explosions.

The second phase troops now moved into the vacated front line to await their turn to go forward. This would be in the late afternoon after the first lot had consolidated the ground they should have captured.

Prisoners started to drift in in an aimless manner. Some had totally blank faces with absolutely no expression on them at all. Others were openly crying. There were those who came in on their hands and knees, whimpering like terrified animals. Yet more were carried back by first phase troops. At first sight, these enemy prisoners who had to be carried were untouched, but something must have happened to them. The impact of their experience in the midst of that inferno must have so damaged their mental faculties as to not only deprive them of the power of speech but also of the use of their limbs.

With glazed eyes and blank faces, they were like zombies, the walking dead. The only difference was that some were incapable of standing, let alone walking.

Was this the face of modern warfare?

By the late afternoon, some of the field guns had been moved forward into what had been 'no-man's-land'. At1500hrs. the barrage was resumed with all its old ferocity, but now, the target was the German second line. Any of the enemy who had been fortunate to survive the first lot of shelling then the explosions of the mines would now have to live through a second lot of shelling.

At 1900hrs, the second phase assault troops passed through and beyond the shattered remains of what had been the enemy front line. Wytschaete no longer existed other than as piles of rubble situated on a map reference.

Twenty minutes was all the time needed to move into and occupy the section of the Oostaverne Line which was the objective of the 9th Mid-Yorkshires. It was the same on both flanks.

Mopping-up parties went on the prowl across the captured ground to the rear of the new British forward positions. They had learned the hard way that any enemy overrun during an advance and left behind had to be dealt with as soon as possible otherwise they would emerge from cover with machineguns and fire into the backs of those who had passed them by.

It was now standard practice to have groups of men following a little way behind the main wave to eradicate this sort of problem. Rather than venture into enemy dugouts, a grenade would be tossed down the steps. If this provoked any reaction, the safest method of dealing with the occupants was to blow in the entrance tunnel.

On this occasion, these parties had nothing to do apart from collecting Germans wandering around in a daze, or sitting in stunned bewilderment. They could not surrender quickly enough. They were too shattered mentally, and too demoralised to want to continue the fight.

Newspaper accounts of the day's events which they would subsequently read said that the blast of the mines had been heard in London. Some even mentioned Dublin. Either way, it must have been the biggest man-made explosion of all times.

Chapter 26

Following the success of the Messines offensive, the captured ground was fortified in anticipation of any counter-attack. Trenches were repaired or re-dug. The parapets and parados had to be reversed so as to give protection from the opposite direction to that which had been required before.

Any captured pillboxes still intact between the Ridge and the Oostaverne Line had the entrance facing towards the enemy. When built, they had been correctly sited, but now that they were in British hands, the openings were vulnerable to fire from the previous occupants. Bullets and shell fragments could enter and ricochet around inside with disastrous consequences for the new tenants. Walls of sandbags were hastily built by the divisional pioneers to screen the doorways, and make these strongpoints suitable for use as H.Q.'s or regimental aid posts.

They then found out just how crafty the enemy had been when building the pillboxes. What had originally been the rear walls of a large number of them were found to be very much thinner than the original fronts and sides. This meant that shells could more easily penetrate into the interior before exploding amongst any troops inside. Once again, the services of the pioneers were called upon. Sandbags were used to reinforce the weak points. If this could be done on the outside without taking casualties, then that was where the bags were stacked. If not, it had to be on the inside.

Any counter-attacks when they came were little more than exploratory, probing efforts aimed at checking the strength of the recently established British positions. They were easily driven off as there seemed to be a lack of any real enthusiasm for the job in hand.

The German artillery did better and spoiled the feeling of satisfaction of the British and Australian troops at what they had achieved. All the old positions on the Ridge must have been registered and ranged by their spotters against a possible withdrawal. They knew every spot to an inch. No matter where they took cover, German shells would find them.

It was about this time that Tom realised that there was something different about Fred. Something had changed in his manner and his attitude to life. All the time Tom had known him, from the day they enlisted and through all they endured, he had been a cheery, happy-go-lucky, talkative character. But now, all that had changed. He no longer made light of the hardships they had to put up with. He had become morose, withdrawn and introverted. He only spoke if spoken to, and then, only with a bad-tempered grunt.

Tom made a point of finding out what was amiss. He discovered that Fred was tense, wound up and unable to relax. He was like a tightly coiled spring. Nowadays, he was worried about anything and everything. But above all, he was jumpy, nervous and twitchy.

Tom suggested that a visit to the M.O. might be the answer to Fred's problems.

Unfortunately, the previous M.O. had just been replaced the previous day after being wounded himself. The grey-haired veteran of the Boer War had gone, and in his place was callow youth who looked as if he should still be at school. It was doubtful if he had even started shaving. This was his first posting. He had had no battlefield experience whatsoever.

He listened to what Fred had to say then scribbled "L.M.F." on the relevant record card. Fred not unnaturally asked what the letters stood for. He was told "Lack of moral fibre. You're a shirker. Pull yourself together, man. You've just got the wind up!"

Fred was incensed at this. How dare this boy, scarcely out of school write him off as a coward? With icy calm, and barely controlled fury he addressed this youngster who presented himself as an officer.

"Wi' luck, you might survive as long as Ah've done. In your position, you'll not 'ave to go through what Ah've had to. If your job gets too much for you, as an officer you will get a nice soft number back at base, suffering from "strain". According to people like you, blokes like me in the infantry are too stupid to 'ave any feelings. Try thinking about what you are doing. Ah hope you can live wi' yersen if your conscience lets you. Aye, Ah am being insubordinate, so put me on a charge. You 'ave all mi details, so ger on wi it!"

With that, Fred left the office without bothering to salute.

So that was the official verdict. Fred was suffering from latent cowardice! Tom was all for requesting an interview with the C.O. intending to take matters further. Fred would not hear of it. "What's the point? They're all bloody officers together. They'll all back each other. We're only bloody cannon fodder!"

June ran into July.

On the Messines front, the fighting had diminished and was now limited to sporadic artillery duels, and what amounted to exchange visits by fighting patrols. It had become what official circles described as a 'quiet sector' of the Front.

Then, during the second half of the month, units were quietly withdrawn and sent north to the Ypres Salient. Another 'stunt' was in the offing. Among those who went were the 11th (Northern) Division taking with it the 9th Mid-Yorkshires.

Their new quarters were to west of Ypres, and once again they were in bell tents with fitted duckboards. Any grass there might have been in earlier days had long since been worn away by the thousands of feet which had pounded it into oblivion. The space between the tents was hard, baked earth, not mud. So far this summer, the weather had been comparatively dry.

As always, bathing facilities for the troops were provided by a requisitioned brewery, this time in Poperinghe. What had been a sugar refinery was now the official delousing centre. The only problem was that there were so many men needing these facilities that it was at least a fortnight before anyone's turn came round again.

The arrangements at the bathhouse were the same as always, uniform off and tied in a bundle with caps and boots. To the bundle were tied the owner's identity discs, just like luggage labels. Underwear was exchanged for laundered, deloused garments less dirty than those handed in. Whether they fitted or not was, as usual, a matter of luck. It usually had to be swapped around until it did, more or less.

Theoretically, uniforms were deloused as well, but hardly ever were. If the weather was half decent, men would sit outside their tents in their underwear running candle flames along the seams of their tunics and trousers which had been turned inside out for the purpose. A crackle or a pop would indicate that unwanted guests had been incinerated *in situ*.

It was at Poperinghe that "Toc H" was to be found. This was a meeting place for all off-duty troops, irrespective of rank. It was run by an army chaplain, the Reverend 'Tubby' Clayton. It had been originally called Talbot House until its initials in signalling code were adopted as its official title.

Meals could be had at reasonable prices. Newspapers were there to be read. There was, of course a chapel where one could spend time with the chaplain or by one's self, but use of this facility was not compulsory. There was a garden to sit in. All in all, it was a haven of peace and sanity where one could relax after the Hell of the trenches.

Immediately opposite the club was a shop run by an enterprising Belgian. He sold everything a soldier could need, or imagine he might need, from candles to solid methylated spirits blocks for 'Tommy' cookers.

On July 16th the artillery commenced another of its tremendous barrages on the enemy lines, across the full width of the Salient. This continued on a daily basis.

On August 1st it started to rain. It was to continue to do so non- stop for the whole of the month. At no point was there a break which might have allowed the land to drain. Instead, the rain fell unabated at twice the normal average for that time of the year.

The artillery of all the combatants engaged in the Salient pounded the area incessantly. Watercourses, be they natural or man-made, were obliterated. Ditch and river banks were breached. Retaining rims of lakes and ponds were destroyed. In short, all drainage of any kind was no more.

The continuous bombardment pounded all the surface water and earth into a quagmire, a bottomless morass. It would be across this that the infantry would be required to advance

In amongst the ironmongery that Jerry was now flinging into this swamp, he now added mustard gas. It was a recent addition to his armoury and would produce over a thousand casualties during the next few days. Contact with it produced painful blistering.

It was an oily liquid with the propensity for sinking into the ground on which it fell, where it would last for some time without losing its virulence. So anyone who got some of this gas-laden mud on his hands or clothing would be covered in weeping blisters before he realised he had been in contact with the irritant. If inhaled, the irritation in the lungs would produce copious amounts of liquid with the victim effectively drowning as a consequence.

'H-hour' was set to coincide with first light on July 31st. Originally set for the 23rd, it had been postponed. As a result of this delay, the arena had been mashed for a further eight days.

Finally, the advance got under way. The ground facing the Mid-Yorkshires was muddy, but not totally impassable. The biggest worry was the sheer number of shells falling all around them and of being on the receiving end of one of them. There was no possibility of dodging them or taking cover in the sea of mud. For one thing, there was the problem of being unable to move quickly enough. If that had been possible, where to go would have been the next question. But what would be the point if you had no idea where the next shell would land? It would all be down to luck be it good or bad.

'Digging-in' and trying to convert one of the countless craters into some kind of refuge if possible became a matter of some urgency. It was some struggle with the ground being like so much porridge, but it was amazing just what could be achieved if you were frightened enough!

The attack became bogged down, literally. The area in front of the troops was under the total control of machinegun nests which were spread in great numbers across the line of advance. Some were in concrete pillboxes, others in strongly built entrenched emplacements.

There were three staggered lines of them, all of which had been set out so as to be mutually supporting. If an attempt was made to outflank one of them, two or more of its neighbours could bring fire to bear on the attackers.

Eventually, by dint of much self-sacrifice, bravery, and, let's face it, sheer madness, forward progress was resumed. This was painfully slow, gains being measured in yards rather than miles.

All the time, the rain poured down on them. Shell holes became death traps. If a man slipped, and it was easily done as he struggled along in the morass, the weight of his equipment was more than sufficient to take him below the surface of the liquid now beginning to fill these holes.

The mud between the holes was of a different texture to the liquid stuff in the craters. It was more like putty or plasticine only much, much softer. It would not take a man's weight. He would go in up to the knees with each step. In the really bad spots, he could be stuck to the waist, or worse. In the really tenacious stuff, he would slowly vanish from sight as he was slowly sucked under the surface.

Two or three men would engage in an often futile struggle to pull their mate out of the trap in which he was caught. If they were unable to drag him out, it was not unknown for the struggling man to be shot through the head by his pal in order to save him from a long drawn-out, agonising death.

In such circumstances as these, the 'blighty' wound, (so much coveted in other parts of the line) became a death warrant condemning a man to slow death by torture. If your time was up, the order of preference was first and foremost to be killed outright. Failing that, the next choice was that of falling into a shell-hole full of water so that a reasonably quick death by drowning was achieved.

A 'blighty', particularly a leg wound was the last thing they wanted. Such an injury would render the victim helpless in the vile conditions now prevailing in the Salient. He would be unable to crawl through the mud either to the rear or to any stretcher bearers who happened to be nearby. They, in any case, would be in certain trouble if they ventured out into the mire in an attempt to rescue him.

Any artillery pieces brought up to support what little forward movement had been made had to be dragged forward through the slough by the superhuman efforts of their crews. It was impossible to find sufficiently stable ground on which to set up the gun either for the wheels or for the trail. When it was fired, it would tip to one side, or sink in the mud where it stood. It had to be dug out each and every time it was fired. It was impossible to range it accurately under those conditions.

To get it to where it was needed, each shell had to be manhandled either by the crews or by infantry coerced into doing so (as if they hadn't enough to worry about with their own tasks). Before it could be used, each round had to be cleaned.

It was now the last week in August, and it was still raining. The 9th.Mid Yorkshires were struggling past, and to the south of Langemarck. To their left, Fred could see into a German pillbox shown on the maps as *"von Bulow's Farm"*. The view was rather intriguing as he was looking through what had been the floor!

Large calibre shells, whilst not damaging the structure, had fallen so close to it that the blast waves of the explosions had gone underneath and inside it. In doing so, they had tipped the edifice onto its side. The open floor space was now in the position previously occupied by one of the walls.

As he was musing on this, he realised that among the incoming shrapnel and high explosive shells falling all around them, Jerry was now mixing gas. These were bursting with a quiet 'plop' which went unnoticed amongst the general clangour of the battlefield, but they were there, right enough.

Both Fred and Tom now had the improved gas masks in the form of the 'box respirator'. The respirator consisted of a moulded face-mask with built-in goggles. This face-piece was connected by means of a flexible pipe to filter elements and packs of charcoal granules through which the poisoned air was drawn. These were all housed in a haversack which was worn high on the chest and held in place by means of a length of cord which passed from one side of the wearer to the other, round his back, just below the armpits, and tied to the 'D-rings' on each side of the haversack.

It only took a moment to don it, but as he did so, Fred found to his horror that a shell splinter had torn a ragged hole through the filter compartment of his haversack. His mask was totally useless!

At precisely that moment, the man just in front of Fred threw his arms above his head and fell forward. Thought Fred, "If 'e's done for, Ah'll 'ave 'is mask!"

Stopping by the fallen man, he bent down and checked for any signs of life. He found signs of death instead, a bullet-hole in the front of the head and the back of the skull missing. The dead man had not even had time to get his mask out of its stowage, let alone put it on, so it was undamaged. Fred had it on his head before he'd untied its retaining cord. His own he cut, discarding the useless item. The serviceable mask he secured in place on himself.

So far, so good! As he stood up ready to move forward again, he found himself in a veritable hailstorm of machinegun bullets, snarling past him from all sides. There was nothing he could do to get out of their way. Even if he could have pulled his feet from the mud quickly enough, they would have been the size of footballs with the amount of mud sticking to this boots. Lord knows how much they must have weighed. Not the sort of situation which encouraged nimble footwork.

He felt a series of hammer-like blows to the thigh as his left leg was taken from under him. As he collapsed on the stinking mud, he knew in terror that his worst fears had just been realised. He would die slowly of suffocation as the mud swallowed him up alive, and smothered him.

He could see it all so clearly in his mind's eye. As he slowly went down, the mud would rise inexorably to cover his chest. He could imagine its cold clamminess as it crept up his neck to reach the underside of his chin. Then, before he realised, it would be up to his lips. He could almost taste it. Then it would be up to his nostrils. He would take one last desperate snort of air in an attempt to fill his lungs before it was too, late. The mud was now passing the bridge of his nose. Then it was at eye level, and his eyes were full of the stuff as he struggled against his inevitable suffocation.

Suddenly, he realised that despite his worst imaginings, it wasn't happening like that. He wasn't sinking! In falling, he had landed flat, spread-eagled. This had effectively distributed his weight over a greater area than if he had been upright. Spread out in this manner, he covered about ten to fifteen times more ground than would have been covered by the soles of his boots.

That was great, but how was he to get back to somewhere safe with his leg in the state that it now was?

As he wrestled with this problem, the point of a bayonet jabbed him in the shoulder and he heard Tom's voice. "Fred. Can tha 'ear me? If tha can, stir thissen. Cop 'o'd o' mi rifle sling, an' 'ang on to it!"

Tom had seen his best mate pitch forward in the mud, and had come back for him. He had brought another man with him to help pull Fed out of the trap. But there was also another reason other than the straight rescue. If Fred was still alive but stuck so inextricably that the two of them could not haul him to safety, Tom intended to shoot him.

After the disastrous meeting with the young M.O. near Messines, Fred had become more and more introverted and morose. As nothing that Tom could do had any effect, he had resolved to keep an eye on Fred in case he showed any signs of doing anything silly. This was why he was able to help so quickly when Fred was felled by machinegun fire.

With Fred hanging onto the sling of Tom's rifle and Tom pulling at the butt end of his own and the sling of the third man's rifle, Fred was slowly but surely dragged from the mud into which he had fallen. The pain that this caused to his wounded leg was excruciating, but at least he was still alive when he was freed.

As he was dragged forward, an idle thought flitted through his mind. "The planners were right for once". When they had been explaining the plan of attack before this particular part of the assault had commenced, the troops involved had been told that their objective was a farmhouse and its outbuildings which had been fortified by their opponents and made in to a strongpoint. It now rejoiced under the name *"Vieilles Maisons"*. They had also been warned that this strongpoint was guarded on the left by *"von Bulow's Farm"*, as well as by *"Pheasant Trench"* slightly to its rear. From the right, it was covered by *"Vancouver Trench"*. These three positions were all well armed with machineguns which could sweep the ground across which the 9th Mid-Yorkshires would be advancing.

Von Bulow's Farm had gone, but the other two were unharmed and still in business. Part of the farm complex had been captured despite heavy casualties, and it was in that direction that the two men dragged the third. Bullets whizzed round them like so many angry bees, but miraculously none found a target. As they made it to the doubtful safety of the captured outbuildings, Tom and his helper collapsed, exhausted with the effort of struggling through the quagmire with Fred.

As if his leg wounds were not enough, Fred was beginning to feel the effects of the small amount of phosgene he had inhaled whilst sorting out his respirator problems. His hands were now blistering badly. The mud in which he had been lying must have been contaminated with mustard gas from previous attacks.

When he got his breath back, Tom set about binding Fred's injuries. These were clean flesh wounds the rounds having gone through the fleshy part of the thigh, missing the artery and the femur as they did so. As he tied the dressing in place, Tom remarked "You lucky bugger. This will get you another blighty bar!" (This was a reference to the newly introduced 'wound stripe' one of which both Fred and he now had on their left sleeves, just below their marksman badges. When they were issued, the rank and file had immediately given them this nickname.)

It would be several hours before stretcher bearers could get through to them. The two trenches which had caused all the problems had had to be silenced before any attempt could be made.

When he was handed over to the M.O., Fred saw that he was the young officer who had written him off as a coward near Messines. Strain had etched deep lines across what should have still been a youthful face.

When asked for his name, rank and number, Fred answered correctly. However, when asked about his religion, it was the original, chirpy Fred who answered. He grinned at the M.O. and said "L.M.F. It's no picnic out 'ere, is it?" At this, the officer looked up and recognised Fred.

Although the youth made no reply, it was difficult not to agree with Fred's summing up of the situation. As the aid post was on the fringes of the battleground, the staff were able to get the full benefit of the assorted noises of the conflict. Whilst theoretically they should not have been within range of the German guns, the odd 'overshoot' of the larger calibre weapons was adequate cause for real concern.

Add to this the state of the casualties on arrival, the filthy muck with which they were plastered usually covered the most gruesome of wounds. It was no wonder the young doctor was showing signs of strain, particularly if he had led a sheltered, pampered life before donning a uniform.

From the aid post, Fred was taken to an advanced dressing station where his hands were dressed. The next move along the chain was to a casualty clearance station. It was all too familiar, just like the children's party game "Pass the parcel!"

Eventually, he was held for a day or two in the emergency holding centre which had been set up in the grammar school in St. Omer. This had been established to regulate the flow of casualties so that the military hospitals in the locality would not be overwhelmed by a sudden rush. Then, at last, he arrived at the 14th General Hospital, Wimereux where he would wait for the hospital ship which would take him back to England once again.

It was one of the supreme ironies of life that around the time that Fred was being carried off the battlefield for medical attention, a field postcard would arrive at his parents' home in Cleckmonsedge. This card limited the sender to a selection of phrases which had to be left or deleted. The one phrase left standing was "I am quite well".

With the wisdom of hindsight, this simple piece of card might have been interpreted as a portent of things to come, and could have indicated that all was not well with Fred, and not just with his bodily wounds.

There was a discrepancy in the two dates the card carried. The sender had dated it 18/6/17 whereas the Field Post Office postmark showed 19/8/17. Somewhere, two months had been lost. This could have been because Fred had carried the card in his pocket for the lost months, but its pristine condition did not show this to be the case. Alternatively, it might have taken the Army two months to deliver it. Again, this was not really feasible as an explanation as the cards usually arrived within two or three days of posting.

No, Fred must have misdated the card either by a simple mistake, or as a result of losing track of time. It was impossible to say which at this stage. If it was the latter, did this presage something more serious? Was this a sign of some impending mental trouble? Only time would tell.

The hospital at Wimereux was just along the coast from the infamous 'Bull Ring' at Étaples. For one brief moment, Fred wondered what had become of the two sergeants the Australians had kidnapped and taken up into the forward area just behind the front line. It was only a fleeting thought which he did not waste time pursuing. What they had got was no more than they deserved.

As he lay in the coolness of the ward, he realised that he had been carted away by the stretcher bearers before he had had a word with Tom. That omission would have to be repaired immediately. As he asked for pen and paper, Fred found that he was unable to write, as he could not hold the pen. After the mustard gas burning they had suffered, his hands had been swathed in bandages. So, the nurse who brought the writing materials was enlisted as his scribe.

In amongst the general chit-chat, Fred promised that when he came back to France, he would seek out Tom and thank him personally for saving his life in front of Langemarck. Above all else, he insisted that they both should keep in touch with each other for the rest of the war and afterwards if they survived.

Of the original six, as far as he could find out, only Tom and he were still alive. While they had been in camp near Messines, he had tried to trace Lt. Richardson and Charlie, as well as the rest of the Ledfords. They had been at Arras in February and March of this year, 1917, providing labour for the New Zealand engineers who were extending the mediaeval tunnels under the city to well forward beneath no-man's-land in preparation for the forthcoming battle.

After that, he was unable to find any trace of the 17th. M.Y.R. What he did not know was that shortly afterwards, the survivors of both the 15th and 17th battalions had been amalgamated to form the 15/17th. M.Y.R. For expediency, the new battalion was always shown on records as the 15th.

The letter finished, it was left unsealed for the censor's attention, and then, posting. This done, Fred felt better in himself, and fell to thinking about his time as a soldier.

It was now September, 1917. He had joined the Ledford Bantams in December, 1914. That meant that he had been with the Colours two years and nine months.

He had landed in France for the first time in February, 1916. He had been wounded in July of that year, and, as a result, was back in England in the August. Then, it was back to France in March, 1917. He had collected this lot last month, August.

So the score was this.

Out of a total of thirty three months, the first fifteen had been spent in training. Then there had been two stints each of six months on active service with the remaining six months in hospital or recovering from his wounds. Presumably some good had come from the time he had spent in France?

On their daily rounds, the doctors at the various hospitals through which Fred had passed had seen how nervous and jumpy he was. His records had been noted to this effect.. The slightest sudden noise would make him shake uncontrollably.

Medical opinion was at last coming round to conceding that even common footsloggers could only take so much before they cracked up. It was not only the officer classes who succumbed to 'shell shock'. However, in their case, it would be referred to as 'battle fatigue', or ' neurasthenia'.

If the question of susceptibility had been pursued to any degree, it could have been determined once and for all, and very simply. For instance, there were many well-educated men serving in the ranks who, although coming from a social background which automatically classified them as 'officer' material, refused to take commissions.

Then there were men who came from the working classes and had been n.c.o.'s. When all their officers had been killed in action, these men had taken over and brought things to a successful conclusion. Such men had often been given 'battlefield' promotions.

A rather provocative question would have been: "Which man would be certified as suffering from shellshock, the upper-class man serving as a private soldier, or the working-class man holding an officer's commission?"

Then came the day when the patients in Fred's part of the hospital were moved down to Boulogne where an ambulance ship lay alongside the quay.

Part Four
"England, Home and --- Now What ? "

Chapter 27

Back in England, they landed in Folkestone where a fleet of ambulances was waiting for them on the quay to take them to a hospital which had been constructed in the grounds of a large, stately home. Where it was, Fred never did discover. The hospital was one of many which had been built in response to the unprecedented demand of the Somme offensive and currently that at Paschendaele.

It consisted of interlinked wooden huts and corridors. All facilities were under cover. The need to transport patients across open spaces in all weather was no longer necessary. For some reason, this form of accommodation was known as 'spiders'.

Fred's hands were recovering from the blistering caused by the mustard gas. The lesions were now covered with a fine, shiny skin which was becoming more durable as the days went by. His thigh wound was also healing nicely. The initial poisoning had burned itself out of his system, and the inflammation was rapidly going down.

What was giving cause for concern was the state of Fred's nerves. Most of the time he was fine, but sudden movements or noises would produce an excessive reaction. If he had a mug of tea in his hand and a door slammed, for example, the violent twitch that the noise provoked would project the hot liquid over anyone who was in the vicinity and happened to be within range.

As his physical wounds were coming along well, he was transferred to Fulford once again. It was only a year since he had last been there. Nothing had changed apart from him being there by himself whilst Tom was presumably still slogging it out in the mud of the Salient.

Once again, he sought and found the arbour. He would take a book out there, but it was not the same somehow, even with other patients for company. He now took all his meals in the dining hall along with all the other ambulatory patients.

When his physical wounds were all but healed, he was moved from the main ward he had been in, to a small side-room holding just four beds. The other three occupants were similarly afflicted in that they all had problems coping with sudden noises or movements, just like Fred.

A neuro-surgeon was, of his own volition, conducting a study of such patients. He knew the cause, had seen the effects and was now intent on devising some form of treatment if he could.

Once again Fred had a suit of blue and was allowed to go into York during the day where he found that the uniform still attracted the sympathy and generosity of the townsfolk. He took to spending long, solitary days just sitting on the banks of the river, or walking the ancient walls of the city. He would frequently forgo his midday meal at the hospital, but never missed the one in the evening.

By now, he had earned himself the reputation of being a 'loner', fond of his own company, but this attitude was being eroded by having to be in the presence of the other three inmates in his room. If any of them was going through a bad patch, the rest would rally round to help in any way they could. Fred found that he was becoming the strong one, the one who made the decisions. He would be the one who took charge in a crisis. While this was going on, the specialist was watching from a discreet distance, ready to step in if it looked as if things were getting out of hand.

It was amazing how well Fred handled most problems. It was even more noticeable the change that this was bringing about in Fred himself. He became steadier, more confident. Anything unusual or sudden did not alarm him as much as it had done during the previous few weeks. Eventually, he seemed to have recovered in all aspects and was discharged from hospital. He was to report to the Mid-Yorkshire Regimental depot as he had done last year.

Apart from what he had on his person, once again, all his kit, and personal belongings were still somewhere in Belgium or France. This time, they could be at Langemarck, Ypres, St. Omer, Wimereux or somewhere in the neighbourhood of any of these places.

Once again he called in at the Q,M.'s stores to be kitted out. This time, he had two 'blighty' bars for his left sleeve. Together with his bedding, he carried all his new kit to yet another bed space. It was becoming a regular occurrence. It was just like old times.

His next call was at the armoury to get a replacement for the rifle he had left behind in the mud of Flanders. This was the third in as many years. Where would this one be left?

Now attached to the depot staff, he was on light duties until further notice, reporting at the hospital for daily check-up. As time passed by, he gradually recovered the stamina and physique he had lost during the time spent in hospital.

At this stage in his recovery process, he was allowed seven days convalescence leave to see if he could cope without the reassurance of daily visits to a medical officer. As well as his leave pass and travel warrant, ration cards to cover his spell in Cleckmonsedge were issued to him. He also carried a sealed envelope to give to his local doctor should he have 'problems' while on leave. If it was not needed, it was to be returned to the M.O. unopened. If it had been used, a receipt was to be obtained and forwarded to Fulford.

All went well during his furlough. In fact, he seemed to be just like his former self. Leave over, he returned to York.

One day, out of the blue and without any prior warning, he found that he had been put back on the "Fit for Active Service" list. He would be going back to the slaughter on the Western Front from which he had just escaped. Where would it be this time? Would he come back from it this next time? Would the war end before there were no more young men to be killed or mutilated? These were the worries which now assailed him.

Notwithstanding the fact that he had only just returned from leave, he was given a further five days prior to posting back to France. His travel warrants and movement orders took him back to Boulogne and the hated Étaples, and thence to a holding camp to the west of Cambrai. On arrival, once again he would not be rebadged. He would still remain with the Mid-Yorkshires, but this time he would go to the 8th Battalion.

During his embarkation leave, his mood changed to one of black despair as he brooded about what lay ahead of him. If he was lucky and lived, he might get away with another 'blighty' wound, although the more he thought about it, the more he convinced himself that this time his luck would run out. The more he despaired, the more withdrawn and introverted he became. He never uttered a word, and only spoke if addressed directly, and then in monosyllabic grunts. He had regressed to a state much worse than ever before. He refused point blank to see a doctor.

One day towards the end of his leave, Fred put on all his equipment and slung his rifle over his shoulder. Announcing that he was going to see Betty, his 'intended', he left the house. Why he had to take all his kit and his rifle, he was not sure. But he knew he had to make for Barnsley because she came from nearby Royston. It made no difference that he had spent yesterday evening with her, drinking tea and eating hot, buttered toast in the kitchen of the big house of one of the local mill owners just up the road from his parents' home. This was where she was in service as a housemaid. He just had this compelling urge which could not be ignored, so Barnsley it had to be.

Off he strode on the twenty mile journey. Wakefield was reached and passed. Next was Barnsley but having got there, he just carried straight on heading in a roughly southerly direction. Trudging ever onwards, he got to Sheffield. By this time, night had fallen and Fred's thinking was even more confused than it was when he set out. "Ah don't live 'ere, neether does Betty. Why 'ave they stopped shellin'? 'Ave they run aht o' shells?" With that comforting thought, he continued to walk ever southwards, out into the open countryside of Derbyshire. It was now raining heavily, and he had nothing to eat for some considerable time.

Full daylight once again, 'Stand-to' was over till dusk, and sentries had been posted. As he had been given no specific orders, he would get his head down for a bit and try to catch up on a bit of 'shut-eye' while nothing was happening. With that, he lay down in the ditch at the side of the road, thinking as he did so, "This trench needs deepening!"

So what if he was hungry and soaked to the skin, that was normal out here in the trenches. Anyway, it's a quiet sector, there's been no shooting of any kind for some time, so it's not too bad a spot. With that, he fell asleep.

When he awoke some time later, the guns were still silent. Neither side was disturbing things. So, taking advantage of the lull, he set off again. He knew he had a long way to go before nightfall, but had no idea as to his destination. No one had told him.

Daylight passed into darkness again without him even noticing the change. Throughout the night he plodded, on through the Stygian gloom. By this time, he was beginning to worry about the continuing absence of gunfire. He hadn't heard a single shot all day. He hadn't seen anyone, not even a British 'squaddy' let alone a German.

Was the war over? If so, why hadn't he been told?

In an ever increasingly confused state of mind, he hurried on across the moors. Another dawn came, and still he pushed on. "I must find the Front, or Betty!" he thought in his panic. Then, "There's summat wrong here. There's no mud!" With that, a wave of blind, overwhelming terror struck him and he broke into a shambling run. He ran until he could run no longer, then collapsed in the road.

He lay there for a while then staggered to his feet. He stood there looking round him trying to get his bearings. The countryside was totally unknown to him. He had no idea where on earth he was. There was nothing to indicate whether he was in England, France or Belgium. All he could see was open moorland stretching to the horizon on all sides. He could have been anywhere.

Then panic struck him once more. Wave after wave of desperate anxiety swept over him. He set off again at a run. Lurching erratically down the road, he soon fell over once again. He tried to get up but it was no good, his legs did not want to work. They refused to support him.

As he lay there in a daze, he heard someone talking to him. A local carrier out on his rounds had seen Fred staggering drunkenly down the road which was miles from the nearest village. He had watched for a while. When Fred had fallen a second time and could not get up, he decided that it was time to investigate.

The first thing he did was smell Fred's breath. If the soldier was drunk, he must have been on a real 'blinder' to get to the state he seemed to be in. But there was not the slightest trace of drink. By now, Fred was shaking like a leaf and gasping for breath. Obviously he was very ill. With that, the carrier picked Fred up and placed him very carefully on a pile of empty sacks in the back of his lorry, thinking as he did so, the customers will just have to wait for once!" His next stop would be at the cottage hospital he had passed ten miles back up the road he had just travelled.

On arrival, Fred was stripped and his soaking clothes taken away to be dried and cleaning, covered as they were with mud from the ditches which Fred had mistaken for trenches. The doctor on call took the opportunity to examine his new patient for any clues as to the cause for his condition.

Fred's face was now ashen-white and clammy, and covered with cold perspiration. He was breathing heavily and unevenly. He was shaking violently. His body was covered with a network of recently healed wounds, both biceps having had slices taken out of them.

As for the left thigh, there were livid signs of very recent injury. On the left front, there were two entry wounds made by bullets, judging by the size of the scars. There was a similar scar on the right, also at the front. All three bullets seemed to have emerged in more or less the same place at the back of the leg. In doing so, they had left an angry-looking depression which could barely be covered with one hand. All these wounds had healed quite recently but were still very tender in appearance.

Apart from the physical damage which seemed to have healed, the doctor could not identify any other reasons for Fred's condition. He came to the conclusion that it must have a deeper-rooted cause, something of a mental or nervous origin. As he made notes of examination findings, he commented on the state of Fred's hands covered in new skin as a consequence of the mustard gas blistering.

In the meantime, the nurse had finished dressing his feet which were so like so much raw meat. The skin had been rubbed off them, and his boots were full of blood. After all, he had just walked the best part of a hundred miles with sixty five pounds weight of equipment hung about him, as well as his kitbag and rifle. That his new boots, recently issued, had not been fully broken-in hadn't helped.

(In the Army, it is said that the soldier does not break-in his boots, they break him in. But once they've been soaked a time or two after river crossings for example, and allowed to dry out on the wearer's feet, they are as comfortable as anything you can get. But not before!)

With all his wounds and injuries freshly dressed, Fred was now put into a single bed side room, away from the hustle and bustle of the main ward.

In order to book him into hospital, Fred's papers were examined when it was seen that he had overstayed his leave. He was, in the Army's eyes, A.W.O.L., or 'Absent without leave'. That would be the substance of the primary charge to be brought against him when he faced the inevitable Court-Martial. As he still had his rifle and all his kit, that would be taken to indicate that he intended to rejoin, eventually. If he had kept none of it, that would have shown that he had had no such intention. In that case, the charge would be one of desertion. If the offence had taken place in France or Belgium, the offender would have been executed by firing squad. That was the way the Army handled such matters in time of war.

Having discovered Fred's position with regard to his leave, the doctor had no choice but to inform the local police. They, in their turn, were obliged to inform the military authorities.

Meanwhile the doctor had come across the letter from the neuro-surgeon at Fulford Military Hospital which Fred was still carrying. This should have been handed in when he had returned from convalescent leave but he had forgotten to do so. The next day, a car containing an escort of Military Police turned up to take Fred into custody. He was to be lodged in Stafford Gaol until appropriate charges had been formulated.

On arrival, Fred went through all the necessary formalities. While these were being dealt with, so, the prison doctor had been reading the covering letter sent with Fred from the hospital he had been taken to by the carrier. He also read the letter from Fulford, after which Fred was given another thorough going-over before he was accepted into the prison's care. On the doctor's instructions, Fred was taken straight into the prison sick-bay.

Fred was now sitting up and talking to all and sundry. Anyone who came within range was told that he – Fred -- had been trying to find his girl in Barnsley. What he couldn't understand was where the trenches had got to, nor why there wasn't any shooting of any kind. In fact, he was sure the war had ended but that they had forgotten to tell him.

During these rambling conversations, he would suddenly go silent halfway through a sentence. It was as if his vital spirit had left his body for a split second. His empty husk (for want of a better description) would remain frozen in the position it had been in when his spirit left him. Then, just as quickly, the conversation would be resumed as if nothing had happened.

Despite Fred's obvious condition, and overruling the prison doctor's protestations, a District Court-Martial was arranged for three days later. When the court officials were being appointed, the prison doctor insisted on being appointed as the "Prisoner's Friend". He dismissed out of hand all objections pointing out that not only was he a qualified doctor, he still held his commission as a major in the Medical corps. He was on the reserve having been invalided out after being shot through one lung at Mons.

The first thing he did was to contact Fulford and arrange for Fred's medical records to be sent down to him by special messenger.

The President of the court was to be a colonel of the North Staffordshire Regiment. He now occupied a desk at the regimental depot in the town after being severely wounded in the trenches. A livid scar ran down the left side of his face. This was matched by an empty sleeve on the same side. He walked with a pronounced limp.

The stage was now set for the trial.. Yet again, one relic of the battlefield was to be defended by another. In charge of proceedings, was a third.

In an attempt to control his shaking, Fred clung grimly to the rail of the dock in which he was arraigned. Apart from one occasion when he suffered a momentary 'absence', the only answers he seemed able to produce were his name, rank and number. He insisted that he was a "Bantam", a Ledford Bantam of the 17th. Mid-Yorkshires. For some reason, any mention of service with the 9th. Battalion of that regiment no longer registered with him.

It looked as if the trial would not be without its problems.

At one point when asked why he had overstayed his leave, Fred replied "What leave? I was on my way back to the trenches. As I was near Barnsley, I thought I'd call on my girl in Royston. Anyway, what's happened to the guns? You'd best ask Tom, he's bound to know!"

What Tom could, or couldn't tell them, no one could discover. Even Fred had no idea.

The Court-Martial was getting nowhere fast, and was in danger of becoming a complete farce. The Prisoner's Friend rose to his feet to request a postponement on the grounds that the prisoner was in no fit state to answer questions being put to him.

Just then, there was a loud bang followed by another one in quick succession.

There was simple explanation for them. The morning of the trial was very muggy, and as the room set aside as the court-room was poorly ventilated, the door had been left slightly ajar to improve things. A sudden gust of wind had slammed the door. This had startled the clerk-to-the court who had knocked the tome containing the King's Regulations and precedents off his desk and onto the floor.

The two bangs had startled Fred who threw himself to the floor of the dock. He wrapped his arms round his head, and tried to take cover behind the panelling. He lay there shaking, but without making a sound. The M.P. standing behind him reached down and grabbed Fred's collar and yanked him back into view. But Fred was unable to stand, his legs refusing to support him. As Fred was hauled to his feet a second time only to collapse once more, the prison doctor in both that role and that of Defending Officer protested and demanded an immediate adjournment of the trial. This was granted. The accused was rushed away to the sick bay and sedated.

The President of the Court now called both the doctor and the prosecuting officer to the front of the court. He remarked that prior to commencing proceedings, he had read the service record of the accused, as well as his medical papers, both official and unofficial. He had read the comments of the neuro-surgeon at Fulford which were now kept with the file. He had also taken into account the notes from the cottage hospital where Fred had been taken when found out on the moorland road, as well as these the prison doctor had made when the accused had been taken into custody.

If all parties agreed, as President of the Court-Martial he intended to rule that while the accused was technically guilty as charged insofar as he had actually overstayed his leave, the Court would award no punishment in view of the circumstances in which the offence had occurred, especially when his service record was taken into consideration.

That the prisoner was suffering from severe memory loss was beyond question. The doctor had certified that on the prisoner's arrival at Stafford. All the doctors from the one at the C.C.S. near Ypres as well as those at St. Omer, Wimereux and Folkestone, had all noted the medical records as to the state of Fred's nerves. Finally, the specialist at Fulford had stated categorically that his patient was suffering from shell shock. He, the President had no doubt whatsoever that Fred had gone A.W.O.L. because of amnesia brought about by this condition.

The comments of the young M.O. at Messines referring to 'Lack of Moral Fibre' were dismissed as balderdash, utterly preposterous. Someone who had spent four months in the flooded trenches in early 1916 in the Laventie–Festubert sector, and then marched most of the way to the Somme, only to be blown up during intense shellfire was not a coward. He was, after all, one of the only four of his platoon to survive.

On recovering from his wounds, he had been sent back to France in time to take part in the Messines offensive. Having come through that unscathed, he had gone up to the Salient to take part in the 3rd Ypres Offensive which would go down in history as "Passchendaele".

Outside Langemarck, he had been gassed (both mustard and phosgene) before being felled by machinegun fire. To him, the President, this did not sound like the record of a coward. A coward would have been dodging the column from the very moment he had first set foot in France, that is, if he had not managed to get out of the posting in the first place.

It was pertinent to note that the first doctor Fred had seen at Langemarck had, in fact, been the self-same man who had made those disparaging comments at Messines. Even he had remarked on Fred's agitated state of mind.

With all this in mind, the President would add 'riders' to the verdict of the Court that if the Army could not find grounds for

Fred's early release on medical grounds, then he should be graded as unfit for further active service, and posted to a home-based garrison.

That was the verdict the Court returned, and was so entered in the official record of the proceedings.

Chapter 28

Once again, Fred found himself back at Fulford. The Military Hospital was fast becoming his second home. Having gone through the now so-familiar routine, he handed in his rifle at the armoury at the depot just along the road from the hospital. That would be the last he would see of that!

The neuro-surgeon was now using a combination of mild sedatives and hypnosis. He was strenuously against the often brutal electric-shock therapy in vogue at the Mental Wing at Netley Hospital. At medical conferences, he would make himself unpopular by inveighing against this 'treatment' on the grounds that it often did more harm than good.

Although Fred no longer suffered the incoherent spell or the mental 'absences', he still could not relax. Although he was still slightly 'twitchy', he was not noticeably so. In order to let him adjust, he was allowed to go into the city. During one period of wandering through the streets and alleyways of the old town, he found himself outside the Minster, so went in. It was a haven of peace and tranquillity. As he had time to spare before it was time to go for his evening meal, he sat down on one of the chairs in the nave. He must have spent at least an hour just gazing at the magnificent vaulting overhead, and at the light streaming through wonderful mediaeval stained glass windows.

He became aware of someone standing at his side, talking to him. One of the clergy was asking if wished to discuss anything, anything he wanted to get off his mind. Did Fred want to talk over any problems he might have? The offer was turned down, politely.

Fred said that although in his childhood he had been brought up to attend church, after what he had seen and been through in France and Belgium, he was not sure he believed in anything anymore. Surely, if there was a Divine Being as all the churchmen insisted there was, why had the horrors of the war been allowed to happen? Why had it continued for so long?

He personally, had been driven to the very edge of insanity by what had happened to him, and he was still clawing his way back. His problems were ones that only he could sort out. He would have to come to terms with them himself, and try to effect some sort of reconciliation. He would have to learn how to close his mind to the past so that he could sleep at nights. If that was not possible, then he would have to find some other way to end things, one way or another. If he needed help from the Church, he would come and ask for it, thank you.

Fred added that if it was any consolation to the cleric, he found that just sitting in the calm and 'holiness' of the Minster did have a calming and beneficial effect on him.

As the days passed by, he became calmer both physically and mentally, and could now get a decent night's sleep. He was now back to helping fellow sufferers as had done during his last spell at Fulford.

Then came the day when he was sent off on a week's leave to see if he could cope without medical support at his elbow. This proved to be no problem at all. It would now simply be matter of time completing the healing process, the staff at the hospital having done as much for him as they could. It was now up to him.

Could he handle life in military surroundings other than in hospital? Would the fact that there was no longer the threat of being sent to the Front again change things? That would now be put to the test.

Once again he was posted to another battalion of the Mid-Yorkshires, this time, the 3rd. As part of the Tyne Defence Garrison, it was stationed at Whitley Bay. Along with Fred's service and medical records, a confidential report was sent to the garrison M.O. advising him of Fred's problems.

Whitley Bay found him on light duties. These consisted of helping in the cookhouse. He assisted with the washing up, serving meals, preparing vegetables and that sort of thing. He had no responsibilities at all. This kind of existence posed no problems apart from that of boredom. As he had more than his share of excitement, it suited him down to the ground.

One morning, early in 1918, Fred was dishing out porridge at breakfast-time. Out of the blue came a voice from the dim and distant past, as if from another life. "Is this Fred's Place?" He looked up, startled, to see Tom grinning at him. He also saw that Tom was leaning heavily on a stick. In explanation, Tom said "Ah needed another 'blighty bar' to catch up wi thee. Now wi''v' gotten two apiece!" That was all he would say about his damaged leg.

For some reason, Fred's letter from Wimereux had never reached Tom, nor had any of Tom's found Fred. After several tries, he had given up. He had been as surprised as Fred had been when he had seen who was serving meals in the mess-hall.

Tom, who had just arrived at Whitley Bay had been given the job of post corporal because, as he said "Ah've 'ad more nor enough running rahnd like a silly bugger bein' shot at! Wi' this leg, ah can just abaht keep up wi' t' letters in t' Post Room!"

Luck was to get Fred a 'cushy' number as well. He had overheard two fitters arguing over a problem which they had in setting up and operating a new gear-hobbing machine in the M.T. workshops of the garrison. The problem was in getting it set up accurately before actually cutting the new gear wheel. Fred, who had recognised the machine from the conversation chipped in and explained what the problem was likely to be. He offered to show them how to overcome the problem.

While he was working on the machine, the captain in charge of the M.T. lines, on seeing this total stranger using one of his precious machines, came rushing over to see what was going on. He saw at once the confidence and familiarity with which Fred was using the equipment. When asked, Fred said that before he had volunteered for the army, he had served a five-year engineering apprenticeship which had involved using that type of machine. He had been employed in the workshops of a factory which had built and repaired wool-combing machinery.

"From now on, you are on my staff" the officer ordered. "I'll square it with the catering officer. There's an empty bunkhouse next to this workshop. Move into that." Fred did so, and found that not only did it have its own ablution and toilet facilities, it was in fact a two-berth unit. The second bunk was empty, so naturally, Tom moved in as well. This was a very satisfactory arrangement, but it was a privilege which had been earned the hard way.

As Tom was unpacking his belongings, a small, square box fell to the floor. As Fred picked it up, Tom snatched it out of his hand. This reaction rather surprised Fred who asked what it was. In a rather embarrassed voice, Tom confessed " It's mi medal".

Eventually, Fred managed to wheedle the full story out of his pal.

Two or three weeks after Fred had been carried back from the conflict. Tom had been going forward along a plank road which had been built so that the artillery could bring their guns up in support of the infantry. He had been in the company of a group of Canadian stretcher bearers. As Tom said, as it turned out, this was as good an arrangement as being knocked down by an ambulance. A shell had landed in the mud to one side of the track way, and they had all been smothered in sludge.

Tom who had been nearest the explosion was the only one injured in the blast. When he recovered consciousness, he was on one of the stretchers he had been carrying just a moment ago for the 'Canucks' who had simply turned round and were now carrying him back to where they had just come from. Both legs had been bound together with bandages, and then to his rifle which was now in use a splint.

When the Canadians had got back on their feet, they had seen that Tom's right leg was sticking out at an unnatural angle. His thigh had been gashed, but the worst injury was to his shin which had been broken in two places. Although a rifle does not make the most comfortable of splints, it did effectively immobilise the limb.

Then followed the usual routine as he was passed down the line of medical centres until he finished up at Wimereux, just as Fred had done. With the passage of time, the broken bone had knitted together, although amputation had been considered at one stage. What had delayed full recovery and caused problems had been severe blood poisoning, probably brought on by filthy splinters from the wooden track having been driven into the wound. This had needed to be opened several times to remove the pus which had accumulated in the damaged area.

The last occasion it had been necessary, Tom had just come out of the operating theatre, still groggy from the effects of the anaesthetic, and was generally feeling sorry for himself. As he lay there, his doctor was gently shaking him. A general in all his glory had arrived at the hospital and demanded to see Tom who was still in the operating theatre. The great man had just had to wait. After many months, Tom had finally been awarded the Military Medal for his sniper-hunting exploits at Festubert. The general was here to make the presentation.

After pinning the medal to Tom's hospital gown, he beamed at him and asked what it felt like to be a wounded hero. Even if he had been fully fit, Tom would still have found this patronising question annoying. Such a question would have been offensive to anyone, wounded or not. The general was rather taken aback to be told that in his job, it would be extremely unlikely that he, the general, would ever be exposed to the risk of being wounded, let alone the circumstances in which wounding occurred in the trenches.

As for the medal, Tom said that he would swap a lorry-load of them if it would get back his mates he had been with when they were killed on the Somme. With that, he had gone back to sleep.

Later, as the doctor recounted all this to Tom, he had a huge grin on his face. Apparently, on being addressed in such a manner, the general had turned bright purple, and nearly exploded. The doctor had had great difficulty in calming him down. He did manage to convince the general that patients coming out from anaesthesia often had this tendency to ramble and to say the wildest things as they surfaced. They often were completely unaware of what they were saying.

As the great man stalked out of the ward in high dudgeon, he was heard to snort "Ungrateful bounder!"

Tom looked the medic straight in the eye and asked if what the general had been told was true. "I've no idea" said the doctor. "It could be! Anyway, it convinced 'his nibs'. He's been under our feet, getting in the way all morning".

Tom then said very quietly "Ah knew exactly wor Ah were sayin' ". "I know" said the medic.

Fred then asked Tom why he wasn't wearing the medal ribbon on his tunic. He was told "Ah'd feel a reight fraud. Ah'm still alive. Like thee, Ah've bin lucky to survive!" When Fred said that he could be put on a charge for being improperly dressed for not displaying the ribbon, Tom's answer was to the effect that 'they' could get on with it if 'they' wanted to.

During his time with the mechanics of the transport lines, Fred made sure that he learned how to drive. With his aptitude for things mechanical, he also made sure that not only did he become proficient at stripping, rebuilding and tuning engines, he also took care to get army proficiency certificates to prove it.

He was, of course, anticipating the end of the war and had been quick to realise that several thousands of men would suddenly be released on to the labour market from the armed forces. All would be looking for work, but not all would be lucky.

Fred wanted to have as many options open to him as possible, and had decided that the motor car would be the big thing in peacetime. Chauffeurs would be in great demand, especially if they knew how to look after the vehicles they drove.

Then there was Betty, the girl who would become his wife. She was now a cook-housekeeper. They would seek employment together as a couple in domestic service. He had got it all worked out. All that was holding them back was the war. It was still not over, and he not been released.

Then, in November 1918, the war ended. Three months after the armistice, Tom and he were instructed to report to a camp at Clipstone, Nottinghamshire. They were demobilised on February 7th. 1919. They were given twenty eight days 'demob' leave in which to unwind, adjust to civilian life and start looking for work.

Tom returned to his haunts in Wensleydale. His 'profession' still had vacancies!

Fred had more weighty matters to take care of, such as a wedding. But first, he had to find a job. As a married man, he would be taking on financial responsibilities. As he was now back in his home town of Cleckmonsedge, he set out and visited every mill in the locality. All vacancies for mechanics had long since been filled, even for those with qualifications. The fact that he was a time-served and fully qualified ex-apprentice counted for nothing. Not even labourers were needed. There were no vacancies whatsoever in this 'land fit for heroes to live in" that Lloyd George was going to create.

Skilled weavers were actually being laid off. Demand for woollen serge which had been at a peak during the war was virtually non-existent now that it was all over. Any required for tram or train drivers' uniforms was available from warehouses on demand, with suppliers dying the material to the required colour free of charge as an inducement just to get rid of it. As the colour required was usually navy-blue, it was not a problem.

With the coming of peace, the bottom had dropped right out of the market, along with any prospects of employment in this field.

Then, a letter arrived from Tom. He too was still unemployed, (officially), but not going hungry. Fred had a good idea why his would be so. Tom had heard that the owners of a large country estate required domestic staff. They were looking for a cook-housekeeper (that would suit Betty) and a coachman. Their present staff were on the point of giving up work as they had only stayed on until the end of the war. There was only one stipulation. The coachman was to accept that in the not too distant future, the gentleman of the house would be disposing of his horse-drawn carriages and buying a car.

Tom had already put in a word for Fred. Would he care to apply himself? This was the opening Fred had been waiting for. He sat down and began to pen his application for the forthcoming vacancy. Then he tore it up. Tomorrow, he would go and apply in person.

During the interview, Fred confessed that although he knew nothing about horses, not only could he drive a car, he knew how one worked. Not only that, he could make sure it kept on doing so. He then produced his aces, his army certificates of proficiency both as a driver, and also as a motor mechanic. When he had got them in Whitley Bay, he had had a shrewd idea they would could in useful.

As regards the housekeeping post, his future wife was more than capable of taking care of that side of things. He had not got any references for her as he had left home on the spur of the moment, and had not spoken to her before he left. In fact, she did not know he had come about the vacancies, he had been in such a hurry to come and get the jobs, if possible. He could give the names and addresses of people she had worked for in and around Cleckmonsedge. If they preferred, he would come back up north again with her so they could speak to her.

If they were offered the posts, Fred said that he would bring the wedding forward. When did the present staff wish to finish? Dates were settled and the posts were theirs if Betty agreed. Despite not having been consulted, she was delighted with the arrangements that Fred had negotiated. They were married within days with Tom as 'best man'.

There was no honeymoon. Apart from the fact that they could not afford one, there was no time available before they were due to take up their new posts.

So Fred and Betty became fixtures in a large house set in a vast expanse of parkland with its own shooting as well as fishing in the river which ran along one boundary of the estate.

They had been there just over six months when the owner remarked that his gamekeeper who was getting a bit long in the tooth was finding it hard work trying to keep up with the local poachers, so was talking of retiring. What the owner wanted was a younger man who was good with a gun, someone about Fred's age. Did Fred know of anyone?

Fred mentioned his army pal, Tom, the one who had recommended Fred and Betty for their present posts. He had been a sniper during the war. He was still out of work. (He kept quiet about the fact that Tom was also a successful poacher. Somehow, it did not seem wise to mention this as he only lived about a mile away down the dale!)

In suggesting him, Fred had a very good idea that if Tom was taken on as the gamekeeper, the level of poaching on the estate would fall. (This also was a fact that it seemed better not to mention!) Once again, the survivors of the Ledford Bantams were looking out after each other's interests.

Tom was given the job, and, as expected, was very successful in thwarting the poachers. All it had needed was a younger man! As he had almost certainly been one of the villains prior to changing loyalties, he would also have the distinct advantage of knowing the job from both sides.

The owner was so delighted with the progress made that he told the two old comrades-in-arms that if they wanted to take the occasional bird or fish, they were to help themselves provided that they did not abuse the privilege, and overdo things.

Tom was now taking legally what he had always taken in the past. "It's not t' same some'ow" he complained to Fred. " All t' fun's bin tekken aht of it!"

In the local pub in the evening, anyone who knew what the two had been through during the war might have been tempted to ask them why they had volunteered in the first place. They would just grin, sheepishly, and remark " Some daft bugger had to go!" But if the questioner persisted and asked if it was because they were patriots, they would take along pull at their pints and say "'Appen, 'appen not". That would be the end of the matter as far as they were concerned, there was no more to be said. Apart from Fred and Tom, no one in the village knew about Tom's decoration. Even Betty was unaware of its existence.

As for the war, it was all over and done with.

But was it? The actual physical struggle, the conflict, 'the war to end all wars', that may well be over, but what about the aftermath, the peace?

After the rapturous celebrations had finally died away, the country at large tried to settle down to what should now have been a normal existence. But it was not to be as simple as that.

Over the past four years or so, manufacturing industry had switched over to full-time production of the goods required to meet the insatiable demands of the military machine. It was now geared up to producing the kind of merchandise not need in peacetime. In any case, al the pre-war markets and outlets had long since gone.

So, as well as converting manufacturing strategy to meet peacetime demands, for its products, those demands had to be established. New markets had to be sought out and won. Till then, not only was there no work for the hundreds of thousands of men now being released from the armed forces, there was no longer any need for those workpeople recently employed on war work. They too were surplus to requirements. Those who had been fortunate to survive the war now found that they had to survive the peace!

The charitable funds of parish or church councils were unable to cope with the overwhelming flood of demands now being made on their meagre resources. Ex-servicemen were reduced to begging in the streets in order to support their families and themselves Campaign and gallantry medals were being offered for sale to anyone who would buy them for what they would fetch.

Ironically, the crippled or the visibly maimed fared better than those who had come through the conflict unscathed. Wound scars, no matter how hideous counted for nothing if they could not be seen. Those apparently unmarked were told in no uncertain terms to go and get a job. The fact that there were none to be had was beside the point.

As a result, hundreds of men tramped the roads in an often vain attempt to find casual work. If they were lucky, seasonal employment would be available on farms or with the highways departments. If not, they went hungry, as did their dependants.

While they were risking life and limb in the trenches, they had been fed reasonably regularly, and from their Army pay, they could make allowances to their families back home. Everybody could eat. Now that they were no longer physically at risk, they were unpaid, unfed and unwanted.

To add to the irony of the situation, the boots which were now pounding the roads of the British Isles were often the same as those which had pounded the roads of France and Belgium.

The estate on which Fred and Tom were fortunate to find themselves was on the direct line of march of large numbers of those itinerants who were down on their luck. Whilst the majority were genuine in their search for work, there were inevitably the 'free-loaders', the scroungers, those who would take all they could get as a matter of right, no matter how they got it.

Fred and Tom had discussed this problem with their employer who was totally in sympathy with the genuine job-seekers. He had lost two sons in the war as well as having a nephew crippled for life. He suggested that on an estate of this size i.e. his, they could surely find something which needed attention. They should be able to do something to help

There was also the question of the two empty tack rooms as well as the stable lad's quarters which were now disused now that there were no horses on the estate. They could be turned into dormitories for any casual workers who had been taken on.

And so it came about that a peacetime version of the Flanders cookhouse came into being, but now it would be known as "Fred's and Tom's Place".

They heard that a wartime transit camp nearby was being dismantled, and that all the furniture was destined for the rubbish dump. A visit by Fred ensured that all he needed would be delivered to the stables by an Army Service Corps sergeant and his driver in a War Department lorry. (This diversion from the tip would be unofficial, of course!)

Payment would be in kind. Meals would be available in the kitchen of the house for both men. There, they could eat their fill. This would be followed by a trip down to the local inn where drinks were 'on the house'. Again, they could have as much as they wanted.

The innkeeper was another veteran of the Somme who had been discharged on medical grounds. He carried a wide variety of scars to show for it. When the project was being discussed one night over a few beers, he had offered this 'inducement' to 'lubricate the negotiations' (as he put it).

The beds were set up in what had been the stable-lad's room as it had its own sink and fireplace. It would be known as "The Doss-house". It came as no surprise that the first two occupants were the sergeant and his driver as neither were capable of standing up at the end of the evening, let alone drive a lorry.

Fred's employer very tactfully (and wisely) made no enquiries as to how the beds had been obtained. He had also diplomatically ensured that he would be away in town, on business, when they were delivered.

Whilst the majority of those who called at the Hall were genuine in their search for work of any kind in exchange for a meal, the scroungers were very plausible. Some of these claiming to have had a hard war would produce medals in support of their 'hard luck' stories. These medals had very likely been bought for a copper or two from some starving individual with nothing else left to sell.

Staff at the Hall were told to refer all job-seekers to either Fred or Tom as they would be able to spot cheats immediately. In this way, only those genuinely in need would benefit. Simple questions would be asked. If, the man was merely on the make and trying to get something for nothing in giving wrong answers, he would be told to leave the area immediately otherwise he would be handed over to the police as a vagrant.

A true veteran would give the correct answers without hesitation. He would not need to produce any medals to back up his story. If he did, then he would be asked to produce his release papers as proof of his identity. At this stage, the medals would be examined. Round the rim of each one produced would be the number, rank and name of the recipient. All the medals should agree with each other. More importantly, they should agree with the details on the discharge papers. If there was any discrepancy, the man would be kept talking.

It had been arranged that the gardener's boy would be lurking in the background on his bicycle. If medals were found on examination to be of doubtful origin, at a signal from Fred or Tom, he would cycle down into the village and get the local 'bobby'. That worthy had been in the Battle Police during the war, and had been wounded several times. He had scant sympathy for those who dodged the column in any way. Any such individual would be swiftly arrested, and brought up before the local magistrate and charged under the vagrancy acts. He would also be charged with attempting to obtain a material benefit by fraudulent means i.e. by using medals to which he was not entitled in backing up his lies. The local magistrate just happened to be Fred's employer.

So it would seem to be a case of all the cards being stacked against the fraudster. Not only had he tried to fool two battle-hardened veterans, he had been arrested by an ex-Front Line Battle Policeman, and had ended up in front of a magistrate who had had both his sons killed in the war.

When the man was convicted as was invariably the case, the point was always made that wearing medals to which he was not entitled was an offence under military law, and that if he was picked up by the Military Police, the wearer would be in serious trouble. Although on this occasion, the accused had been arraigned before a civil court, that aspect would be reflected in the sentencing. Its custodial nature would provide the man with his board and lodgings, which would be at the Crown's expense for the length of his incarceration.

If possible, a genuine man would be found work on one of the local farms by Fred or Tom. This had been agreed with most of the local farmers. Failing anything locally, there was always something to be done on the estate itself, (even if it was not really necessary). It was a bit like the army, when you think about it. The stone-flagged courtyard must have been the best washed and brushed in the country.

There was usually a pile of logs to be split. By coincidence, the fireplace in the Doss-house used logs! At Fred's suggestion, the gardener always had a spare plot of ground which needed digging. Acres of lawn needed mowing.

In this way, the meals and accommodation were earned, they were not charitable handouts. In the case of the 'invented' jobs, the dividing line was very thin, but it saved face which was the main consideration. In this way, the man's self-respect was preserved, if only on the surface.

All this time, an epidemic of so-called "Spanish Flu" of frightening proportions was sweeping across the British Isles. People were dying like flies in numbers which even exceeded the casualty rate on the Somme.

The local villages and farms were to be spared the ravages of this frightful visitation, probably due to their comparative isolation. None of the job-seekers brought the illness with them.

This was probably due to the fact that they were out on the open highways most days, and not in contact with the general population of the towns and cities. In a twisted kind of way, their present hardships almost certainly saved their lives as they escaped the 'flu.

The routine established by Fred and Tom helped many a deserving veteran through a bad patch. However, as things gradually got back to normal, the number of callers died away to a trickle, until ultimately, they stopped coming altogether.

Fred and Tom decided to call it a day. They had done all that they could when their kind of help was needed.

Now they could say that the war really was over!

And so it would be until the next one reared its ugly head.

Appendix I.
How This Book Came To Be Written

After the death of my mother, I was going through a boxful of old papers when I came across a letter at the bottom of the box. It was dated July 20th. 1916 and was originally sent to my grandmother by Lt. O'Brien, my father's platoon commander on the Somme, In it, he told her how my father had been wounded but at the same time reassuring her as to his condition.

When I retired, I decided to trace my father's time in the army during the Great War.

I had various bits and pieces which had references to some of the various units of which he had been a member.

So, at first sight, it seemed as if it would be straightforward. I soon discovered that was not to be so.

The first obstacle I encountered was finding that during the Second World War, when the Public Records Office in London had been fire-bombed during the *blitz,* about half the service records of World War I had gone up in smoke, amongst them those I was hoping to examine.

So, it became a matter of haunting libraries, bookshops and museums in Yorkshire, or wherever a scrap of information seemed to be leading. The museum of the West Yorkshire Regiment in York proved to be invaluable, producing the War

Diary of the 17th Battalion and other papers from their archives. The staff were most helpful.

If it might have anything to do with the West Yorkshire Regiment, any scrap of information from whatever source would be followed up as far as possible. If, as was often the case, the wrong unit of the W.Y.R. was being traced, the frustration was intense. When the end result was relevant to the 35th Division, and to the 17th W.Y.R. in particular, the satisfaction was tremendous. One such occasion was when I came across the name of the troopship which took Dad to France in 1916. Armed with that information, an approach to Lloyds Registry produced full details of her specification and history.

The "Yorkshire Evening Post" produced photocopies of the initial announcement in the paper, as well as a later article detailing how the recruiting campaign was going.

Leeds Town Hall provided a copy of the relevant section from a book "Leeds at War" dealing with specifically with the Leeds Bantams.

Ultimately, after about ten years, it became more and more obvious that if there was any more information on the 17th, it must be buried in private records and the like, to which I could not gain access, even if I could find out where they were.

In one last effort before calling off the chase (so to speak) I engaged the services of a London-based professional researcher into matters historical. The "Burnt Records" were checked on the off-chance that there might just be something of use, but this was not to be the case. (These records are, of course, the remnants salvaged from the bombed P.R.O. and whose details had been transferred to other media.) In addition, all avenues in the new P.R.O. would be checked, again on the remote chance that something might come to light. When nothing new was found, I decided that I had done all I could as regards the research side of things.

I could now compile Dad's service record for the other members of our family and for me. On completing this, I think all aspects of his military service had been covered, at least, that is, the official side. What happened in his off-duty time we shall never know.

While I was doing this, a fascinating story started to emerge, so I decided that in addition to the formal record, I would write it up as a continuous narrative. This was to prove more difficult than I had anticipated. Although all elements had been covered, some were just bald, statements of fact which, as such, do not lend themselves to the making of a good story.

I decided therefore to write it up as a work of fiction but to base it firmly on what I had discovered. So, where there were just statements of fact, I decided to draw on my own experiences during the part of my period of National Service with the West Yorkshire Regiment. I therefore wrote up situations and characters I met with, but as if contemporary with the First World War. After all, I doubt whether the character and outlook on life of a Yorkshireman, a "Tyke", would have changed much over the years, if at all. In fact, it was once said that " You can always tell a Yorkshireman, but you can't tell him much!"

One thing of which I can be certain is that his evaluation of the higher ranks in the Army, the "Top Brass", would be just the same in the 1950's as it was in the Great War. Feel free to decide what that was!

Appendix II

Appendix II
Transcript of the Letter from The Somme

17th. West Yorkshire Regt.
B.E.F.
FRANCE.
July 20th. 1916.

Dear Mrs. Brooke,

It gives me the greatest pleasure in the world to have to inform you that your son Pte. Brooke has been wounded.

You will wonder why it gives me pleasure. I will tell you.

At this time all regiments out here are going through a very trying time facing many dangers and many discomforts. The most fortunate people are those who are wounded provided that they are not seriously hurt. They are taken away out of it all, well cared for, surrounded by everything that the best medical and surgical skill can give them. Also, they do not come back to the fighting area for some time.

Your son I am happy to say is one of them. He is wounded in both arms, in the left arm just above the elbow and in the right arm just below the elbow. He had a lucky escape, though. I as the officer commanding the platoon was taking the men into some trenches. Your son was quite close to me. Suddenly a great shell dropped close to us. When the smoke cleared, I saw that your son and two other men standing near to me were wounded. I saw that your son's coat and shirt over the stomach were all torn and I feared that he had been hit in the stomach, a very dangerous place. However, he didn't look much like a dying man and I soon discovered that he had sustained only slight wounds in the arms and that the stomach was only bruised. The stretcher bearers attended to him as he walked away smoking a cigarette to the dressing station quite happy.

I myself have been twice wounded in this war and I can assure you that your son will now be having the time of his life and you need have no anxiety on his behalf. In fact, you should be very glad that he is out of it for some time. His friends in the platoon are sorry to lose him, but we are all I am afraid rather envious of him.

I have the honour to be

Yours sincerely

Raymond O'Brien. 2nd. Lieutenant,
17th. West Yorkshire Regiment.

P.S. A parcel arrived for your son today and I gave it his chum Colin as it would probably be lost if we sent it to him from here.

Appendix IV.
Did You Know ------- ?

During the lengthy and involved research undertaken which ultimately lead to the writing of this story, some strange but fascinating facts came to light. Rather than let them sink back into obscurity, they have been presented in no particular order in the form of this appendix.

1/. British troops in Belgium and France were not as popular as contemporary records suggest. Some farmers went as far as refusing British water parties access to their wells. The lids would be padlocked and pump handles removed to prevent any water being taken. Not surprisingly, members of the British Expeditionary Force took the view that as one reason (amongst their other responsibilities), they were in that part of the world was to protect the farmer's property they were entitled to a drop of water. The locks were shot off as necessary. Pump handles were manufactured in the army Engineers' workshops.

Tradition inbred over the centuries is hard to break---- the English and the French had been sworn enemies for the best part of eight hundred years, from 1066 until Waterloo in 1815. For a lot of that time, our allies had been the Germans.

2/. Some German infantry regiments had the same or similar battle honours as British regiments. These stemmed from the times when British and German troops had fought alongside each other, usually against French and / or Spanish armies.

3/. When the Mills bomb was introduced, it was thought that some of them were 'duds' because they failed to explode when thrown. It was then realised that the so-called duds were 'failing' because in the heat of the moment, the fuses had not been inserted. The boxes which held the grenades prior to issue carried them un-fused as a safety measure. The fuses were held in a separate package within the main box. When grenades are to be used, the troops involved draw and insert the fuses themselves. Without them, throwing the bombs is akin to throwing stones at the enemy.

4/. When gas was used for the first time, the victims had no means of protection against the chlorine used. It was found that urine-soaked handkerchiefs tied over the nose and mouth gave some degree of protection. Funnily enough, it seemed to be more effective than just plain water. There was, however, no protection as yet for the eyes.

5/. When rifles have been fired, the burnt cordite fouls the rifling in the barrel of the weapon. Normally this is removed by pouring boiling water through it from breech to muzzle. In the trenches, this was not possible. It was found that with the muzzle temporarily plugged and the bolt removed, if the rifleman urinated into the breech so filling the bore of the rifle, then if it was left in the weapon for a short while, the natural product worked almost as well as if the rifle had been 'boiled out' correctly. When the rifle was drained and 'pulled through' as usual, the result was a weapon of acceptable cleanliness.

6/. When the Bantams took over sections of the Front Line from regulation-sized troops, they would find that the parapet of the trench was too high, whilst the firing step was too low. What did they do? They filled in the trench bottom, and cut a new firing step to accommodate their lack of height. When, however, the trenches were handed back on being relieved, if the incoming troops were not Bantams, they would find the trenches were now too shallow, thus exposing their heads and shoulders above the parapets. This was worse if Guards regiments were involved!

Orders were therefore given that all Bantam units going into the Line were to carry two empty sandbags per man. These were to be filled on arrival in the trenches and placed on the firing step. Trenches were not to be filled in! Relieving troops of regulation size could then put the sandbags on the parapet, and use the original firing step.

7/.Along some stretches of the Line, there seemed to be an unofficial arrangement regarding 'Breakfast Time'. From roughly 0630hrs.until 0730hrs., a lull would descend on the trenches when the first meal of the day was being taken by friend and foe alike. After that, it was business as usual. This custom depended on which regiments were in the Line opposite each other. Not every regiment (be it British or German) recognised this informal arrangement.

8/.German Intelligence always seemed know when a Bantam unit was coming into the Line. On arrival, they would often be greeted with clucking and cackling noises together with cries of "Cock-a-doodle-doo".

9/.The first and last British fatalities of the war occurred at locations within a mile of each other. They are both buried in the same cemetery at St. Symphorien, Mons.

10/.Millions of the shells fired at the enemy during the war were fitted with a Type 80 fuse. This could be set to "Airburst" so as to explode in flight after a pre-set time delay when attacking troops in the open. On this setting, shrapnel shells would used.

It had an alternative setting, "Impact", when defence-works were the target. In this case, H.E. (high explosive) shells were the projectiles.

The fuse had been designed by the German armaments manufacturer, Friedrich Krupp, about the turn of the century. Before the outbreak of hostilities, Britain manufactured these fuses under licence on payment of royalties. After the war, in the 1920's, Krupps sued the British government for the unpaid fees due on all the fuses used during the conflict, and fired against the

German armies. The International court found in Krupps' favour, and ordered the United Kingdom to hand over the monies owing.

The sum paid was assessed by use of a complicated formula(!) which calculated the number of shells required to kill one German soldier. This was offset by reference to the number of British soldiers killed by the Germans. Very much a case of "How long is a piece of string?"

11/.It was realised early in the war that officers were easily spotted by snipers because of their fitted uniforms, badges of rank embroidered round their tunic cuffs and the fact that they carried revolvers. Their tunics, riding breeches and leggings also marked them out as officers, and as such, prime targets. The solution was to wear private soldiers' uniform with rank badges marked on the shoulder straps when in the front line, and to carry rifles. Out of the line, the correct attire was worn. This practice was officially frowned on until about 1917 when it was realised that it had become an established fact.

Another 'give-away' for both officers and men was the wire grommet in the crown of the cap. This gave, and maintained, the sharp, circular outline to the headgear. As such, it is a totally unnatural shape, and immediately obvious to anyone such as a sniper on the lookout for such things i.e. targets, in the forward areas of the enemy. When these wire rings were removed from the cap, it could be crushed and crumpled to give an irregular outline in keeping with battlefield surroundings.

12/.When tunneling was taking place, infantry 'resting' or in reserve would be employed as labourers to remove the spoil from the working area. In 1917 when the mediaeval tunnels under Arras were being extended under 'no-man's'land' towards the German lines, the actual tunneling was being done by New Zealand engineers. One unit deployed for this work was from the 17th.West Yorkshire Regiment, "The Yorkshire Bantams".

It seems that they were paraded in the open outside the entrance to the workings. This would happen irrespective of weather conditions anything up to an hour before they were actually needed. It was not unusual to be soaked to the skin before starting work. As if that was not enough, they would frequently miss a meal due to parading too early.

The New Zealanders took a dim view of the way in which the Bantams were being treated. On raising the matter, they were told that it was nothing to do with them. It was the *British* Army's problem.

For some reason, the rate of forward progress of the tunnel fell off markedly. When this was investigated, the New Zealanders said that they could not concentrate on their work because of worrying about the manner in which the "little blokes" were being treated.

As a result, in future the Bantams (and all subsequent infantry labourers) were paraded under cover and given a meal before starting their shift. Coincidentally, the rate of progress went back to what it had been previously.

13/. In the early days of the war, it was soon discovered (the hard way) that the sound of wooden posts being hammered into the ground would pinpoint the location of wiring party. Even though the mallet blows were muffled by using an empty sandbag as a pad, the noise could be heard by the enemy.

Screw pickets were introduced. These were essentially steel rods with loops in the main length to carry the barbed wire, and terminated in a corkscrew-like end section. These could be silently and quickly screwed into the ground without alerting the opposition. The ones used by both sides were identical. This was not surprising as the bulk of those used were manufactured in Sweden and sold on demand to all belligerent nations.

14/. Tsar Nicholas II of Russia sent two brigades, the 1st. and the 3rd. to assist the French on the Champagne-Ardenne front.

"So what?" you might ask. Rather bizarrely, all the personnel in the 1st. had dark hair and grey eyes, while all of the 3rd. were blond with blue eyes! The men were deliberately selected accordingly.

15/. They fought heroically alongside the French in 1916/17 during which winter scores died during a gas attack. However, *Mischka* ('Bruin'), their bear cub mascot survived by burying its muzzle in the snow. The cub survived the war then spent the rest of its life in the *Jardin des Plantes* zoo in Paris.

16/. During the recruiting drive for Kitchener's 'New Army', men from the similar backgrounds, areas or interests formed what became known as "Pals Battalions". Hull raised four battalions of the East Yorkshire Regiment. They were the 10th.(Commercial), the 11th.(Tradesmen), and the 12th.(Sportsmen). However, when the recruiting office clerk enquired as to the designation of the 13th. Battalion, the recruiting officer casually referred to them as " 't Other Lot". From that day on, all official records have them as the " 13th.Battalion ,East Yorkshire Regiment, ('t Other Lot)."

17/. One of the Canadian Bantams stayed on in the United Kingdom after the cessation of hostilities and founded a well-known chain of holiday camps. His name? ---------- Billy Butlin.

Although born in South Africa, as the Butlin family had emigrated to Canada, Billy enlisted as a bugler in one of the Canadian Bantam battalions.

18/. When Archduke Franz Ferdinand was assassinated in Sarajevo, it was at the second attempt. Earlier in the day, a bomb had failed to do the job. As a consequence, the return route had been changed but the driver had not been told. As the official car approached, the would-be assassin managed to get his gun entangled in his clothes when producing it from its concealment. By the time he had freed it, all he could see was the back of the car as it drove away. But then the car had been stopped and the driver informed that he had over-run the new official route. He reversed in order to regain it, then stopped before turning onto the correct road. The car was now opposite the killer thus presenting him with the ideal opportunity for the shot.

So, if the official driver had NOT missed his road, WW1 might not have happened.

19. The official photograph of Gavrilo Princip, (the assassin), is NOT him. It is actually that of one of the innocent bystanders arrested at the time of the incident, but subsequently released as he had nothing to do with it.

And finally ---------- When the call for men for the Local Defence Volunteers went out in 1940, two men were waiting at the local recruiting office when it opened for business. Both were former soldiers of the West Yorkshire Regiment in the Great War. One was one of the original Bantams. His name? Norman F. Brooke whose *alter ego* is Fred Booth in the main narrative. This time, height did not matter. He was accepted without hesitation.

He was to find that his less than good health due to the wounds and gassing suffered during World War I restricted his ability to meet the physical demands of the L.D.V. / Home Guard activities. For instance, on one of his now frequent visits to hospital, he was to find that he was still carrying shell splinters in his body from his time on the Somme.

He became the unit armourer, and, by arrangement with his employer, was able to put his skills to good use.

Initially, all firearms issued to, or 'acquired' by his local unit were either well-worn or faulty in some respect. Being the skilled mechanic/machinist that he was, he would make replacement parts as and when necessary. If all parts were in place on a deactivated weapon, a replacement for the damaged piece would be machined from the raw metal if at all possible. If a piece had been removed at some stage in the past, then nothing could be done.

It became a normal, everyday sight to see him leaving his place of work, and boarding a 'bus with a couple of rifles tucked under his arm, or perhaps a Lewis gun over his shoulder.

ONCE A "BANTAM", ALWAYS A "BANTAM"!